A Practical Guide to E-commerce and Internet Law

A Practical Guide to E-commerce and Internet Law

2nd Edition

Osborne Clarke

ICSA Publishing

Published by ICSA Publishing Limited
16 Park Crescent
London W1B 1AH

Professional advice should be sought before acting on the guidance contained in this publication. Osborne Clarke cannot accept responsibility for any damage or loss sustained through acts or omissions arising from a reliance on the information contained herein.

Typeset in Sabon and Franklin Gothic by
Hands Fotoset, Woodthorpe, Nottingham

Printed and bound in Great Britain by
TJ International Ltd, Padstow, Cornwall

British Library Cataloguing in Publication Data
A catalogue record for this book is available from the British Library.

ISBN: 1-86072-305-5

Contents

The Contributors

Andrew Braithwaite – Partner *Date of qualification: 1985*

Andrew's experience covers a wide range of non-contentious IP and IT transactions and technology issues. For 20 years, he has given specialist advice to the high-tech sector and has been a leading advisor in the emergence of internet and e-commerce businesses in the South West. Andrew also handles a range of IP licensing transactions, including trade marks and merchandising, sponsorship and TV production and has acted as legal adviser to a number of sport businesses, including Ryder Cup and the PGA for the past ten years.

James Pond – Lawyer *Date of qualification: 2001*

James is a commercial lawyer who specialises in all aspects of intellectual property and commercial work relating to the advertising, interactive media and entertainment industries. He has extensive experience of providing copy clearance advice and drafting, negotiating and advising on all forms of commercial agreements for advertising agencies and brand owners. James originally qualified as a barrister in 1998 before joining Osborne Clarke's London office in 2000. He has also worked in-house at one of the world's leading internet companies.

Victoria Powell – Lawyer *Date of qualification: 2001*

Victoria specialises in non-contentious commercial, regulatory and intellectual property issues within the technology and e-commerce sectors. She has wide experience of drafting, negotiating and advising in relation to a variety of commercial contracts, for example, software licences and technology agreements, participation agreements and card processing agreements. Victoria also advises in relation to data protection issues including drafting data processor agreements, notifications and privacy policies and has conducted a number of Europe-wide data protection audits of large organisations in conjunction with more widely focused business operations audits.

Emily Utley – Associate *Date of qualification: 1999*

Emily deals with all aspects of transacting online, from setting up websites with appropriate terms and conditions and privacy policies, to ensuring compliance with e-commerce and Distance Selling Regulations. Emily has advised on, and drafted agreements for, e- and m-commerce transactions including global software development and licensing agreements, supply and installation, support and maintenance; content agreements; and web-based frameworks. She also advises technology clients on appropriate sales channels taking into account competition law and the Commercial Agents Regulations 1993.

Clare Robinson – Partner *Date of qualification: 1987*

Clare specialises in IP disputes and has been a partner since 1992. Since qualification she has advised many companies both in the UK and overseas on a full range of contentious IP issues. She has dealt with significant IP disputes involving patents, copyright, design right, database rights, trade marks and passing off. She has also devised and managed strategies for the enforcement of IP rights in the UK and across Europe for several major companies.

Douglas Peden – Associate *Date of qualification: 1996*

Douglas is a senior associate in the litigation department and deals with IP and general commercial disputes. He acts for a wide range of clients in all types of intellectual property disputes, including patent infringement claims, trade mark and passing off claims, copyright infringement, domain name disputes, database right issues and misuse of confidential information. He has particular experience of working with clients to develop and pursue anti-counterfeiting campaigns. He is also experienced in handling a wide variety of general commercial and contractual disputes, including IT disputes, warranty claims and disputes relating to commercial agencies.

Mark Antingham – Associate *Date of qualification: 1991*

Mark is an associate solicitor based in our Thames Valley office. He has 13 years' experience of advising on all aspects of intellectual property. He has particular expertise in the creation, protection and exploitation of trade marks and brands, as well as merchandising, sponsorship, franchising and anti-counterfeiting. He frequently advises on IP strategy and portfolio management as well as the IP implications of mergers and acquisitions and other commercial transactions. His experience spans many international markets and both traditional and electronic media.

Anna Keeling – Associate *Date of qualification: 1998*

Working for the Commercial department in Bristol, Anna is an Associate solicitor with wide experience of non-contentious IT transactions and technology issues. She has advised on and drafted agreements relating to global software development, reseller and licensing; supply and installation;

support and maintenance; content and web-based frameworks. She has worked closely with a number of universities and technology companies in relation to the development of spin-out and innovative technologies advising on patent and know how licensing, funding and competition issues. Anna also specialises in: advertising and marketing services; data protection; intellectual property and publishing.

Russell Bowyer – Partner *Date of qualification: 1986*

Russell joined our Thames Valley office in August 1998 to head up its IT and Telecommunications group, which the independent legal directories have described as 'first rate' and 'highly talented'. His expertise spans three interconnected areas of law: information technology, intellectual property and competition law – vital subjects for the region's thriving technology sector. He acts for both technology suppliers and major users and has 18 years' experience in advising on the commercial and legal issues relating to software development and licensing, facilities management and outsourcing, telecommunications, e-commerce, channel and partner relations and the development and commercial exploitation of intellectual property.

Eva Krogh – Lawyer *Date of qualification: 2003*

Eva joined Osborne Clarke having spent ten years in commerce. She specialises in commercial law, with emphasis on contracts within the regulatory framework of the technology and telecommunications sectors. She has experience of a broad range of commercial matters, including outsourcing, software licensing, IT and e-commerce matters. Eva also advises on distribution and agency arrangements involving cross border issues. Her work includes outsourcing deals for major UK telecommunications operators and advising a global provider of information and support in relation to services provided to OEM resellers. Eva has also advised a US internet security provider in relation to its localisation of an on-line subscriber and certification arrangement within the UK and project managing same within the EU. Eva also writes numerous articles for legal publications which have dealt with a variety of topics including data protection.

James Mullock – Partner *Date of qualification: 1996*

James specialises in technology and telecoms issues such as e-commerce business contracts, encryption and data protection and Freedom of Information issues (in particular compliance audits), technology and telecoms supply, procurement and outsourcing arrangements, IP licensing, establishing MVNOs and telecoms regulatory issues. He is the co-author of The Data Protection Act 1998 Explained (published by the Stationery Office), is an editor of the publication Data Protection Law and Policy and is regularly asked to comment on technology issues by trade and national press. James became a partner in 2001, and is based in our Bristol office.

Piers Leigh-Pollitt – Associate *Date of qualification: 1997*
Piers specialises in Data Protection and employment issues. He has advised on the human resources aspects of a European-wide data protection audit and has also co-ordinated the introduction of IT security and related policies on a pan-European basis. With James Mullock, he co-authored the book 'The Data Protection Act 1998 Explained'. On the employment side, he regularly advises on a wide range of employment law issues, assisting clients in HR teams with disciplinaries and grievance hearings, equal opportunities and advising on redundancies and TUPE issues.

Rachael Wright – Associate *Date of qualification: 1994*
Rachael is the Training and Know-how Lawyer for Osborne Clarke's employment, pensions and incentives department and Head of Knowledge Management at Osborne Clarke. A qualified solicitor specialising in employment law, Rachael worked for seven years as a fee-earner with a City firm where she gained particular experience in High Court and Employment Tribunal litigation, including industrial disputes, sexual harassment cases, and restraint of trade injunctions.

Emma Wills – Lawyer *Date of qualification: 2004*
Emma regularly deals with a broad range of employment issues, from drafting contracts, service agreements and policies to dealing with employment tribunal claims and handling dismissals. She also has experience of drafting various employee incentive schemes and reviewing schemes as part of corporate transactions. She has worked with and advised several plcs and large multinational companies as well as US companies looking to start up in the UK.

Catherine Shepherd – Associate *Date of qualification: 1999*
Catherine advises public and private companies on a full range of employment and work-related issues, including day-to-day workplace problems, wrongful and unfair dismissal claims and discrimination issues. She has also advised on the employment aspects of business transfers, share acquisitions, large-scale relocations and collective redundancies. Catherine is currently a visiting lecturer in employment law at the University of the West of England (Bristol Business School) teaching on the Masters in Human Resources Management.

Philip Moss – Partner *Date of qualification: 1983*
Philip is head of Tax at Osborne Clarke and a partner in the Corporate Tax unit. He deals with all areas of direct tax, stamp duty and VAT for business clients. Philip also leads the Property Tax function at Osborne Clarke. He advises UK and overseas companies and institutions on all taxation aspects (including VAT and stamp duty) of corporate and property matters and transactions. In addition to general day-to-day tax issues arising on the four

management, acquisition and sale of property portfolios, he has advised on many other matters, including property finance and finance leasing transactions, joint ventures and developments.

Graham Roe – Lawyer *Date of qualification: 2002*

Graham specialises in corporate taxes, including the sale and purchase of companies and businesses. He advises selling shareholders and purchasers on relevant tax issues such as capital gains tax, VAT and stamp duty and how to structure and implement transactions in a tax efficient manner. Clients range from smaller owner managed companies to listed Plcs in a variety of industry sectors such as media and entertainment, support services and finance. Graham is also member of the Chartered Institute of Taxation having qualified as a Chartered Tax Adviser in 2001.

Miles Trower – Lawyer *Date of qualification: 2001*

Miles advises on all aspects of both UK and EU competition law. This includes advising on and making UK and EU merger filings as well as co-ordinating notifications on a wider international basis and seeking confidential guidance and informal advice from the OFT. He has also advised a leading distributor in relation to the Competition Commission's recent inquiry into the supply of prescription-only veterinary medicines. Miles has extensive experience of reviewing commercial agreements from a competition perspective, as well as drafting and negotiating a wide range of agreements, including distribution, outsourcing, franchise/master licences and dealer agreements. He also specialises in the area of motor vehicle distribution and after-sales operations.

Mark Webber – Associate *Date of qualification:* 1999

Mark advises on commercial matters in the technology, licensing and privacy fields. His areas of expertise include: transactional technology deals including outsourcing; IP and software licensing, and development deals, procurement, channel and partner relationships and wireless ventures. He gained a valuable insight into the US technology industry as head of Osborne Clarke's Silicon Valley office, and has substantial experience of organising and managing pan-European projects in multiple jurisdictions for both European and US clients. He is currently based in our Thames Valley office where his work includes: advising on European expansion for US technology businesses (including Vonage, Good Technology, JamdatMobile and Melodeo), negotiating deals in the wireless space and acting for technology outsourcing providers.

Simon Rendell – Partner and Commercial Practice Group Head
Date of qualification: 1991

Simon has worked within the technology sector for over 17 years, advising on legal strategy for business growth through the exploitation of intellectual property. He is a non-executive director of three technology companies and a director of Technology Venture Consulting Ltd, an advisory company to technology SMEs. Simon is recognised in The Chambers Directory and The Legal 500 as one of the UK's leading practitioners of IT & telecommunications law. He has practised in this field since 1986, as well as advising on EC regulatory and competition law, intellectual property and all aspects of commercial law. Simon is responsible for the co-ordination of Osborne Clarke's North American business alliances and assists in the development of the firm's European Alliance. He has assisted in the legal development of global businesses such as Yahoo!, VeriSign, Apple and Electronic Arts.

Paula Staunton – Partner *Date of qualification: 1991*
Paula specialises in technology and commercial law. Based in London, she heads the Commercial department's sales channels team and advises clients on their distribution/reseller and agency agreements. Paula regularly advises both suppliers and users on the legal issues associated with intellectual property, outsourcing, ownership/licensing, IT procurement, software development, service level agreements and e-commerce. Other work has included advising on: outsourcing contracts in respect of a €400m securitisation of a hardware provider's leasing contracts; and, the anglicisation of an American IT company's reseller/distribution agreements, including an analysis of the impact of the European block exemption.

Truda Borthwick-Stevens *Date of qualification: 1995*
Truda Borthwick-Stevens edited both this edition of the book and the original version which appeared in 2002. She is also responsible for researching and re-writing the section on Criminal Liability in Chapter 4. Before entering the law, Truda worked as a commercial journalist. She qualified as a solicitor in 1995 and gained a broad range of experience in both commercial and IT law, working both in-house for Sun Life and NPI and for private practice. She also worked as a professional support lawyer for Osborne Clarke for four years where she developed and wrote a number of on-line legal updates for fee-earners and clients.

Table of Cases

Table of Statutes

Foreword

There has been a tremendous upsurge in e-commerce activity since the last edition of this Guide. This has been facilitated by faster internet connections and more people having access to the internet. These days many people prefer to shop from the comfort of their own home or office rather than venture out to crowded stores. Besides, internet shopping can offer better value. And it hasn't just been the consumer that has benefited, business to business e-commerce trade has transformed all areas of procurement supply.

A few years ago, it was mainly dotcom businesses that traded online. Now most stores have a website offering their goods for sale. Such websites often provide a greater variety of products than are available in-store, and provide a convenient way to search or sift through what's on offer. Companies are also increasingly diversifying the products which they offer on the internet, for example, Amazon.com, which is primarily known for specialising in selling books and CDs, now sells a vast range of products, from kitchen appliances and electronic goods to home and garden furniture. Amazon also encourages customers to sell their unwanted items through its website.

As e-commerce becomes ever more prevalent, so does the need for further legal regulation. Although initially many countries' governments and legislative bodies found ways to adapt existing laws in order to make them applicable to the internet, they are increasingly implementing new regulations to fill the grey areas. Unfortunately, as it has been hard to predict how internet activity and e-commerce would grow, these new regulations have often been introduced slowly, and in a fairly piecemeal fashion. This makes it extremely difficult to navigate your way through all the legislation with which one needs to be familiar before embarking on an internet business or expanding a business to trade online.

The authors of this Guide have attempted to collect the essential information and put it in one short, accessible text that is interesting and easy to understand. It will enable you to familiarise yourself with the 'legal' requirements so that you can make the right risk assessments before deciding whether to offer your products and services on the internet. It will also help you ensure that you structure your legal relationship with the customer appropriately, which can sometimes be more demanding than the challenge of getting the right business plan and obtaining funding. You will find a lot of practical and useful information in this Guide.

Michael Miller
UK General Counsel at Amazon.co.uk

Preface and Acknowledgements

The internet is one of the most powerful tools available to modern businesses. It allows traders to advertise and sell products online. It permits customers to browse virtual shop windows from their homes, select goods and place an order at the touch of a button. If used properly, it can significantly extend a business's reach and reduce costs and increase efficiency.

However, the internet is not a magic formula; it is a business medium. As such, it is necessary to understand both its benefits and pitfalls. For instance, the internet offers far greater scope to marketeers, permitting them to reach a much larger audience at a significantly lower cost than traditional methods of advertising. Unfortunately, there are also disadvantages which have to be considered. For example, as exposure to consumers is increased – often across international borders – so are the risks.

This book is aimed at company secretaries, finance directors, IT managers, in-house lawyers, students, and anyone in need of a broad-ranging introduction to the legislative and commercial issues related to doing business online. While the amount of legislation dealing specifically with e-commerce issues has increased in recent years, much of the relevant law affecting this area is still drawn from general commercial legislation and the common law. For this reason, the book offers a number of chapters dedicated to subjects such as tax, competition, media, employment, data protection and intellectual property, covering both general principles and specific, e-commerce applications.

Chapter 1 provides a general introduction to the key elements of contract law which are as relevant to contracts made online as to paper-based agreements. However, it also highlights areas of uncertainty regarding e-commerce (for instance the acceptance of offers by e-mail) to which online traders should pay particular attention.

Setting the context for the rest of the book, Chapter 2 uses the example of a fictitious company to enable readers to understand how and when various legislative elements affect different aspects of an online business. Chapters 3 to 10 then expand upon the subjects introduced in Chapter 2, setting out the basic principles of relevant legislation and then applying these to specific circumstances likely to be encountered by online businesses.

The book's no-nonsense approach aims to help readers get a better understanding of the legal implications of doing business on-line. Apart from practical information, the book provides a number of checklists and summaries to facilitate the identification of some of the pitfalls commonly encountered by e-businesses. For instance – What are the key elements to be covered when drawing up an online privacy policy? What factors should be considered in an ISP agreement? What are the main issues to be addressed in an email/internet policy for employees?

Finally, the appendix provides useful sources of information, which should allow readers to perform further research of their own.

✳

We would like to thank all contributors to *A Practical Guide to E-commerce and Internet Law* for their hard work and patience. These include not only the contributors, whose biographies appear at pp. xv–xx, but also those responsible for advising, editing, researching, proof-reading, amending and collating the book. They are: Simon Rendell, Andrew Braithwaite, James Mullock, Nick Johnson, Mark Culbert, Truda Borthwick-Stevens, Anna Blackden, Joanne Lee, Jenny Withnall, Fiona Hunt and Chloe Swift.

Introduction: The Legal Context

Introduction

This chapter seeks to introduce the reader to some of the concepts and issues relating to e-commerce that will be covered in greater depth elsewhere in this book. It starts with a review of the basic principles of contract law. While these are still relevant to modern business, the formation of contracts online has presented some interesting problems.

E-mail and click-wrap contracts, the two main methods of contracting online, are discussed; and the question of how to incorporate terms and conditions into a website is considered.

In addition to a brief overview of some of the relevant statutory and case law, this chapter also highlights some items of specific interest to online traders. These include: warranties; dealing with returns and refunds; consumer protection; payment and security on the internet; and law and jurisdiction.

1. Basic principles of contract

Every day, we enter into contracts without realising that we are doing so. For example, successful deals made by the sales force may comprise the 'contractual steps' set out below.

Under English law the formation of a contract requires the following elements:

- an *offer*;
- unequivocal *acceptance* of the offer, which is communicated to the person making the offer;
- *consideration*;
- an *intention to create legal relations*; and
- *capacity* in each party to be legally bound.

A contract is formed when an offer has been accepted and, following acceptance, the offer cannot be withdrawn. In general, contracts may be made verbally or in writing. However, there are some exceptions; these include formal contracts made by deed and other types of contract, such as contracts for the sale of an interest in land, which must be made in writing.

It is very important to be able to identify, and control, exactly when a contract has been formed. For instance, in the case of an international contract, this will decide which country's laws will be used when interpreting and enforcing the agreement. In the context of online trading, it is crucial to control when a contract is created, to minimise business risk.

1.1 Offer

English law distinguishes between an offer and an 'invitation to treat', such as an advertisement that promotes the sale of products but is not an offer. Under traditional contract law, the display of goods in a shop is not an offer but an invitation to treat (*Pharmaceutical Society of Britain* v. *Boots Cash Chemist Ltd.* [1952] 2 QB 795). Accordingly, when the purchaser asks the seller if he can buy a product, this constitutes the offer. At this point, the seller is free to accept or reject the purchaser's offer.

A business intending to trade online will be concerned to control the contract by ensuring its customers make offers, open for acceptance by the website owner. It should construct its website so that it is, in effect, a shop window. The site should carry a clear statement that the supplier will not be bound to a contract unless the supplier accepts the offer of the customer. (Statements to this effect are often seen on traditional terms and conditions and are regarded as an invitation to treat.)

The online business will also be keen to ensure it knows to whom it is making offers, and is in a position to target only those it wishes to accept. For instance, an online liquor store may target adults only; and a geographical limit on territories is often set on a retailer, who will only be able to target customers in its territory.

1.2 Unconditional acceptance

Under English law a contract is formed when the offer is unconditionally accepted. Acceptance may affect both the timing of the contract and the place it becomes effective. In the case of timing, it may be crucial for an online auctioneer to clarify which bid was accepted first; and in the case of location, this will affect the law that governs the contract and the tax treatment of the transaction. There are two rules of acceptance:

1. The *receipt rule*: this states that a contract is formed at the time and place

when the acceptance is received by the offeror. This applies to instantaneous forms of communications such as telephone, fax and telex.

2. The *postal rule:* this applies to communications by post, according to which acceptance is effective at the time of posting of the communication. The postal rule does not apply to instantaneous communications.

Legal opinion continues to be divided on whether the postal rule applies to e-business, that is acceptance via a website or e-mail. Interestingly, provisions expressly dealing with contracts made over the internet were included in a proposal for an EU Directive but were subsequently dropped from the final Electronic Communications Act 2000 passed in the UK. The proposal suggested that e-mail was not an instantaneous form of communication. The reason given for this was that often, external e-mails are routed through a number of servers located in different jurisdictions before reaching their final destination and thus receipt can be delayed.

It has been suggested that out of office auto-replies may have an important role to play in this area. This is because an e-mail may be deemed to have been accepted when it reaches the intended recipient's machine, even if it is not read or acknowledged. This means that it is possible for a contract to exist even where one party is unaware of it, as long as the e-mail has reached their inbox. An out of office auto-reply would stop this situation arising as the sender would be made aware that the recipient had not accepted the contents of the e-mail. Given the current uncertainty, a supplier is advised to override the postal rule by using a clear statement in its website terms and conditions as to how acceptance can be made, and when it becomes effective. One suggestion has been to state that the offer is not accepted until payment has been taken from or charged to the customer.

Acceptance of an offer is normally communicated, but can also be inferred by the conduct of the parties, which may amount to performance (for example, carrying out the service requested or paying the price for the relevant item). So it is also important that the seller makes it clear which acts (if any) will amount to acceptance.

1.3 Consideration

Consideration is essential to create a contract. In simple terms it is the exchange of promises, normally for the supplier to give up something of value, in exchange for the customer making payment. The requirements are the same in online business.

Consideration need not be money. For example, an online business may offer an information service that provides information to subscribers. In return, the person receiving the service agrees to supply the provider with his or her profile and other relevant data. Such data may be valuable in itself and will therefore amount to consideration.

1.4 The intention to create legal relations

Although intention to create a binding contract is a requirement, it is generally not an issue in day-to-day business – if a party alleges a lack of intent on their part, they face a hefty burden of proof. Just consider what arguments Argos raised following a computer error, which resulted in the company advertising televisions for sale on its website for £2.99 instead of the correct price of £299.99. The intention of the parties to enter into a legally binding document can be inferred from surrounding circumstances – for example, the payment of money or compliance with certain obligations in return for goods or services.

Letters of intent (unless otherwise stated) do not create legal relations since they indicate only an intention to negotiate rather than establish contractual obligations. As we will see, the same principle applies to electronic commerce.

1.5 Capacity

A number of difficulties may arise for online suppliers over the identity of the other parties to a contract. Such difficulties generally fall into two categories: legal capacity and mistake.

1. *Legal capacity*: Under English law, contracts made with minors are generally voidable at the minor's option under the Minors' Contracts Act 1987. However, adults who do not seek to take unfair advantage of a minor with whom they have entered into a contract are entitled to uphold a contract for certain necessary items covering a variety of goods and services excluding luxuries. Generally speaking a contract with a mental patient is valid unless the other contracting party knew of the other's disability in which case the contract is voidable. Online suppliers therefore need to ensure they have certain basic information about the person with whom they are making a contract.

2. *Mistake*: Generally, a mistake does not invalidate a contract unless it is fundamental. A fundamental mistake is one which means that the intended offer and acceptance do not coincide and therefore there is no true consensus. There are three general circumstances where a mistake will be fundamental. These are:

   a) where a reasonable person could not infer the intention of the parties from the circumstances surrounding the transaction; or
   b) where one party knew of the other's mistake; or
   c) where one party negligently induced the other's mistake.

A fundamental mistake occurred in the old case of *Raffles* v. *Wichelhaus* in 1864 which involved a contract for cotton on board a ship called *Peerless* sailing from Bombay. In fact, there were two ships of that name sailing from Bombay, one in October and one in December and the parties had different ships in mind. The contract was void for mistake in this instance. However in a more recent case, *OT Africa Line Ltd* v. *Vickers Plc* in 1996, a typing error meant that $155,000 actually appeared as £150,000 in the final contract. The judge in this case held that the contract was binding because the offer made sense in the circumstances in which it was made. He went on to say that there was nothing in the claimants' conduct making it inequitable for them to hold the defendants to the contract. The rules relating to mistake are clearly heavily influenced by the circumstances surrounding the contract and each case will have to be decided on its own particular facts. This area of law can affect online suppliers, for example where a person is seeking the goods of one company and mistakenly visits the website of another company with a confusingly similar domain name or, as in the case above, a typing error occurs.

2. The E-Commerce Regulations

The Electronic Commerce (EC) Regulations came into force on 21 August 2002. They are a brave first attempt at setting out the basic requirements of e-contracting. The purpose of the Regulations is to ensure that what are described as 'information society services', i.e. broadly e-commerce, benefit from the EU internal market principles of free movement of services and freedom of establishment. The Regulations cover online services such as trade and advertising but do not apply to non-commercial interactions or the offline elements of online transactions. They may apply to companies that sell or advertise goods or services both to businesses and to consumers through websites or via e-mail or to those who convey content using e-mail or provide access to a communications network. The Regulations define 'Information Society Services' as 'any service normally provided for remuneration, at a distance, by means of electronic equipment for the processing and storage of data, and at the individual request of a recipient of a service'.

The basic position under the Regulations is that any person providing an information society service must make the following information available to the recipient:

- the name of the service provider;
- the service provider's geographic address;
- details of the service provider, including an e-mail address;
- details of the service provider's trade registrations, if any;
- particulars of any relevant supervisory authority.

The use of e-mails on their own is not classed as an information society service. However, a service provider does need to provide certain additional information when sending e-mails if they form part of an information society service. This includes:

- clear identification of the person on whose behalf the e-mail is being sent;
- clear details of any promotional offers, competitions or games.

The Regulations also state that, where a contract is to be concluded by electronic means, details of the following must be provided:

- the steps required to conclude the contract;
- the point at which it will be deemed to have been concluded;
- how any errors will be identified and put right; and
- the languages offered for conclusion of the contract.

Similarly, when electronic orders are placed the service provider must:

- acknowledge receipt of the order to the recipient of the service promptly; and
- make available means to allow any errors to be corrected prior to the placing of the order.

Breaches of the Regulations could result in claims for damages or the contract being invalidated. Where a breach affects the collective interest of consumers, a service provider may also be subject to a 'stop now' order obliging them to publish corrective statements. Failure to comply with such an order will be treated as contempt of court, punishable by fines or imprisonment.

3. Electronic negotiations

The development of e-mail and the World Wide Web has not affected the application of the current principles of contract law, nor is it expected to do so. However, there are peculiar technological issues regarding the formation of a contract online.

The supplier's website must act as a virtual shop window, allowing him the freedom to accept or reject the customer's offer. By this means, the supplier will have the flexibility to choose with whom to contract.

He will also be able to avoid an embarrassing and costly situation where he is contractually bound to fulfil an order but is unable to do so due to a stock shortage. For instance, the supplier may state, as a term of trading, that he will not accept an offer until payment has been taken, which, in turn, will depend on the goods being ready for despatch. In the event that the goods are not available, the supplier will not take payment and will be able to refuse the order.

3.1 Making contracts online

There are two main methods of electronic contracting, each with its own characteristics and each requiring to be treated separately.

The first method is *electronic mail*. E-mail is considered to be the digital equivalent of a letter. It can be used to make an offer or to communicate acceptance; it can be used for advertisements and for sending unwanted communications ('spam'). As mentioned in section 1.2 it is not yet certain which rule applies as to when e-mails are accepted, so online suppliers are advised to make this clear in their terms and conditions.

The second method of contracting on the internet is often known as the *click-wrap contract*. This is where, before downloading or using software online, a message on screen requires the user to agree to the terms of the licence agreement. The user must then indicate that they agree to the terms by clicking on the 'I Agree' button (or similar) before proceeding. In practical terms, the design and structure of the website are important, as is the navigation. Consider where the terms of contract will be displayed, whether part of them will be invisible 'below the fold', and where the 'I agree' button will be located.

3.2 Incorporation of online terms and conditions

There are a number of ways of incorporating contract terms into a website:

1. By referring to the terms with a hypertext link, which means that a customer can click on the link if he/she wishes to read the terms.
2. By displaying the terms on the website where they can be seen before entering into the contract.
3. By displaying the terms on the pre-contract web page and including a dialogue box.

The best method for ensuring the customer is aware of all the terms is the last one, which requires the customer to scroll through the terms and acknowledge acceptance by ticking a box or clicking on an icon before he/she can proceed with the transaction. As a general rule, the customer will not be bound by the terms unless they have been brought to his/her notice prior to the conclusion of the contract. Any changes to the terms must be brought to the customer's attention immediately. It is good practice to allow for a reasonable period of time to pass before the new changes become effective. The period will depend upon the seller's business.

7

It is important to prevent the customer from being able either to amend existing terms in the electronic form or inserting new ones.

Whether the supplier deals with consumers (business-to-consumer or B2C transaction) or with other businesses (business-to-business or B2B transaction), he/she must consider whether the terms and conditions normally relied upon in his/her traditional commercial dealings may need to be adapted to reflect any e-commerce issues.

The following issues should be considered by online suppliers when drafting their online trading terms:

Delivery

It is advisable to let the customer know the steps and time that will be required for the order to be dispatched. When dealing with consumers the provisions of the Distance Selling Regulations need to be taken into account (see chapter 2).

Liability

If a limitation or exclusion of liability clause has not been freely negotiated between the parties, then, depending on the details of each case, the limitation/exclusion may be regarded as unreasonable. Great care must be taken in drafting such clauses.

Under the Unfair Contract Terms Act 1977 (UCTA), whether a company is dealing with consumers or other businesses, it is impossible to exclude or limit liability for death or personal injury resulting from negligence. If the supplier is (i) contracting with a consumer or (ii) requires another business to contract on his/her standard terms of business, then the supplier must ensure that any exclusion/limitation of liability is reasonable. In order to determine what is reasonable each case must be judged on its merits. The following may provide some guidance:

- the negotiating power of the parties (inequality in the parties' bargaining positions may mean that the relevant clauses are regarded as unreasonable);
- whether the e-customer was induced to enter into the particular contract;
- having regard to standard industry practice and the parties' previous dealings, whether the e-customer ought to have known or be aware of the exclusion of liability;
- if the restriction is conditional upon the non-performance of a certain obligation, whether at the time of the conclusion of the contract it would have been reasonable to expect performance of such obligation;
- whether the goods were custom made;
- the resources of the party relying on the exclusion/limitation of liability available to meet the liability under the particular contract; and
- insurance cover for the party relying on the exclusion/limitation of liability.

At this stage, it is important to refer to the significant case of *Watford Electronics Ltd. v. Sanderson CFL Ltd.* [2001] EWCA Civ 317. This was decided in the Court of Appeal and supports the view that businesses should be free to negotiate such terms as they agree are appropriate. The Court based its decision on the following issues:

- the parties had equal negotiating power;
- the key terms including the entire agreement and liability clauses were subject to negotiation;
- the parties negotiated the price and the customer received substantial reductions;
- the parties also negotiated as to which of them should bear the risk of making good indirect, consequential losses and the loss of profit the customer may suffer if the product failed to perform;
- the customer's own terms and conditions excluded liability for indirect or consequential damages. (See also *St. Albans DC v. ICL* [1997] FSR 251; *South West Water v. ICL* [1999] BLR 420; *Pegler Limited v. Wang (UK) Limited* [2000] BLR 218.)

Warranties

According to the Sale of Goods Act 1979 and subsequent amendments, certain warranties will be implied in contracts unless expressly excluded. Such terms include fitness for purpose and satisfactory quality and title. As discussed in relation to exclusion/limitation of liability, attention should be paid to the provisions of UCTA. For example, while it may be reasonable to exclude all warranties in relation to software licensed free of charge, it may not be reasonable to do this in relation to software for which a licence fee is charged.

Where there are any guarantees applied to the goods, the supplier should ensure compliance with the terms of the Sale of Consumer Goods and Associated Guarantees Directive (the Guarantees Directive). Among the other requirements, the Directive provides that the consumer has statutory rights that the guarantee cannot displace.

Dealing with returns and refunds

This is an important provision especially when dealing with consumers and also in view of the latest legal developments and the E-commerce Directive. The Consumer Protection (Distance Selling) Regulations 2000 ('the Distance Selling Regulations') require an online business supplying consumers to offer a minimum seven days' 'cooling-off' period, or right of cancellation. If properly handled, it could provide an excellent marketing tool for the supplier.

For instance, depending on the nature of the goods and whether the goods were faulty when dispatched or were damaged by the customer, the supplier could allow the customer to return the goods within a specified time limit with the cost of post and packaging refunded to the customer.

Law and jurisdiction

Under the Contracts (Applicable Law) Act 1990, the parties may choose their own governing law. In the absence of choice, the Act provides that the law governing the contract will be the one with which the contract was most closely connected. This will be the country where a party effects 'characteristic performance'.

The characteristic performance is the performance for which payment is made. The location of characteristic performance depends on whether the party performing it is a business or individual. For a business it will be the place of business; for an individual it will be its habitual residence. An e-seller's place of business is likely to be where physical activities are carried out – for example, from where goods are dispatched or services arranged – rather than the location of the server.

However, it is possible that mandatory rules (that is, laws that cannot be contracted out of) of another country may also apply. This is particularly likely if the purchaser is a consumer. It is therefore important to take advice on the potential applicability of other laws. Consideration should also be given to refusing to supply in some jurisdictions. A choice of law clause should usually be included in a contract, which provides which law is to apply to the contract. However, if the contract is made with a consumer, consumers have the right to choose the law of the territory in which they reside, despite the inclusion of such a clause.

As we have seen in section 1.2, the place of the contract could determine which jurisdiction applies. Generally, the contract is made where the acceptance is made. For example, if a buyer places an order with an overseas supplier who faxes an acceptance, the contract is made in England where the fax is received and is therefore presumed to be subject to English law. In the case of contracts formed over the internet the position remains unclear. In order to avoid problems, a business in the UK would normally include a clause that stipulates that English law governs the relevant contract and that English courts will be able to hear a dispute arising out of the subject matter of the contract. However, this may not always be the case, especially if the supplier is selling to consumers.

Place of performance

Under English law, where a contract is for delivery of physical goods, the performance obligation takes place at the delivery address. However, when the delivery is electronic – for example, software sent as an e-mail attachment, or music download or streaming – the position is less clear. The place of receipt could be:

- the location of the purchaser's server;
- the purchaser's mailbox; or
- where the purchaser downloads and/or reads the e-mail.

The best tactic is to specify the place and time of performance in the agreement. If the contract is subject to English law, the usual rules concerning exclusions, limitations and standard form contracts apply. However, the Unfair Contract Terms Act (UCTA) will not generally be applicable when one of the contracting parties is not in England.

4. Practical considerations for suppliers

In addition to reviewing their standard terms and conditions, suppliers need to consider the following:

1. When information is made available via a website, users may try to copy and use that information; in the standard terms and conditions for accessing the website the supplier should restrict what users can do with such information.
2. If the supplier is in the business of software licensing, as licensor he needs to ensure that the potential licensee is bound by the terms of the licensing agreement. The issues already covered in this chapter in relation to the incorporation of terms and conditions will be relevant to these circumstances.
3. The consequences of collecting and using personal data need to be addressed in the terms for accessing the website. Adequate privacy policies need to be put in place.
4. If the website contains third party content, the supplier will need to obtain relevant disclaimers/warranties from the content provider in relation to the content and will also need to restrict what a user can do with the content.

The risks to businesses of ignoring basic contractual principles in their online dealing have been brought sharply into focus in the US case, *Christopher Specht and others* v. *Netscape Communications Corporation and America Online Inc.* (3 July 2001, United States District Court, Southern District of New York).

Netscape allowed its users to download software electronically. To download the software, website users were transferred to a particular page containing a button labelled 'Download'. The only reference to a licence agreement was in a sentence, which came into view on the next screen if the user scrolled down to it, and which read: *'Please review and agree to the terms of the Netscape Smart Download software licence agreement before downloading and using the software.'*

However, users were not required to read the licence agreement or even indicate that they agreed to it before downloading the software. The download could occur without the user even seeing a reference to the licence at all. The licence agreement contained terms indicating that by clicking the 'Accept' button or installing or using Smart Download the user accepted the terms of the licence agreement. In this case, the claimants alleged that Netscape's software Smart Download unlawfully transmitted to Netscape private information about the users' internet activity.

One of the issues before the court was whether the required arbitration clause in the licence agreement was binding on the user. Ultimately, this depended on whether or not the licence agreement itself was binding.

The judge looked at values and methods of software licensing including shrink-wrap, click-wrap and browse-wrap methods. In brief, shrink-wrap licensing is commonly used with off-the-shelf software that is in a package that advises the purchaser that use of the software is subject to a licence agreement that is contained inside the package. Click-wrap licensing is an online version of shrink-wrap. Before downloading or using software online, a message on screen requires the user to agree to the terms of the licence agreement. The user must then indicate that they agree to the terms by clicking on the 'I Agree' button (or similar) before proceeding. Browse-wrap licensing is the third method and was used by Netscape for Smart Download. The user is not required to read the terms or even acknowledge the terms exist, let alone agree to them. In the *Netscape* case, the judge thought that the main purpose of downloading was to obtain the software rather than to indicate consent. It was also observed that the user was not made aware that he or she was entering into a contract. For the licensing agreement to be binding, the user should have had to click on a button marked 'I Agree' before being allowed to download the software.

Netscape's failure to require its users to indicate their consent to the licence agreement before downloading the software was critical to its case. The judge concluded that the licence agreement was not binding on the users.

5. Electronic data interchange

Online trading between businesses is generally implemented by adopting an agreed method of communication, which involves defined method structures known as electronic data interchange (EDI). EDI is key to certain business methods such as just-in-time procurement where orders for the purchase of products are closely co-ordinated with suppliers. EDI is also the method used for bank automated payment systems.

Traditional EDI requires communication in a structured format, which involves significant investment in software and related hardware. It also involves modifying internal IT systems to make them compatible with the chosen format of EDI. Given the investment required, it tends to be adopted in trading relationships between large organisations. However, many small and medium enterprises (SMEs) are coming under increasing pressure to support EDI. This pressure usually comes from larger suppliers, customers or distributors (collectively known as trading partners) that have invested a great deal in EDI in order to cut their trading costs, and are looking to deploy such automation more widely.

In an attempt to make EDI available to SMEs, new web-based tools have been developed to interact with traditional EDI tools. Many such applications are written in Extensible Mark-up Language (XML), being the more powerful offspring of Hypertext Mark-up Language (HTML), the language used to describe web-page contents.

XML used in relation to EDI (XML/EDI) provides much more flexibility and allows many desirable practices for data management and exchange to be applied both more broadly and at a lower cost than traditional EDI. Because it removes the requirement to synchronise all data formats, the hope is that XML/EDI will drive wider adoption of EDI for business to business transactions. It is unlikely that XML/EDI will replace traditional EDI, it will simply make EDI more accessible to more businesses. Indeed, based on the current level of deployment, EDI will continue to play a key role in supporting external data exchange for many years to come.

Another factor that has made EDI on a global basis much more complex is that, traditionally, different regions of the world have used different technical EDI standards (the US primarily used technical standard ANSI X12, and Europe and Asia used EDIFACT). However, this situation has changed in recent years, and EDIFACT is fast becoming the global EDI standard.

Since EDI involves the exchange of electronic messages without human intervention, the need for a clear contractual basis is particularly important. It is usual for both parties to enter into a framework agreement governing the way in which trading contracts are formed, and their terms.

The EDI agreement normally specifies:

- the communication protocols which are to be applied in the relevant communication;
- the procedure which is to be adopted if messages are unintelligible; and
- the time at which an electronic message is deemed to be received.

In 1998, the International Chamber of Commerce (ICC) published the

Uniform Rules of Conduct for Interchange of Trade Data by Teletransmission (UNCIT Rules), which set out key principles to be addressed in interchange agreements such as storage of data.

The European Commission published a recommendation on EDI in 1994. This includes a European model EDI agreement (European Model). The UK EDI Association has also produced a standard electronic data interchange agreement (UK Model), which can be adopted by parties engaged in EDI. Interchange agreements do not have to follow exactly the terms of a particular standard; the parties can agree to modifications, so there is scope to take provisions from various standards. These agreements tend to be in addition to contracts setting out businesses' contractual trading terms and conditions.

The key issues addressed in an EDI agreement are as follows:

1. *Technical*: The European Model requires compliance with the EU-approved version of the European technical standards (UN EDIFACT). Any further technical issues should be specified in the agreement.

2. *Contract formation*: Where contracts are concluded using EDI, it is necessary to specify when and how the contract is formed. The European Model identifies the point of contract conclusion as the time and place where the EDI message constituting acceptance reaches the computer system of the offeror. There is no obligation to acknowledge receipt unless requested. The UK Model does not address contract formation and so this would need to be added, otherwise the formation will be determined in accordance with the governing law of the contract concluded via EDI.

3. *Contract validity and admissibility*: The European Model states that the parties waive any right to contest the validity of the contract affected by use of EDI on the sole ground that it was affected by EDI. Also the parties agree that the records of EDI messages shall be admissible by the courts. Again, if EDI is used to form contracts these issues should be inserted into any agreement based on the UK model.

4. *Security*: Under the European Model the parties agree to implement and maintain security procedures and measures in order to guard against unauthorised access, alteration, delay, destruction or loss of data. These procedures and measures include in particular, verification of the origin and integrity of the data. Specific procedures and measures may be set out in the technical annex to the agreement. The UK Model requires the parties to respect the integrity of messages subject to exceptions such as where an error is reasonably obvious to the recipient.

5. *Confidentiality*: Both the European and the UK Models provide that the parties may agree to use a specific form of protection such as encryption for certain messages.

6. *Recording and storage of EDI messages*: Both the European and UK Models

require each party to store a complete and chronological record of all EDI messages in a readily accessible form. The UK Model also requires each party to designate a person to be responsible for these obligations.

7. *Liability*: The European Model provides that no party is to be liable for special, indirect or consequential damages or for events beyond that party's control. The UK counterpart contains a *force majeure* clause, but does not otherwise address liability for breach on the grounds that loss is not likely to be caused by breach of the model itself. This does not preclude inclusion of such a clause.

8. *Governing law and jurisdiction*: The European Model does not impose a particular European national law and gives a choice between arbitration and reference to national courts. The UK Model assumes that English law and courts will apply unless otherwise agreed by the parties.

6. Consumer protection and regulatory compliance

When a company is dealing with consumers, as well as issues already covered in this chapter, it needs to take into consideration consumer protection laws, such as sale of goods legislation and product safety requirements, which apply just as much offline as they do online in e-commerce. The extent to which suppliers can restrict their liability under a contract is also restricted. An e-business will also have to take into account the Distance Selling Regulations (see chapter 2). The nature of some e-businesses increases the likelihood of contravening laws of other jurisdictions. For example, particular care is required in relation to heavily regulated products, such as betting, alcohol and pharmaceuticals. Care is also required when dealing with products that raise safety issues such as food and motor vehicles.

The Data Protection Act 1998 is an important development in the area of privacy and its implications should be carefully considered. There are eight principles put in place by the Act in order to make sure that information that is personal to one individual is handled properly. They state such data must be :

- fairly and lawfully processed;
- processed for limited purposes;
- adequate, relevant and not excessive;
- accurate;
- not kept for longer than is necessary;
- processed in line with consumer's rights;
- secure;
- not transferred to countries without adequate protection.

Compliance with data protection law has resulted in the majority of e-tailers adopting the use of a privacy policy in its dealings with consumers, which are considered in chapter 3.

7. Payment and security on the internet

Strong security mechanisms are essential for developing confidence in electronic transactions. Encryption is the process by which messages or data in readable form are encoded into unreadable cyphered data by the use of an encryption algorithm and a key, which is used to prevent others reading confidential, private or commercial data. Initially, encryption technologies were used by governments, the military and intelligence services. However, recent changes in legislation and increased use of the internet mean that there is likely to be an increase in the availability and use of strong encryption products, initially by large corporations and then by the public at large.

Encryption, of course, does not solve the problem entirely. It transfers the problem of keeping the data secret to that of keeping the key secret. The keys used to encrypt or decrypt data are essentially passwords made up of numbers. All key-based encryptions can be broken on the basis of systematic trial-and-error methods. Accordingly, the strength of a key depends on the range of numbers that can be used by the encryption algorithm. The length and strength of the key is measured by the number of the binary digits or bits. The bit length of the key used in an algorithm determines how long trial and error will take to decrypt the message and thus whether it is possible to crack a key within a practical time period.

Of course, if a sender encrypts a message, the recipient must to be able to decrypt it. The same key will be needed to encrypt and decrypt the message. This means that the parties need to agree in advance which key to use. Alternatively, they need to have some means of exchanging the keys before or after the message is sent. Since this area of the law is still evolving, the reader is advised to keep an eye on any legislative changes in this respect.

8. The Electronic Communications Act 2000 and the Electronic Signatures Regulations 2002

Under the Electronic Communications Act 2000, electronic signatures are admissible as evidence in relation to any question as to the authenticity of the communication or data or as to the integrity of the communication or data.

An electronic signature is defined as anything in electronic form that:

- is incorporated into, or otherwise logically associated with, any electronic communication or electronic data; and

- purports to be so incorporated or associated for the purpose of being used in establishing the authenticity of the communication or data, the integrity of the communication or data or both.

While electronic signatures are admissible in legal proceedings in the UK, they may not yet be afforded in all cases the same status as handwritten signatures in relation to paper-based data as they are not presumed to be legally binding. Again, the reader is advised to keep an eye on legislative changes in this respect.

Together with the Electronic Communications Act, the Electronic Signatures Regulations complete the UK implementation of the European E-Signatures Directive. The Regulations mean a public register of 'certification service providers' who can offer 'qualified certificates' is now kept. According to the Regulations, a 'qualified certificate' is an electronic confirmation that a particular e-signature belongs to a named individual that meets the standards set out in the Regulations. This means that parties to an e-commerce transaction know with whom they are dealing and this helps the execution of online contracts. The Regulations also make certification service providers liable to anyone who suffers loss as a result of reasonably relying on the certificate.

9. Electronic payment systems

At the height of the internet bubble, many minds and significant financial resources were directed towards developing an electronic alternative to cash and credit and debit card payments. The aim was to develop a virtual payment system, referred to as a 'digital purse' (essentially, smart cards on which a cash value is held electronically) that would be the currency of the internet. Various schemes were piloted but, save for a couple of exceptions, there was a conspicuous lack of success and some high profile casualties: DigiCash filed for bankruptcy in 1998 and the future for Mondex's smart card remains unclear.

Nevertheless, the development of a viable digital purse system is still viewed as an essential progression in the future of e-commerce. Currently, in relation to transactions conducted over the internet, a supplier of goods or services is at risk, because the cardholder is not present at the point of payment, leaving the merchant with no practical means of verifying either the cardholder signature or requesting the input of the relevant PIN number. In the future, credit and debit card issuers may amend their rules so as to accommodate electronic signatures in an attempt to limit the opportunities for fraud.

The Financial Services and Markets Act 2000 ('FSMA') did look to the future however and under the provisions of the FSMA Regulated Activities Order 2001 (Electronic Money), the issuance of electronic money is a regulated activity and issuers must be duly authorized and comply with the provisions of the FSMA. Under the FSMA, electronic money is defined as monetary value as represented by a claim on the issuer which is:

- stored on an electronic device;
- issued on receipt of funds; and
- accepted as a means of payment by persons other than the issuer.

Despite regulatory recognition for electronic money, the real growth area in this space is the development of systems to facilitate 'micro payments', e.g. the payment amounts necessary to purchase drinks, or items from a vending machine. These systems do not involve a digital purse as such, but will enable payments to be made using a mobile telephone. Briefly, it is envisaged that the mobile telephone will become a cash or card substitute, with the relevant telephone number being offered as the means of payment and the customer's mobile telephone account being debited with the cost of the purchase. A system of this type could be used for internet transactions, but also it has the key advantage of being truly universal and, depending on the type of contract between mobile operator and customer, not necessarily subject to top up. Most of the major mobile telecoms companies are actively seeking to develop systems of this type.

CHAPTER 2

Getting Down to the Business of Going Online

Introduction

This chapter takes the approach of a case study, by providing a step-by-step example of how a fictitious traditional, trading company goes about developing its business online. The subject of this case study, Trading Company Limited, typifies many other companies interested in using the internet to improve their competitive edge.

The types of concerns and issues raised by Trading Company's directors regarding such issues as domain name registration, data protection and liability for website content are likely to be shared by directors and managers of actual companies. It is therefore hoped that the solutions and action points offered to Trading Company Limited will be of value and relevance to other companies and organisations as they make the transition from traditional business to e-business. It may also serve as a checklist for businesses with a more established online presence.

The main issues for Trading Company Limited are set out below:

1. Obtaining a domain name
2. Signing up with an ISP
3. Setting up a website
4. Protecting trade marks
5. Advertising online
6. Web linking
7. Selling online
8. Defective goods
9. Data protection
10. Employment
11. Tax
12. Competition law

Cross-references appear throughout this chapter to other areas of the book in which particular legal issues are dealt with in more depth.

Meet Trading Company Limited

In 1990 Trading Company Limited was incorporated in the UK. Since that time the company has been successfully selling widgets through its twenty UK retail outlets.

Despite the fact that the widget industry is thriving, Trading Company Limited has experienced a reduction in turnover during the past twelve months. It is therefore prompted to conduct a customer survey to ascertain the reasons for that downturn.

The results of the survey reveal that the way the market operates has changed. Many of Trading Company's competitors now operate websites, selling their widgets online. Unfortunately for Trading Company, many of its previous customers have been lost to such competitors, as they find it less expensive and more convenient to shop online.

Trading Company Limited's board meet to discuss the survey results and come up with a plan to become more competitive and to recoup lost sales. After much discussion, the board decided on a web strategy, which will involve it setting up a website to promote its products and sell its widgets. Additionally, it decided that advertising on its new site might be a good way to generate additional revenue for the online business. However, the board was not sure of the best way to proceed. This chapter charts their progress.

1. Obtaining a domain name

1.1 Some domain name basics

What is a domain name?

A domain name is a unique Internet Protocol (IP) address in an easy-to-remember alphabetical form. IP addresses are individual 32-bit numbers used to identify computers connected to the internet. A computer user will type a domain name into a web browser to locate a particular website. The computer will translate the domain name into the IP address, retrieve the data (text and pictures, etc.) forming the website from the computer on which it is stored and display it on the user's own computer. The various elements of a domain name are discussed in chapter 7.

Why should I register a domain name?

The ideal domain name provides an address for a company's website which is easy for its customers to remember. Domain names are typically allocated by the domain name registrars on a first come, first served basis.

Like company names and logos, domain names can be effective marketing tools and become valuable assets in themselves. This is particularly the case where the company is, or becomes, synonymous with the domain, e.g. ebay.co.uk, scoot.co.uk, or lastminute.com. More generic domains can also be valuable: cinema.com fetched $700,000, if.com $1,000,000 and business.com $7,500,000.

How do I choose a domain name?
- You cannot register a domain name if it has already been registered. To find out which domain names have been taken and by whom you can do a 'whois' search (see chapter 7). Alternatively, an Internet Service Provider (ISP) might be able to suggest some appropriate domain names that are available. See www.whois.net/suggest.cgi.
- You should not register a domain name in bad faith (see chapter 7) or in order to 'cyber squat'.

1.2 How do I register a domain name?

ISPs
You can register a domain name online through an accredited ISP, who will deal with the registration requirements on your behalf, and will often provide domain name hosting services. See www.icann.org/registrars/accredited-list.html, www.nominet.org.uk/Members/ListOfMembers/ListOfMembers.html and chapter 7. It is important to remember that an ISP will act as agent between you and the relevant registrar. Therefore, in registering a domain name, you will, in effect, be entering into two contracts: between you and the registrar in respect of the registration of the domain name, and between you and the ISP in respect of any additional services provided by the ISP (such as e-mail). The registrar is not a party to the second contract and therefore has no power over these provisions.

The specific information which a registrar will require will vary to some extent. However, it will include:

- name, address and contact details of the person or company the domain name is to be registered to;
- name, address and contact details for any queries, etc.;
- name, address and contact details for billing details:

It is important to ensure that the details submitted are accurate, as any inaccuracies will delay or invalidate the registration process.

Costs
Registration charges vary between ISPs. Typically, for a one year registration, you could expect to pay approximately £40 for a .co.uk and £50 for a .com.

Time

It usually takes between 24 and 48 hours, although a .com can take up to five days. Once registered, it can take up to 36 hours before your domain name is fully visible across the internet.

1.3 Someone has already registered my choice of domain name – what can I do?

How do I find out who has registered my choice of domain name?

You can perform a 'Whois search' to discover the contact details of the registrant. This search is not reliant on whether a website has been constructed at the domain name in question. Website addresses for some Whois search engines are included in chapter 7.

First come, first served

Traditionally, domain names are registered on a first come, first served basis. However, this has meant that some companies have discovered that they have been too late to register their name as a domain name. Unlike trade marks, where the same mark can be owned by two or more people in any of 45 different classes, there is no equivalent system for domain names. Therefore, where a domain name has been registered and is being used in good faith, a complainant may well be unable to force a transfer of that name.

Obviously, as a first step, it is important to work out the use to which the domain name is being put. This is simply a matter of viewing the website through a browser. You then have the following options. They are discussed in greater detail in chapter 7.

Buy the domain name

You could investigate the possibility of buying the name from the registrant, although if the registrant is a cybersquatter you may be able to obtain the domain name through other means.

The courts

If you have enforceable trade mark rights that pre-date the registration of the domain name, you may be able to sue the registrant to achieve a transfer of a domain name that is identical or similar to your registered trade mark. If you do not have registered trade mark rights, it may be possible to rely on unregistered rights in a claim for passing off. However, in a situation where you do not have a well-known mark or a reputation under the relevant name in the UK, it is likely to be difficult to obtain an order from the court that the registrant transfer the domain name to you.

Dispute resolution procedures

Alternatively, you may decide to follow the dispute resolution procedures of the relevant registration authorities, which are incorporated into the agreements with the registrants. This can be cheaper and quicker than going to court, although it is not suitable for all cases.

2. Signing up with an ISP

2.1 What is an ISP?

An ISP is a company that provides third party access to the internet. It is front-end access to all that the internet offers and is made up of a network of servers, routers and modems attached to a permanent high-speed internet 'backbone' connection. Businesses can simply use their modem to connect to the ISP, which then links them to the internet automatically.

Although the prices and facilities of ISPs differ, they should all offer some standard services such as 24-hour internet access, a unique e-mail address for your company, storage space for your own website and basic software programs for browsing the internet.

ISPs (also called online information providers) can potentially provide extra services such as access to databases of business information.

2.2 What should you look for in selecting a particular ISP?

The choice and number of ISPs is immense. It is recommended that businesses choose an ISP that is a member of an industry association, for example, an organisation such as the ISPA (Internet Service Providers Association http://www.ispa.org.uk/). This is because ISPA members sign up to a code of conduct, which is intended to ensure that they will provide a certain level of service and abide by an industry-approved set of standards as well as providing for a standard complaints procedure.

Such industry associations are useful if you have a complaint against your ISP as they have a high rate of success in solving any problems between customers and ISPA members without the need to enter into any official legal proceedings. If your ISP is not a member of an industry association, although it is possible to refer any problems to the local Trading Standards office, this is likely to be a more time-consuming process and more expensive since in all probability legal advice will be required.

Since ISPs offer different services it will depend on your business requirements which of these you most want to take advantage of. As a general rule, almost all ISPs act as e-mail hosts and allow access to the internet (see below on what to look for in an agreement with your ISP for hosting and access). Some also act as content providers and gather together useful information, which can be accessed by their subscribers only.

The larger ISPs have their own high-speed leased lines so that they are less dependent on the telecommunications providers in order to provide a better service to their customers.

2.3 What to look for in an ISP agreement

The following checklist sets out some of the key factors to consider before signing an ISP agreement:

- *Price*: What set-up/on-going fees are payable? Do you get unlimited access for your price?
- *Reliability and service availability*: Is it a well-established and well-regarded ISP? Is its size or quality of service offered appropriate for your business? Does it offer guarantees of availability of access or connectivity that will be sufficient for your business requirements?
- *What security measures are in place*? An ISP should at the very least have secure servers and encryption technology for transmission of your information to ensure it is safeguarded.
- *Features*: Do you have sufficient available bandwidth and web space for your business purposes? Check any restrictions on storage space for websites or e-mails. What is the user-to-modem ratio and what type of connection does the ISP use to the internet?
- *Support, service levels and response times*: You should ensure that there is 24-hour support service with sufficient response and repair targets. Check if the ISP has included any permitted downtime, and if so, whether the times are acceptable.
- *Cancellation*: If you are unhappy with the service, are there any cancellation charges or options for a refund?
- *Law enforcement requirements*: Given the current climate, it is likely that an ISP will reserve the right to forward your user details to the police or regulatory authorities when requested for law enforcement or compliance purposes.
- *Content*: Where you are providing content for your business site, it is likely that a contract will include restrictions/exclude liability for your content.
- *Website development*: You can either use your ISP or a specialist developer to develop your website to your specification. Website development is detailed in section 3 below.

2.4 Acceptable use policies

An ISP contract will normally incorporate an acceptable use policy. This consists of guidelines relating to misuse of the service by anyone other than the ISP. Typically, this will include any online behaviour of a criminal, libellous, defamatory, obscene, pornographic, threatening, abusive or illegal nature, as well as the use of the service to spread unsolicited e-mail ('spam'). It will generally exclude all liability on behalf of the ISP for such behaviour and will explicitly state that you should comply with its acceptable use policy.

You should pass these requirements on to your users, especially as there may be ISP sanctions associated with a breach of the guidelines, for example, suspension or termination of the service, or compensation or an 'indemnity' may also be payable for any loss suffered by the ISP associated with such breach of the guidelines.

2.5 Use of website 'chat rooms'

If your ISP hosts a chat room or bulletin board for use by your staff or external partners, you must be prepared to accept responsibility for illegal or offensive material (see chapter 4). You should, therefore, make sure your employees or any other users of your website who are posting information in the 'chat room' are aware of these restrictions and comply with them. This can be achieved by including specific terms of use and disclaimer statements on the website – these terms must be clearly visible to users and must be in plain English.

3. Setting up a website

Trading Company Limited now has a domain name and an agreement with an ISP. Before it can trade online it will need to design and create its website, taking into account at all times its web strategy and any legal requirements associated with the operation of the website.

Unless a business has its own skilled IT personnel, it will usually outsource the development work to a website developer, who will design, build and possibly host the website. Trading Company Limited does not have the internal skills to develop its own site so is looking to an external developer to carry out the design and development work.

3.1 What type of website?

First impressions are very important.

- *'Brochure ware' websites*: These act as a product or services brochure. The key thing is to ensure that the navigation and design makes the site attractive and easy to use. Over the past few years research has shown that web users want sites to be informative, easy to navigate and fast to load. Avoid using gimmicks, introductory 'movies' or flash/animated graphics, especially if they don't add to the experience.

- *A content-rich site*: This contains useful information that encourages repeat visitors. Depending on the perceived value of information, it is often wise to control access to it by use of a simple registration and password login feature. This also means you gather data on users and can keep in touch with them.

- *E-commerce site*: If your products or services are suitable, you can choose a full e-commerce site, where customers can order online. This clearly entails greater development in terms of checkout procedures and it is essential that any order processing is secure.

Trading Company Limited must ensure it selects the correct developer to assist with these decisions. Practically, Trading Company Limited should meet several developers before selecting one that it feels it can work with closely. It should also ask to see examples of the developers' work and obtain references from past clients.

Trading Company Limited wishes to maximise its potential customer base by ensuring that its online information is accessible to visually impaired people. Trading Company Limited's HR director is also keen to comply with The Disability Discrimination Act 1995, which places duties on those providing goods, facilities and services not to discriminate against people with disabilities. Trading Company Limited's HR director is familiar with the Royal National Institute of the Blind's (RNIB) 'See it Right' campaign (www. rnib.org.uk), and is keen for the chosen website designer to follow the RNIB's recommended content accessibility guidelines (see www.w3.org/WAI/ resources/).

3.2 Is an agreement necessary?

It is tempting for both parties to start work on the website design and development without signing a written contract. However, this is ill advised. Once work has begun it will become increasingly difficult for Trading Company Limited to extricate itself from working with the developer if the website specification is not met.

Trading Company Limited should be wary of signing the developer's standard terms and conditions which will be favourable to the developer. These can be reviewed and amended, or alternatively Trading Company Limited may prepare its own terms and conditions based on its requirements, which will then be ready for negotiation with the developer. This may appear to be holding up the progress of the website development, but ultimately will be worth it.

3.3 Will Trading Company Limited need a detailed website specification?

Trading Company Limited will need to develop a website specification, which will set out what it wants the website to do and how it will do it. This may include how it wants the website to look and feel, so if particular colours and fonts are required, these should be stated in the specification.

If you require password registration, information sign-up or other customer interactive features such as e-mail, 'my account details', or call-back functionality, you will need to describe and specify this in as much detail as possible, in order for the developer to: a) quote and b) write the code required. In addition, since Trading Company Limited will be selling over the internet, security of the website, importantly keeping the financially sensitive material of its customers secure, will be need to be addressed.

The specification is a key document – it is against this that the performance of the developer is measured.

3.4 How much will it cost?

The price may include not only the website development work but also any charges for future hosting and support and maintenance, if these are to be provided. Where possible Trading Company Limited will wish to ensure that the price is payable only on the website meeting the requirements set out in the specification. Alternatively, part-payment can be made against achieved milestones set out in the contract.

Judging whether the specification has been met can be achieved by means of a clear acceptance testing procedure. Failure to meet the acceptance tests can lead to a variety of remedies:

- the developer is usually given a grace period within which to make any necessary changes to meet the specification;
- liquidated damages (usually either payment or service credits) may be payable for delays to the 'go live' date – please note that these damages will only be enforceable if they are a genuine pre-estimate of Trading Company Limited's losses; and
- repeated failure of the acceptance tests may result in termination of the contract.

3.5 IPR ownership

The development agreement must clarify who owns the intellectual property rights (IPRs) in the website. This will be the main area of value in the website and is certainly central to the ability of Trading Company Limited to exploit fully its use of the website both now and in the future.

It is a common misconception that when a party has paid for an external consultant to design and build a website, or even to create a piece of bespoke software, that all the IPRs in the website or software automatically belong to the commissioning party. This is not accurate, since under the Copyright, Designs and Patent Act 1988 (CDPA) the IPRs (in this case copyright) in the commissioned work will belong to the creator of the work (subject to any trusts that the commissioner may be able to allege) unless they are assigned (i.e. transferred) to the commissioning party by the developer in writing.

Unless there are some underlying IPRs of the developer/third party in the website (use of which should be licensed indefinitely to Trading Company Limited – see below), an assignment of all IPRs in the website from the developer to Trading Company Limited must be included in the website development agreement.

Below is a more detailed analysis of the possible IPRs associated with the development of the website.

Copyright

The main IPR that arises in the development of a website is copyright. Separate copyright will arise in the following: overall design, the page templates, written text of the website; photographs and graphics; sound recordings and musical works; animation and film footage; and the computer program which runs the website. In each case the work must be original work if it is to be copyright protected. In fact, a copy of an existing work will not be granted copyright protection and is likely to infringe another party's copyright.

Trade marks

Please refer to section 4 below, which discusses trade marks in more detail.

Patents

Although computer software is not patentable in the UK, an invention implemented by means of a computer program is patentable so long as the technical aspect of the invention represents an inventive step previously unknown.

Database rights

Database rights were introduced by the Database Directive. A database can attract copyright protection where the selection and arrangement of content is the result of 'personal intellectual creativity'. In addition, or alternatively, if the database does not attract copyright protection, there may be available a database right, which is not linked to creativity but requires substantial investment in obtaining, verifying or presenting the content.

Background IPR and foreground IPR

A further complication is that IPR in a website can be divided into two elements: pre-existing IPR and new IPR, known also as background and foreground IPR.

- *Background IPR*: The pre-existing or background IPR will usually be made up of content which is owned by Trading Company Limited, or licensed to it by a third party and pre-existing software and tools which are owned by the developer, or licensed to it from a third party, and used in the development and operation of the website.
- *Foreground IPR*: The new IPR will usually be made up of the software, tools and content that the developer creates specifically for Trading Company Limited, either at its request or in the course of developing the website in accordance with the specification.

Ownership of background and foreground IPRs

Clearly, Trading Company Limited will want to obtain ownership of all the IPRs associated with the development and operation of its new website, but in practice this may not happen for the simple reason that the developer's own business is built around the use and re-use of elements of its background IPR. In addition, where any third party software or content is included in the website, the third party owner will not want to transfer ownership of its 'crown jewels' to the website operator.

In this instance, Trading Company Limited should secure a non-exclusive, world-wide, royalty-free, perpetual licence from the developer (or possibly the third party owner) to use its and the third party's background IPR.

Trading Company Limited will, however, require an assignment to it of the foreground IPR in the development agreement.

Where Trading Company Limited already owns any background IPR (e.g. its content, logos, etc.), it must ensure that it does not unwittingly assign these rights to the developer in the agreement. The developer can be licensed to use Trading Company Limited's background IPR solely in connection with the development work.

Warranties in respect of the background/foreground IPR

In the development agreement Trading Company Limited will need to protect itself as fully as possible against possible infringement of the IPRs of a third party through the operation of its website. This can be achieved in the agreement by securing warranties from the developer that the use by Trading Company Limited of the background and foreground IPRs will not infringe the IPRs of any third party and that if Trading Company Limited suffers any loss in respect of any alleged or actual infringement, the developer will indemnify Trading Company Limited against such loss.

Moral rights

In addition, the development agreement should include an express waiver of the developer's moral rights in respect of any copyright (but excluding copyright in any computer programs since it is not applicable) assigned under the agreement.

Escrow

Where any background software of the developer or any specialist third party software is licensed to Trading Company, it is advisable to enter into an escrow agreement, to enable Trading Company to access the source code in certain key circumstances, e.g. the insolvency or failure of the developer to maintain and support the software. An escrow agreement is usually between the licensor, the licensee and a third party (e.g. The National Computing Centre: www. ncc.co.uk).

Additional costs will have to be borne by Trading Company Limited to set up and maintain the escrow agreement but where non-proprietary software is fundamental to the operations of a business, it is money well spent!

4. Trade marks

In addition to its existing marks, Trading Company Limited wishes to use a new trade mark specifically for its website. There are a number of issues regarding the choice, clearance for use and protection of any new trade mark that it will need to consider before doing so. Changes in the somewhat unlikely field of design law introduced by the Community Design Regulation (Council Regulation (EC) 6/2002) mean that Trading Company Limited should also consider this area as well. Once it has decided on the trade mark that it intends to use, the company will need to deal with registration procedures and put in place a strategy to ensure that its rights are protected and properly used.

4.1 What is a trade mark?

The UK Trade Marks Act 1994 defines a trade mark as any sign that can distinguish the goods and services of one trader from those of another and be represented graphically. Traditionally, the term 'trade mark' identifies a mark that is used in respect of goods. 'Service mark', as its name suggests, is a mark used in relation to services. The term 'trade mark' is used here to include both trade marks and service marks. Essentially, a trade mark is used as a marketing tool so that customers can recognise the product or services of a particular trader. A trade mark may consist of words, logos, slogans, three-dimensional shapes and sometimes sounds and smells. The apparent breadth of what can function as a trade mark may even include trade marks that give the appearance of motion such as an icon that 'morphs' or moves on screen. Trade marks are divided into 45 internationally agreed classes of goods and services (see http://patent.gov. uk/tm/reference/&search/index.htm). It may be necessary to obtain a registration in one or more classes depending upon the goods and services in which Trading Company Limited is interested.

National trade marks

Each country has its own national trade mark registry. In general, a national trade mark registration is only valid in that particular country to which it relates. Before applying for or using its new trade mark, Trading Company Limited should carry out a search in all the countries in which it intends to trade to avoid any conflict with pre-existing national rights, bearing in mind that a website has a global reach, unless access can be restricted to certain territories. Details of searches are detailed below.

Community trade marks (CTM)

The European Union operates an EU-wide trade mark system: this means that a CTM is valid across all twenty-five member states (however, Monaco is excluded). A CTM is competitively priced when compared to filing separate applications in the national registries. The downside is that if it fails in one country, it fails in all twenty-five, although it is possible to convert the application into separate national applications.

International trade marks

The World Intellectual Property Organisation operates an international trade mark system known as the 'Madrid Protocol'. This provides an economical, simple and centralised application method for obtaining international protection of trade marks. Such a trade mark will be valid in certain countries which can be nominated by the applicant, including the UK, US (since November 2003) and the European Union (as of 1 October 2004). This can be cheaper than applying for individual national trade marks. However, an international mark can be filed only once a 'home' or national application has been made and the mark applied for must be the same as that in the home application, and for the same goods or services.

Community designs

The Community Design Regulations came into force in March 2002 and creates a new 'Community Design' that is similar in many respects to the Community Trade Mark. This allows for the registration of the appearance of all or part of a 'product', with 'product' being defined broadly as including 'get-up and graphic symbols' and 'packaging'. Trading Company Limited should consider this as an adjunct to formal trade mark protection.

What is a good trade mark?

In choosing its new trade mark, Trading Company Limited would be advised to settle on a trade mark that:

- can be registered;
- will function as a good business tool; and
- does not conflict with existing third party rights.

Invented words, devices or trade marks that consist of arbitrary words, which are not descriptive or suggestive of the goods or services they cover, are the best trade marks.

What is a bad trade mark?

A 'bad' trade mark is one which cannot be registered, or which may conflict with third party rights, e.g. a mark that is:

- the same or similar to a trade mark that someone else uses with similar goods or services;
- not capable of distinguishing goods or services from those of your competitors;
- devoid of any distinctive character;
- descriptive of the kind, quality, quantity, intended purpose, value, geographical origin or other characteristics of the goods or services;
- in customary usage (i.e. generic);
- contrary to public policy;
- made up of laudatory words, that is, expressing or containing praise, e.g. 'The Best of . . .';
- made up of words in common usage, e.g. 'war', 'car'.

Trading Company Limited should try to avoid adopting a mark like this. This is because, unless it is able to show that it is using the mark honestly and concurrently with another trader, not only will it be prevented from registering that word as a trade mark, it may also be sued for trade mark infringement by the other trader.

In some situations it may be possible to obtain consent from the owner of the other mark to defeat an objection from the Trade Marks Registry to register the mark. However, consents are often refused or are sometimes offered at a very high price, and generally take a long time to secure.

Also, until that word becomes synonymous with its goods through *use* (which can take five years or more), the protection that will be afforded to such a mark will be weak: it will not be granted a trade mark registration; and will not acquire exclusive rights in the mark. (This means that it will not be able to prevent its competitors from using the same mark.)

4.2 Trade mark registration

Searches

Before applying for or using its new mark, Trading Company Limited should carry out a trade mark search to determine whether a third party has already registered an identical or similar mark for the same or similar goods or services or is using an identical or similar trade mark without either registering it or applying to do so. The types of search available are:

Identical-only search

This will identify registered marks only or pending applications that are identical to Trading Company Limited's chosen mark for identical goods or services. It will not identify similar marks for similar goods or services. However, this provides a relatively quick and inexpensive method of determining whether its chosen mark has already been registered. Such searches are often carried out at the design stage to help eliminate any proposed trade marks that might be clearly objectionable were they to be used or applied for.

Full search

This will identify all marks that are identical and similar to the chosen mark for goods and services in all classes. Ideally, a full search should be carried out prior to any application being submitted or any use of the trade mark being made.

Common law search

Neither an identical-only search nor a full search will identify any marks which have not been registered, but which are nevertheless being used. In the UK in particular, the owner of such a mark may have 'common law rights' and therefore may be able to prevent Trading Company Limited from using its chosen mark. Although it is possible to perform a 'common law search', it is not possible to search all sources cost-effectively, so they cannot be guaranteed or treated as definitive.

4.3 Registration procedures

Registration procedures vary from country to country. However, as a general guide once a trade mark application has been submitted to the relevant registry it will be examined by that registry to determine whether the mark is capable of registration (e.g. whether it is descriptive of the goods or services for which it has been applied for, and whether there is a prior mark which is identical or confusingly similar to the proposed mark for identical or similar goods or services). If the application is accepted by the registry, the mark is published in a trade mark journal and interested third parties will have a period of time (three months in the UK and under the Community Trade Mark) to oppose the application. If there are no oppositions, the mark will be registered shortly thereafter.

4.4 Using trade marks

Trade marks can be a very valuable asset. A trade mark can distinguish Trading Company Limited's goods and services from those of its competitors. It is vital, that it uses its trade marks correctly to ensure that they receive the maximum protection possible, and do not become vulnerable to challenge by a third party.

Trading Company Limited should remember the following:

- Ensure the trade mark is continually used.
- Always use the trade mark in the same format to that in which it was registered. When the appearance of the trade mark changes, any new or revised form should be registered.
- Use the appropriate trade mark symbol in each country where the trade mark is used/registered. For example:

  ® if the trade mark is registered;

  ™ if the trade mark is not registered.

However, if its website is available in many different territories, Trading Company Limited should list those countries it is registered in and those where it is not.

4.5 Protection of trade marks

An unregistered trade mark can be protected by the law of 'passing off' in the UK, or the laws of 'unfair competition' in other jurisdictions. In its most simple form, these laws mean that a trader may be able to prevent the same or similar mark (or 'get-up') which he uses on his goods or services from being used on the same or similar goods or services by another trader. However, an action for passing off or unfair competition can be expensive and time-consuming as there are various evidential hurdles which have to be jumped.

By contrast, obtaining a registration of a trade mark and protecting that trade mark once registered can be relatively simple and economical. For example, a trade mark owner does not have to prove that it owns the trade mark as it can rely on the entry in a relevant national Trade Marks Register as proof of ownership. Furthermore, the complainant does not need to prove confusion where there is 'classic' trade mark infringement, that is, where an identical mark is affixed to identical goods or services.

Trade mark registration is purely territorial and in order to obtain maximum protection a registration must be obtained in each territory in which the goods and services are used. In the European Union a trader can apply for a 'Community Trade Mark' (see above). In the US, it is possible to obtain one or more State registrations providing protection in those States, or a Federal trade mark which provides protection in all States.

4.6 How else can Trading Company Limited stop infringements of its trade mark rights?

Trading Company Limited should stop infringement of its trade mark rights as quickly as possible when these come to its attention. The longer an infringement is allowed to continue, the more damage will be done to its trade mark rights. If infringement is allowed to continue for too long a period, Trading Company Limited may be unable to enforce its rights against the infringer.

Trading Company Limited should also consider using a trade mark watch service. A trade mark agent will usually provide this service by reviewing the trade mark journals and looking out for applications to register identical or similar marks in the UK and overseas. This will give it the opportunity to try to prevent the registration (and use) of similar marks.

5. Advertising online

5.1 Deciding to introduce advertising

Allowing other companies, individuals, clubs or groups to advertise their products or services on your site can generate revenue for your business. When setting up and maintaining your website this revenue can contribute towards the costs of running and development. It should be noted however that few sites rely solely on the income generated from advertising to fund their entire online business.

5.2 First step

Once the decision to introduce advertising is made, the first step you need to take is to communicate the decision. Just because you have decided to make advertisement space available on your site doesn't mean that people will automatically know that your site sells advertising space. Therefore, you need to do some advertising of your own. Prominently display the advertising opportunities available on your site, and until your advertisement programme takes off, use the spaces designated for advertisements to advertise your own services or products.

In order to attract advertisers to your site you should work towards:

- standing out from other sites;
- offering advertising space that meets the needs of advertisers;
- building relationships with potential advertisers;
- developing a pricing structure and terms that work for you and your potential advertisers; and
- keeping up-to-date with technological developments so that your site can carry all types of advertisements.

Alternatively, rather than selling advertisement space on your site yourself, you could join an advertising network, such as fastclick.com or burstmedia.com. These networks connect advertisers and sites by buying and selling a high volume of adverts, in return for a commission (which can be as high as 50 per cent). A further alternative could be to join a free banner exchange – these are exchanges where each member agrees to run adverts from other members on their site, and in return their advert is displayed on other members' sites. These are attractive where you are more interested in driving traffic to your site as opposed to generating revenue.

5.3 Advertising agreements

For any advertising that you attract to your site, an agreement should be signed by the parties involved to cover the terms under which the advertisement appears. The agreement should cover such things as how the advertisement is to be paid for, practicalities such as the size of the advertisement, where it is to be positioned and whose responsibility it should be to ensure compliance with the relevant laws governing the advertisement.

This section looks at the clauses that should be included in the terms and conditions of an online advertising agreement. The terms look at the best position for the owner of the website as opposed to that of a potential advertiser.

5.4 Terms of payment

The terms of payment clause will be one of the most important in the agreement as it will set out how you are to be paid for the advertising that appears on your site.

There are a variety of ways in which payment for advertisements can be structured. These include:

Flat fee	a set amount charged either monthly or yearly for advertisement placement on a site
Cost per click (CPC)	the price of placing an advertisement on a site is determined by how many times the advertisement is clicked on by users
Cost per lead (CPL)	the price of placing an advertisement on a site is based on how many leads the advertisement generates for the advertiser
Cost per sale (CPS)	the price of placing an advertisement on a site is determined according to how many sales result from the advertisement
Costs per thousand (CPM)	advertiser is charged a set fee for every 1,000 impressions of their advertisement delivered on a site

To decide which method is best for you and appropriate for your site, you need to take a realistic look at the value of the advertising you are offering.

To do this you should consider the following:

Site audience

Most sites cater for an identifiable group, for example teens, people with an interest in a certain hobby, people of a particular profession, and so on. Such targeted sites create access to niche markets for advertisers. It may therefore be possible to charge a higher rate if your site is the best opportunity for advertisers to reach a particular audience.

Types of advertising offered

Advertising on sites can appear in a number of different formats, for example through sponsorship of a site or the more traditional form of banner advertisements. The vast majority of sites use a form of banner advertisement. Banners vary in size and style and can be, for instance, full banners, half banners, vertical banners, buttons or micro buttons. Full banners obviously tend to be charged at a higher rate than buttons or micro buttons. Other common formats include pop-ups, pop-under, invue (where an inline advert scrolls into the center of the browser window) and interstitial (full page adverts launched between pages, where the user is returned back to the next page after viewing the advert).

Positioning and number of advertisements

If an advertisement is to be prominently displayed, or is to be the only advertisement to appear on the page, its impact will be greater and subsequently its worth to the advertiser greater.

It is more common for high traffic sites to sell their advertising packages on a CPM basis, whereas lower traffic sites tend to price using the flat rate.

For sites in the process of being developed or updated that require advertisers to provide some of the working capital for their site building, a flat rate has some advantages. In particular, it allows for earlier invoicing for the relevant advertisement than the calculation of methods such as CPC and CPL allow.

As with agreements for other services, the payment clause should include details of when you are to invoice, whether VAT is included in the price quoted, and whether interest is to be charged for late payment.

Whichever method is chosen, it is recommended that as much detail of the pay structure as possible is provided in the agreement so as to avoid uncertainty.

5.5 Licensing

Intellectual property rights

Intellectual property rights (IPRs) in any advertisement will (usually) be owned by the advertiser or by its creative agency, and it will usually incorporate specific items that are the advertiser's intellectual property, for example their trade mark. Under the agreement you will be required to carry the advertisement and therefore it is likely that you have an implied licence to display the trade mark on the site. However, it is also common in online advertising agreements to expressly state that you have a licence giving you permission to display the trade mark and other intellectual property in the advertisement. This acts as an added protection for you as the site owner, and clarifies the extent of your licence.

Type of licence required to reproduce and display the advertisement

The licence referred to should be a world-wide licence as access to your site can be achieved through a computer with internet access in any country in the world.

The licence should also be non-exclusive as you do not want, or need, to prevent the advertiser from using their own trade mark elsewhere, for whatever means they choose.

Screen shots

Once you have developed your website you may choose to publicise its existence through reproducing in paper format, for example, pages from the site, or incorporating images from the site in advertising for your own business.

In order to reproduce the page ('screenshot') as it appears on the site, the licence you obtain from the advertiser needs to cover your use of screen shots. Without such a licence you will need to edit the printed page so as not to infringe the advertiser's IPRs.

Trade marks and copyright are more specifically dealt with above.

5.6 Data protection

Depending on the type of advertisement (e.g. interactive or html banners which allow for the input of data) it may be possible for personal data to be collected about visitors and customers. If this is the case, the agreement should deal with the obligations of the parties concerning data protection and privacy to ensure compliance with the Data Protection Act 1998. Data protection is discussed more fully in chapter 3.

5.7 Legislation

There is no single statute that codifies the laws applying to advertising. There are, however, numerous legislative provisions that impact on this area that online advertisers need to comply with. Relevant legislation is discussed in chapter 6.

Similarly, industry self-regulatory codes need to be considered. The Advertising Standards Authority (ASA) has confirmed that its code of practice applies to some forms of advertising and promotion on the internet, and in particular to banner advertisements. See chapter 6 for further details of the code and how it applies.

As part of the terms and conditions, the parties should state who is responsible for compliance with these laws and codes, so that both parties are aware of whose obligation this is.

5.8 Advertisers' obligations under the agreement

Applicable law/regulations

The advertiser should be required to give assurances regarding the advertisement it has produced. It should be asked to warrant that:

- the advertisement does not violate any applicable law or regulation; and
- it has complied with the code of practice issued by the Committee of Advertising Practice in the UK in respect of electronic and online advertising and all other relevant industry codes of practice.

Third parties' rights

As noted above, it is common for the advertiser to grant a licence for intellectual property use. In order to ensure you have some right of redress in the event of third party claims, the advertiser should be required to warrant that it has the right to publish all of the contents of the advertisement and can lawfully grant you such a right. The advertiser should also confirm that the advertisement does not infringe any other rights of third parties including all IPRs and rights of privacy.

Financial promotions

In the UK, a person is prohibited from communicating an invitation or induce-ment to engage in investment activity unless that person is an authorised person or the communication has been approved by an authorised person (as defined by the Financial Services and Markets Act 2000 (the Act)). Failure to comply with this provision is a criminal offence. It is therefore important to have the advertiser warrant that the advertisement either:

- does not constitute a financial promotion under the Act; or
- has been approved by an authorised person or is otherwise permitted under the Act.

Where financial services advertisements are carried, it is also prudent to put in place compliance systems to ensure that all advertisements are properly signed off by the relevant compliance officer(s) within the advertiser's business.

Indemnity

To give additional teeth to the warranties that the advertisement does not breach relevant laws or codes, does not infringe any third party rights and does not breach the Act, advertisers should also be required to indemnify you against any claim resulting from the advertisement. This should ideally extend to holding you harmless against any expenses (including legal costs), damages or losses (including loss of profit) in connection with any claims arising from the advertisement.

5.9 Limitation of liability

Having covered the advertiser's obligations and duties, you should state in the agreement what your liability to the advertiser will be. In particular, you should state what the consequences will be if you fail to publish an advertise-ment or deliver the advertisement for the required amount of time. You should aim to limit your liability as you would not wish to be responsible for the costs of a whole advertising campaign or any indirect or consequential loss that the advertiser claims. It is common to find terms providing that liability is expressly limited to publishing the advertisement or a replacement advertise-ment, or refunding the advertising fee. While one cannot say with certainty that it would always satisfy the requirement of reasonableness in the Unfair Contract Terms Act 1977, it is probably not a bad position for most website owners to adopt in practice.

5.10 Usage statistics

In return for paying to advertise on the site, the advertiser may typically want assurance on a range of issues, in particular the number of visitors to the site. However, it can be difficult to measure the exact number of visitors to a site due to such practices as the creation of web caches (whereby ISPs store copies of popular sites for access by their customers) and mirror sites around the internet to improve access times. It is also an issue over which the host party has no control. It is therefore advisable to note in the terms and conditions that any usage statistics referred to or discussed are estimates only, and that no guarantee is given with regard to usage.

5.11 Format of advertisements, etc.

The terms and conditions should set out practical considerations such as the format in which the advertiser should provide the advertisement. This can help avoid situations where you may have to reject the advertisement (if the agreement allows) or spend time converting it into the correct format in order to carry the advertisement. Provisions dealing with operational requirements should ideally deal with format, file size, manner of transmission between the parties, lead-time prior to publication and any other relevant technical or operational specifications.

From the point of view of the website owner, it is advisable to allow for rejections of the advertisement if the advertiser does not comply with the relevant requirements (see below).

5.12 Positioning

Discretion as to positioning of advertisement
It is usual for the website owner to retain the right to decide where to position an advert within their site. However, as with all agreements, this will be open to negotiation depending on the bargaining power of the parties.

Competitors' advertisements
The agreement terms may also include a provision dealing with the placement or inclusion of advertisements for an advertiser's competitor. As a site owner your main aim is to attract as many advertisers as possible and not limit opportunities. Advertisers, on the other hand, may not want their advertisements

displayed alongside their competitors. The standard position in your advertising terms should be that no exclusivity is granted and that competitors' advertisements may be displayed. However, in certain cases, this position may be varied by express written terms

Any agreed restriction should be limited. It could be stipulated as being, for example, for the length of the agreement or the time during which your site is carrying a particular advertisement. It should also clearly define the categories of competitors who are covered.

5.13 Assignment or resale of advertisement space

In order to maintain control of the advertisements carried on a site, it is possible to include in the agreement a clause that restricts the advertiser from assigning, transferring or reselling any of their rights under the agreement to another party. Without this clause, you may be obliged under contract to carry advertisements that are inappropriate for your site.

This term could also be used to prevent an advertiser with whom you have an agreement making a profit from the sale of advertising space on your site by reselling for more than you charged.

5.14 Right to reject advertisement

As with preventing the right to resell the advertising space, you should keep ultimate control of your website content by retaining a right to reject an advertisement or remove it from the site at any time. The right should not be unreasonably used, but having it will clarify from the beginning the conditions under which an advertisement may be rejected or removed, helping to prevent problems later on.

5.15 Other things to consider

The terms outlined above would be suitable for use in most online advertising agreements. However, when accepting advertisements for your site, special care and consideration should be given to advertisements for products and services that attract specific legislation or codes of conducts. Such products and services include:

- tobacco advertising;
- alcohol advertising;
- advertising aimed at children;
- advertising for medicines and medical products; and
- financial services.

In some cases, such products may not be advertised or are subject to restrictions. Even where an advertisement is permitted, additional terms may have to be incorporated into the agreement. Further details regarding the advertising of specific products and services is dealt with in chapter 6.

Lastly, when considering the content of an online advertising agreement, reference should be made to chapter 1 which deals with contract formation and other relevant clauses, such as jurisdiction and governing law, that need to be included to complete the agreement.

6. Web linking

6.1 Web link – friend or foe?

Links are vital to the interaction between your site and others. internet users use links frequently to access both other websites and to move around a single site. Links are used by search engines to point users and advertisers to your site. A link will build brand awareness and drive potential revenue. But care needs to be taken in implementing and using links.

How links work

A link, at its simplest and most straightforward, is an embedded electronic address, or hypertext link, that points to another web location. The link stores the electronic address of the destination site or page, and clicking on the link sends the address to the browser, which then moves the user to the new destination. The new website is shown in its entirety on the screen, usually with the full web address.

A simple hypertext link, while it has some potential problems, is relatively straightforward. The use of an embedded address is usually viewed as part of the intrinsic structure of the Web. Legal rights to link are granted by an implied licence to link to the second site and reproduce and distribute the material contained on that site. It is only where use of the link creates difficulties for the linked site – for example, by driving so many users to the site that its infrastructure cannot cope, or by encouraging users to copy third party material – that the linked party will want to regulate more formally or prohibit this type of link.

A second type of link is more complex. This link acts as a 'pointer' to a document, image or audio clip (or other content) contained in another website, which 'pulls' in the image, text or audio clip from the other web page into the current web page for display. The user's browser still points to the original site.

It is possible for the material from this form of link to be displayed within the frame or border of a page on the linking website. This type of use is known as 'framing' or 'in-line linking', and content from a number of sites may be pooled on one web page. A banner containing the original site's branding is likely to be viewed along the top and down the side of one or both sides of the linked page. In some cases, all of the linked site's branding is obscured. Many search engines use this type of link to pull images or content into 'thumbnails' that enable the user to open a full size content via a new website or browser. A connection is likely to be created in the mind of the user between the framed material and the linking website, which may dilute or damage the goodwill or branding of the originating business. Use of third party marks or advertising ('ambush marketing') to boost the profile of one site can impact on advertising strategy or contractual commitments, for example, exclusivity agreements.

Action may be taken to prevent this type of link on grounds of passing off (trading on another's goodwill so as to create confusion between businesses), copyright or database infringement. No cases have been finally decided in the English courts but the general weight of legal opinion is that a passing off action may be successful.

In January 2001, Haymarket issued proceedings against Castrol Burmah for passing off, when Castrol framed links from the Haymarket sites, autosport.com and whatcar.com, within a Castrol site, without Haymarket's permission. Castrol dropped the links. In July 2003 restrictions in the US on the use of in-line links by search engines were loosened when the courts overturned a 2002 decision that the creation of new windows to display images linked from third party sites was a copyright infringement. The 2003 ruling upheld the view that there was no copyright infringement where images were taken by a search engine for use in an 'image search' as this was 'fair use', and removed the references to in-line linking being an infringement (*Kelly* v. *Arriba Soft Corp (now Ditto.com)* US Ninth Circuit Court of Appeals, 7 July 2003). This case reflects the view that use of copyright material by search engines is generally beneficial but does not open up the use of these types of links where there is no 'fair use' – and there is unlikely to be fair use if one is linking without permission to the site of a potential competitor.

A related category of link that has been in the forefront of recent disputes is the 'deep link'. This is a type of link which links to material contained on another website, but bypasses its homepage and other proprietary pages, depriving that website of brand recognition. Material accessed by a deep link may be framed with a bundle of other content within a third party website.

In March 2000, Ticketmaster Corp (Corp) brought an action in the US against Tickets.com for deep linking to Corp's website, Ticketmaster Online (*Ticketmaster Corp* v. *Tickets.com*, US District Court, Central District of

California, 54 USPQ 2d 1344 (2000). Tickets.com had created thousands of links, which led users to Ticketmaster online web pages. Corp claimed unfair competition, breach of terms and conditions, unlawful interference (as the linking prevented its website from operating commercially), and passing off (as the user would be confused as to the relationship between the two sites). The judge allowed the claims of passing off and unlawful interference to remain, although he did not allow the claim of unfair competition. He did, however, not exclude the possibility that deep linking could amount to unfair competition in particular circumstances.

The *Stepstone* case (*Stepstone* v. *Ofir*, AZ 280 692/00) highlights the possible danger of a claim for database rights infringement.

Other sub-categories of link include 'page jacking' when users believe they are going to a particular website and are diverted to (for example) a pornographic website; and 'mouse trapping', when users close a page and it takes them to another page, which they cannot exit.

6.2 Practicalities

Linking, even at the simplest level, can create risk for a website owner. The cases demonstrate that there is no clear guidance (as elsewhere on the internet) on the legal and commercial parameters governing their use.

Some businesses have taken the view that the benefits of deep-linking outweigh the risks, but any links should be implemented only with an understanding of the potential liabilities. Preferably sites should play safe and avoid accusations of passing off, unfair competition and trade mark, copyright or database infringement by following basic guidelines.

6.3 Think before you link

If linking:

- Check the sites you are linking to. Are there online terms regulating or restricting links? Has the site owner taken action against third parties before?
- Are you intending to frame or deeplink to material and in what context?
- If framing or deeplinking, minimise risk by:
  a) notifying visitors of the relationship between your site and the linked sites;
  b) identifying third-party trade marks and copyright ownership;
  c) including disclaimers of liability for content and make sure that they are brought to the attention of the user; and
  d) ideally, agreeing a proper linking agreement (see below).

If linked:

- Place notices on your site restricting links. Specify that any links can only be made with prior approval and include an e-mail address for approvals.
- Monitor links to your site.
- Evaluate links. Has any material or trade mark been copied? Is there any possible passing off? Take professional advice if necessary.
- Implement a common gateway interface to encourage linkers to go to an agreed home page.
- Preferably, regulate all deep or framed links with a proper linking agreement.

Example: Site disclaimer

[We] *do not represent or warrant that any information which may be obtained* [on this site] *or through any link to or from this site is accurate, complete or current. We do not accept any responsibility for any loss that may arise as a result of relying upon such information or for any damage caused by software viruses. Material contained in any third party site or web page accessed from this site is outside our control and will be subject to third party intellectual property rights, separate terms of use and policies covering data use and privacy. You are advised to read applicable terms and policies before use of this website or any other.*

If you wish to link to this site please send an e-mail to [e-mail address] *for express authorisation.*

6.4 Linking agreement

A properly drafted linking or framing agreement is the most secure way of lessening risks in linking content in or to your site where content is intended to be incorporated within another web page. It is also likely to be operative in establishing partnership relationships and driving and creating revenues.

From the framer's viewpoint, the agreement should include service levels to ensure that the framed site will be available to the framer's users. Content may be specified, or certain types of content excluded. The display of both parties' branding will need to be considered. If the framed content is to appear as the content of the framer's site, it may be appropriate for the provider to use 'mirror' or 'white-labelled' web pages with a different URL, stripped of all provider branding or other identifiers.

It may be necessary to include development provisions and acceptance procedures if, for example, bespoke web pages are being created. There may in addition be e-commerce add-ons, enabling users of one site to order from the other, possibly with commission payments.

Framing agreements may of course, also be two-way.

6.5 Key provisions for a linking or framing agreement – where one party is framing content taken from another's website

- Include as a schedule a detailed specification of the type of link required and associated service level agreements (SLAs). You may also need to schedule development milestones. The following points are key:
  a) Specify the relevant URLs of the sites. What are the visual requirements? What constitutes the frame (e.g. this may be as simple as a branded banner across the top of the screen)? What URLs are to be visible? Where on the web page is the link to appear? Above the fold (i.e. on the visible screen) or below the fold? Where are scroll bars to appear? Is there to be a menu down one side of the framed material?
  b) If it is necessary to create specially developed web pages or content, who will be responsible for development? Who is paying for development? Set out a timetable for development and acceptance.
- SLAs should specify who has responsibility for maintenance, response times and security provisions, including possibly password access to specific areas of the other's sites.
- The SLAs should also set standard web performance targets for uptime, response times for maintenance, and so on.
- If possible, agree detailed specifications and SLAs before entering into the agreement. It is these areas that are most likely to give rise to a dispute later – and signing an agreement where these issues are 'to be agreed' will weaken its effectiveness.

Branding

- What use is to be made of the other party's trade marks? Specify what trade marks or logos are to be used.
- Where are these to appear? Are all trade marks cleared for use? Potential infringement liabilities may be lessened by obtaining warranties and indemnities from the other party, but it is also sensible to ask the question at the start.
- Are there to be express acknowledgements of trade mark ownership on the web page incorporating the link?
- From the point of view of the trade mark owner, an acknowledgement of trade mark ownership should be included, either on the page or by a further hypertext link.

Intellectual property right licences

- Has each party reserved rights in their own intellectual property rights and granted a licence of copyright or trade marks to the other party, for the purposes of the link?
- An express grant of rights is important in defining the scope of use that the other party is entitled to make.
- Ensure that suitable copyright notifications appear in any content provided or on linked web pages.

Controls and approvals

- What control is each party to have over the other party's site or content?
- Is one party allowed to veto certain types of content or third party links?
- What practical arrangements are needed to approve content? Copy may be submitted by e-mail 24 hours before posting, possibly combined with an editorial right to amend copy when posted. Include a right to amend if either party is made aware of any infringement or regulatory breach.
- If links to third party sites (or corporate intranets of either party) are envisaged, where are the links to be held?
- Is the linking arrangement to be exclusive between the parties in relation to a particular area of trade? This type of provision may at first sight be attractive, but may limit the potential usefulness of a site to users, who wish to see a wide range of links.

Data use and protection

- What use is either party to be allowed to make of the other party's data? Is particular use of data to be prohibited? For example, it may be preferable for data to be used on an aggregated basis within either party's entire database, not targeted as a specific visitor sector.
- Provisions should cover compliance with data protection legislation, ensuring, for example, that both parties have a full online privacy policy and that all necessary consents are obtained from users to transfer of data.

Advertising

- Are the parties to be given access to the other's advertising? If so, ensure that any third party terms are not breached.

Payment

- If commission is being paid, does the party paying have full audit rights? Include detailed provisions for the calculation of commission, payment terms and review clauses.

Term

- What is the term of the agreement? In general, short-term agreements are preferable, to give the parties scope to re-evaluate.
- Is there a right to terminate on notice? Make sure termination rights also include a right to terminate in the event of insolvency or breach of warranty.
- Include a right to remove the link immediately on termination or if the other party is in breach.

Consequences of termination

- How are the parties to deal with post-termination issues, such as transferring data to the other party? Provide that all data is returned or deleted as soon as possible and that all licences to use intellectual property rights terminate.
- If one party is paying commission to the other, the Commercial Agents (Council Directive) Regulations 1993 (SI 1993 No. 3053) may apply. If so, have measures been taken to ameliorate their effect, such as express indemnity payments? The regulations also set minimum notice periods that must be observed.

Liability

- Include limitations on liability, bearing in mind the provisions of the Unfair Contract Terms Act 1977 that such limitations must be reasonable. Other statutory legislation will apply if the parties are dealing with consumers, such as the Unfair Terms in Consumer Contracts Regulations 1999 and the Distance Selling Regulations 2000.
- Include disclaimers of liability, particularly in relation to the provision of professional advice by the content provider.

Warranties

- It is normal practice for both parties to warrant ownership of their own intellectual property rights, and that all content provided will comply with relevant legislation and not be defamatory or negligent.
- Warranties are particularly important if content may be relied on by the user. The framer will wish to see a warranty that the content is in accordance with best professional practice, while the provider will want to disclaim responsibility for reliance (to the greatest extent possible).
- Warranties may need to exclude content provided by third parties or be made subject to a specific disclaimer or online terms and conditions.

Insurance and disaster recovery

- If the provision of the link requires substantial investment or carries any unusual risk or high value transactions, have the parties considered insurance for downtime or other loss? What disaster recovery mechanisms are in place?

Confidentiality

- Mutual confidentiality provisions should be included.
- Specify governing law but bear in mind the problems of enforcing these types of clauses.

6.6 How to prevent unwanted linking

Discourage parasites by stating on your website that:

- any link can only be made with approval and provide an e-mail link via which approvals may be sought;
- links are to be made only through a designated home page; and
- material on the website is subject to trade mark, copyright and database right and any unauthorised reproduction of this material is prohibited.

If troublesome illegal links are made to your site, notify the third party as soon as possible that the link is unauthorised and ask for it to be removed. Do not threaten trade mark or copyright infringement without taking legal advice as making groundless threats of infringement may result in a claim being made against you.

If possible, avoid taking legal action by negotiating a properly regulated linking arrangement that will benefit both parties, but if there is no option, take legal advice. It may be possible to claim passing off or trade mark, copyright or database infringement. You will also need advice on the most appropriate jurisdiction. Bear in mind that any legal claim is, as a general rule, only worth doing if you are suffering or are likely to suffer measurable damage.

7. Selling online

Trading Company Limited will need to ensure that its online contracts for the sale of its widgets are legally binding.

The development and operation of Trading Company Limited's website needs to take into account the legislation governing e-commerce sales to consumers in the UK and Europe including, but not limited to, the Unfair Contract Terms Act 1977 (UCTA), the Unfair Terms in Consumer Contracts Regulations 1999 (the UTCC Regulations), the Consumer Protection (Distance Selling) Regulations 2000 (the Distance Selling Regulations) and the Electronic Commerce (EC Directive) Regulations 2002 (the E-commerce Regulations). Trading Company Limited should also bear in mind the Sale and Supply of Goods to Consumers Regulations 2002 which came into force in the UK on 31 March 2003 and which are dealt with in more detail in section 8 below.

Trading Company Limited also needs advice on its obligations under the Data Protection Act 1998 and associated regulations (particularly the Privacy and Electronic Communications (EC Directive) 2003) and what it should do if its widgets are defective. This last issue is addressed in section 8 below and chapter 3 looks at the subject of data protection. (Chapter 1 provides an overview of the basic rules of contract.)

7.1 Terms and conditions

Trading Company Limited will need to publish online terms and conditions for the sale of the widgets on its website. As Trading Company Limited will be selling widgets to consumers, under the UTCC Regulations it must ensure that its terms are fair and reasonable or they will not be enforceable.

If Trading Company Limited uses terms that are deemed unfair pursuant to the UTCC Regulations, the Director General of Fair Trading can investigate the terms and conditions and request that the unfair term and any similar term is removed.

If necessary, the Director General can seek an injunction from the courts to prevent the unfair term being used. In addition, bad publicity can result from any involvement of the Office of Fair Trading (OFT): the findings of the OFT are published and are available to the public and any adverse findings are likely to be highly damaging to the reputation of a company.

What does 'fair' mean?

The following list sets out some examples of what may constitute unfair terms under the UTCC Regulations and the associated guidance issued by the OFT:

General

- Terms that are misleading.
- Terms that are not in plain English.

- Use of legal terms or other terms that are not generally understood by the public.
- Terms that exclude or limit any terms implied by law (e.g. that the company owns the goods they are selling).
- Stating that the written terms incorporate the whole agreement (i.e. do not include pre-sales discussions).

Liability

- Terms where the parties have different liability levels.
- Terms that exclude or limit liability for personal injury or death caused by negligence (such a term would also be prohibited under UCTA).
- Terms that exclude or limit liability if the goods do not match their description, are not of satisfactory quality or are not fit for the purpose for which they are usually used.
- Terms that exclude or limit the buyer's statutory rights.
- Terms that limit the types of redress that are available to the buyer.
- Terms that limit or exclude loss which the parties could have been expected to foresee at the time they entered into the contract.
- Terms that state that the goods are sold as seen or disclaim responsibility for failure to meet any reasonable standard.

Delivery

- Terms that allow unduly long periods for delivery.
- Terms that exclude or limit liability for non-delivery/delay.
- Terms that pass the risk of loss or damage before delivery.
- Terms that deem that the goods are accepted by the customer on delivery.

Payment/Cancellation

- Terms that request full payment in advance.
- Terms that give the supplier the right to vary the price after the contract has been concluded.
- Terms that place excessive penalty/compensation obligations on the buyer.
- Terms that give the buyer unequal/inadequate cancellation rights.
- Terms that allow the supplier to cancel the contract without refund/notice.

The E-commerce Regulations, which are mentioned in Chapter 1, were implemented in the UK on 21 August 2002, their aim being to drive forward the development of e-commerce. They provide that where a contract is to be concluded by electronic means, except when parties who are not consumers have agreed otherwise and except for contracts concluded exclusively by exchange of e-mails or concluded off-line, the service provider must communicate in a 'clear, comprehensible and unambiguous manner', prior to the placement of the customer's order, the following information:

- the different technical steps to follow to conclude the contract (so that the customer is made aware of the process in which they are involved and the point of the process at which they will commit themselves);
- whether or not the concluded contract will be filed by the service provider and whether it will be accessible (filing is a legal concept in other Member States and will apply in the UK only where contracts are made with service providers established in those Member States);
- the technical means for identifying and correcting input errors prior to the placing of the order; and
- the languages offered for the conclusion of the contract.

If a service provider fails to provide the above information, a customer may bring an action for damages against such provider for breach of statutory duty. The service provider must also provide the customer with details of any relevant codes of conduct that he subscribes to and details of how these can be accessed electronically.

Where the service provider provides terms and conditions applicable to the contract to the customer, it must make them available to the customer in a way that allows him to store and reproduce them. If a service provider fails to do so on request, the customer may seek a court order requiring the service provider to do so.

7.2 Governing law/jurisdiction

Trading Company Limited is keen for English law to apply to its online contracts. As discussed in chapter 1, Trading Company Limited should make it clear in its terms and conditions of sale that the sale of the widgets is subject to English law.

However, since Trading Company Limited is dealing with consumers, potentially in many jurisdictions, the choice of law clause will not be able to override any mandatory rules of law in the consumer's home state.

In addition to the EEA countries, Trading Company Limited has four or five key countries to target for the sale of its widgets and so decides to take local legal advice in respect of these countries. If it has been decided that because of the laws which apply in those countries, Trading Company Limited does not wish to sell widgets there, the website should make it clear that it is not targeting customers within those states.

To minimise its risk, the practical solution for Trading Company Limited is to limit sales of the widgets to consumers in countries whose laws have been checked. This may be achieved, for example, by requiring the consumer to select a delivery address from a drop-down list of acceptable countries. In addition, the site can include protective mechanisms such as requiring all visitors to state the jurisdiction in which they are based before allowing further access or including a statement on the website that buyers in certain states are precluded from purchasing the widgets.

As well as expressing a choice of law in the contracts with its customers, Trading Company Limited may wish to increase the likelihood of the English courts having jurisdiction to hear any dispute. If so, it would be well advised to state specifically in its terms and conditions that the English courts will have exclusive jurisdiction.

7.3 Easy access

The terms and conditions may not be enforceable unless they are easily accessible and specifically brought to the consumer's attention. Practically, users of Trading Company Limited's website should be able to click through to the terms and conditions from each page of the website and must be required to click to accept such terms and conditions before using services or ordering goods available from the site.

7.4 Information

Information on the website
By law, all companies must include the following information on their company website:

- company name;
- company registration number;
- registered office address;
- where the company is registered; and
- VAT number.

This is often included in a 'Contact Us' page on the website.

Information to be provided to the consumer
The Distance Selling Regulations and the E-commerce Regulations aim to enhance website transparency and Trading Company Limited must provide the following information in a clear and comprehensive manner which is easily, directly and permanently accessible:

- identity of supplier;
- supplier's geographical address;
- supplier's details including its e-mail address, so that it can be contacted rapidly and in a direct and effective manner;
- supplier's company registration number;
- VAT number;
- authorisation by or membership of any professional bodies;
- the characteristics of the goods;
- price of goods (including all taxes) and payment arrangements;
- where applicable, the period for which the offer or price remains valid;
- arrangements for payment, delivery or performance, including any delivery costs;
- the existence of the consumer's right to cancel the contract (including cancellation procedures and conditions);
- whether the supplier may provide substitute goods if the requested goods are unavailable and, if so, that the cost of the consumer returning such substitute goods in the event of cancellation will be borne by the supplier;
- the cost of ordering the goods via the website where the cost is other than the basic rate;
- where appropriate, the minimum duration of the contract, in the case of contracts for the supply of goods or services to be performed permanently or recurrently;
- information about any after sales service and guarantees.

Accurate and up-to-date information

It is important that any information published on Trading Company Limited's website is accurate and kept up-to-date (e.g. catalogues or price lists).

If, at any time, information is not up-to-date, the site should clearly say this. A phrase commonly used on websites is '*Prices are valid at the time of posting*', but this wording is not recommended as the customer is unlikely to be aware of the date on which the information was published on the site. '*Prices are valid until 5pm on 24 December 2005. For a free price list after this date please call [0800 XXX XXX]*' may be used as an alternative.

7.5 Sales process

Trading Company Limited needs a clear sales process and has suggested that the website developer takes into account the following process whilst carrying out the development work:

Consumer is provided with the information set out above and access to the terms and conditions of sale and privacy policy.

Consumer completes order form following a clear and easy to follow step-by-step guide, which enables him/her to change items in the order at any time, check details he has inputted and correct any input errors.

Consumer is obliged to view and click to accept the terms and conditions of sale before submitting order.

Consumer submits order form.

Trading Company Limited sends consumer a return e-mail without undue delay acknowledging receipt of, and the details of, the order and highlighting any returns policy/cancellation rights and after-sales services information. (The consumer will have seen these already in the information provided during the ordering process.)

Trading Company Limited despatches goods to consumer and notifies consumer of despatch date.

It is important that Trading Company Limited ensures that a sales transaction on its website follows the above process. If Trading Company Limited fails to acknowledge receipt of the order without undue delay, it risks an action being brought against it for damages for breach of statutory duty. Moreover, if it fails to permit a customer to identify and correct input errors, the customer (having entered into a contract with the company) is entitled to rescind, i.e. cancel the contract.

7.6 Delivery of goods

Unless the parties agree otherwise, Trading Company Limited must deliver the goods within a maximum period of thirty days from the day after the day on which the consumer submitted his order. If Trading Company Limited cannot do so, it must inform the consumer and reimburse any sum paid as soon as possible or, at the latest within thirty days beginning with the day after the day on which the period for performance expired or, if the possibility was provided for in the contract with the consumer, provide substitute goods of equivalent quality and price.

7.7 Cancellation

Right to cancel

Under the Distance Selling Regulations, subject to a few exceptions, a consumer has the right to serve a *notice of cancellation* to cancel the online contract within a cancellation period which is usually a period of seven working days after the day on which the consumer received the goods. (See chapter 6 for further details.)

Consequences of cancellation

If a consumer does cancel an order, Trading Company Limited must refund any sum paid by the consumer as soon as possible and, in any case, within thirty days from the day on which the notice of cancellation was given. Trading Company Limited may charge for the direct cost of recovering any goods supplied if a term of the contract provided for the consumer to return goods if he cancels the contract and the consumer does not comply with that provision, or returns the goods at the expense of the supplier. However, this right may not apply if the consumer has the contractual right to reject the goods or has the right to reject under a term implied by law (for example, if the goods are not of a satisfactory quality).

Following cancellation, where a consumer does have goods in his possession, he has a duty to retain them and take reasonable care of them and either make them available for collection or deliver or send the goods to Trading Company Limited.

Cancellation of the contract also has the effect of automatically cancelling any related credit agreements.

Please note that the information and cancellation period will differ if Trading Company Limited provides services rather than goods.

7.8 Domestic Electrical Goods

Extended warranties

Let's assume for the purposes of this section that the articles being manufactured by Trading Company Limited are domestic electrical goods, such as kettles, laptops or camcorders. If Trading Company Limited also offers for sale extended warranties in relation to those goods, to cover, for example, the cost of repairing the electrical product in the event of a breakdown, the company should be aware of the Supply of Extended Warranties on Domestic Electrical Goods Order 2005 (the Order). The Order came into force on 6 April 2005. Its aim is to ensure that consumers are given more information about extended warranties so that they are better placed to decide whether or not they need them.

The Order imposes a number of new obligations on Trading Company Limited, one of which is that whenever it publishes the price of an electrical product on its website, it must also publish the price and duration of at least one applicable extended warranty adjacent to the price of the electrical product. This obligation will not apply once the consumer has opted to purchase domestic electrical product but no extended warranty.

The Order does not specify a precise format for this requirement but the price and duration of the applicable extended warranty must be published in a clear and legible manner. When selling through a website, there is no obligation to make it clear that the purchase of the extended warranty is optional, but Trading Company Limited may choose to do so.

Trading Company Limited must, however, ensure that further information relating to the purchase of extended warranties offered by it for sale is published on its website and must include a hyperlink on its home page, as well as on each introductory page offering domestic electrical goods, directing customers to such further information.

This further information must state, amongst other things, that extended warranties may be available from other persons; that extended warranties do not have to be purchased at the same time as a domestic electrical product; and that household insurance may be relevant to the purchase of a domestic electrical product. The website should also indicate the rights that a consumer has under the sale of goods legislation and where further information in relation to such rights can be found.

Trading Company Limited should also bear in mind that the Order introduces new cancellation and termination rights in relation to any such extended warranty purchased by a company. If the extended warranties have an initial duration of more than one year, the company must offer its customers a minimum 'cooling off' period of 45 days, beginning with the day on which the extended warranty is purchased, in which the consumer can cancel the policy and obtain a full refund where no claim has been made. Consumers must also be given the right to terminate the warranty after the cooling-off period has expired and receive a pro-rata refund regardless of whether a claim has been made.

Furthermore, Trading Company Limited must inform its customers in writing of these rights at least 20 days before the cooling-off period expires, although this does not apply if the price of the extended warranty is £20 (inclusive of taxes) or less.

This piece of legislation will certainly have a significant impact on businesses selling domestic electrical goods and associated extended warranties, as it represents a further step in the direction of consumer protection in the UK.

8. Defective goods

Trading Company Limited also needs a refresher on where it stands if the widgets are defective.

8.1 Sale of Goods Act 1979

Under the Sale of Goods Act 1979 (the Act), it is a condition that the widgets must be of 'satisfactory quality'. This means that whilst the widgets do not need to be perfect, they should be of a standard that a reasonable person would regard as satisfactory in all the circumstances, such as concerning the price and any description of the widgets (including public statements made by the manufacturer or the seller about the characteristics of the goods).

Quality means appearance, finish, safety, freedom from minor defects, durability and fitness for the purpose for which they are supplied. The widgets will need to be of a satisfactory quality for a reasonable amount of time. The exact amount of time will depend on the type of goods and their usual life expectancy. For example, food will not be expected to last as long as a car.

Under the Act, if Trading Company Limited's widgets are not of satisfactory quality, the customer is entitled to a 'hierarchy of remedies' that may overlap. It can:

- reject them and terminate the agreement and claim compensation provided the widgets have not been 'accepted' by the customer. This right applies whether the customer is acting as a business or a consumer, although business customers cannot reject in full and terminate the contract if the breach is minor. Acceptance occurs when the customer intimates to the seller that he accepts the goods, when the goods have been delivered to the customer and he does an act in relation to them which is *inconsistent with the ownership of the seller*, or he retains the goods after a lapse of reasonable time without intimating to the seller that he has rejected them. The right to reject and terminate the contract will therefore generally be lost if the customer has not acted within a relative short period of delivery (e.g. by informing the seller that they are rejected) although a recent case (*Clegg* v. *Andersson* [2003] EWCA Civ 320) has held that this period can be extended (in this case up to eight months) provided the customer initially notified the seller that the widgets are defective.
- require the repair or replacement (at the customer's option) of the widgets free of charge. This right applies since 31 March 2003, when the Sale and Supply of Goods to Consumers Regulations (the Regulations) amended the

Act. They apply to customers acting as consumers as well as businesses acting outside their trade, business or profession. If however such repair or replacement has not been completed within a reasonable time (and without causing significant inconvenience to the consumer) or it is impossible or disproportionate to carry either out, then the consumer may instead be entitled to 'rescind' the contract (and claim a refund) or keep the widgets (e.g. if the widgets have been used) and obtain a reduction in price. This option also applies if the widgets do not conform their contractual specifications. The additional remedies introduced in March 2003 overlap somewhat with the original remedies.

If the consumer opts for the second option above that does not of itself deem him to have 'accepted' the widgets and does therefore not preclude him from exercising his rights under the first option above for example if the repair/replacement does not remedy the defect and/or if the customer wishes to claim damages in addition to the repair/replacement. The customer cannot however reject and/or terminate the contract whilst the seller is in the process of repairing or replacing the widgets unless such repair or replacement has not been completed within a reasonable time or causes inconvenience to the consumer.

A benefit to the consumer of the second option above is that if the defect arises during the six months from the time of delivery of the goods (provided the goods would ordinarily be expected to last that long) they are presumed to have been defective on delivery unless the seller can prove otherwise, i.e. there is no need for a customer to prove that Trading Company Limited is at fault. After this time the burden of proof is reversed. Contrast with the first option above, where the burden of proof is on the consumer and the right to reject can be lost in a comparatively short time. Trading Company Limited will be responsible for the costs of returning the faulty goods to it under either option.

Trading Company Limited cannot repair, replace or provide a credit note instead of allowing the customer to reject the widgets unless the customer agrees.

It is important to note that the customer can only claim a remedy under the Act from the seller. Unless the manufacturer and seller is the same entity, the customer cannot usually claim redress from the manufacturer, unless the goods are under guarantee (see section 8.5 below).

8.2 Consumer Protection Act 1987

In addition to the above, Trading Company Limited may be liable as the manufacturer of the widgets under the Consumer Protection Act 1987 if the widgets are defective and cause damage.

The Act imposes direct liability upon manufacturers, own branders and importers of products in favour of anyone injured and in respect of any damage above £275 caused to private property as a result of the defects.

If Trading Company Limited is sued under the Consumer Protection Act 1987, there are a number of defences it can rely on including if:

- the defect is attributable to compliance with a statutory or EU requirement;
- the defect did not exist at the relevant time, i.e. when the widgets were supplied by one producer to another; and/or
- the state of scientific/technical knowledge at the relevant time was not such that a producer of products of the same description as the product in question might be expected to have discovered the defect.

8.3 The General Product Safety Regulations 1994

The General Product Safety Regulations 1994 apply to new and second hand (but not antiques) consumer products, except products covered by specific European legislation. They place a duty on all producers of consumer goods to supply safe products. There is a lesser duty in the Regulations for distributors (i.e. someone whose activities do not affect the product's safety).

Safety takes into account factors such as the product's characteristics, instructions and warnings and the categories of consumer at risk when using the product, particularly children. Any relevant British or European standards should be taken into account in assessing safety.

A breach of this legislation can result in fines, imprisonment or prohibition and suspension orders.

A revised General Product Safety Directive should have been implemented into UK law in January 2004, but is now expected to be implemented sometime in the summer, most likely at the end of July 2005. The regulations will impose new obligations on both producers and distributors (who know or ought to know that a product poses risks to the consumer that are incompatible with the general safety requirements) to inform the authorities immediately giving details of action taken to prevent risk to the consumer. They also introduce new powers to the authorities to recall products which they have reasonable grounds for suspecting to be dangerous. This is only to be used as a 'last resort'.

8.4 Liability in tort

Under the law of tort, those who use a defective widget may be able to claim damages for personal injury, death and/or damage to property. This may arise where injury or property damage is caused as a result of Trading Company Limited's negligence in designing or manufacturing the widgets.

8.5 Guarantees

Many manufacturers provide guarantees to their customers in which they agree to replace or repair defective products for a specified period of time, usually for a year.

In England and Wales, there is no requirement on the manufacturer to give a guarantee. If a guarantee is given by the manufacturer/seller it needs to comply with certain requirements. The Regulations requires that any such guarantee is a legally binding contractual obligation with effect at the time the goods are delivered. The Regulations however only apply to consumers and do not extend to businesses/companies even if acting outside the purpose of their trade, business of profession.

The Regulations require any such guarantees to be in plain and intelligible English and to include the essential particulars necessary for making claims under it, e.g. its duration, territorial scope, as well as the name and address of the guarantor. If it does not conform to these requirements, the Director General of Fair Trading can ask the guarantor to amend the guarantee. Failure by a guarantor to comply with such a request could result in an injunction, and if broken, ultimately a fine or imprisonment for contempt of court.

8.6 What steps can Trading Company Limited take to minimise its risks for defective products?

Product safety bureaucracy
A robust, paper-based monitoring system will enable it to demonstrate compliance with its legal duties. Procedures also need to be put in place to ensure customers are informed about the life-expectancy of the product (if relevant) and to monitor safety so that any necessary product recall can be carried out slickly and with the minimum of economic and commercial damage.

Quality control, warnings and instructions
It should ensure there are pre-delivery checks to ensure compliance with the various product safety requirements. Instructions and other customer literature should contain appropriate warnings as to possible safety dangers. The bodies who enforce safety legislation, such as the Department of Trade and

Industry or the local trading standards office, are also often willing to give guidance as to the adequacy of safety procedures.

Purchase of raw materials
Where possible, appropriate indemnities should be sought from component or raw material suppliers.

Insurance
Take out appropriate product liability insurance.

9. Data protection

Once up and running, Trading Company Limited's online activities will mean that it will be processing many more details about individuals and in many different ways than was the case when it was purely operating off line. For instance:

- Online customers will be likely to register their names and addresses and pass credit card details for payment of products bought off the website.
- The company's sales and marketing department may want to analyse the business's customer base as part of its schemes and wheezes which seek to squeeze greater sales from the company's existing clientele.
- If the company wants to learn more about those who use its website (including those who do not necessarily buy its products), it may well ask visitors to register further details about themselves so that it can inform them of new product lines or offers that may be of specific interest to them.
- Potentially, the company may want to exchange these details with another business in return for details about that other business's customers.
- Customer information may need to be passed to third parties to whom the company outsources elements of its operations (e.g. those who run call centres which are established to answer customer enquiries).
- The company may want to advertise job vacancies and accept applications for those vacancies on line.
- Cookie technology may well be used on the company's servers to make the process of using its website more convenient (a cookie is the name given to technology which enables a website to remember information given by individual visitors who have previously used that site).
- Finally, it may well be that the company needs or wants to transfer customer details abroad, perhaps because it has overseas operations or because a partner with whom it wishes to share the details is based overseas.

Chapter 3 introduces the subject of data protection laws and explain the likely consequences of not complying with those laws and some of the specific obligations imposed by them that an online business should consider in relation to its operations.

The obligations apply to any use that is made of information from which it is possible to identify a living individual. They apply not only to computerised data, but also to many paper-held records. Therefore, Trading Company Limited should not assume that data protection compliance is a new issue. The company is always likely to have processed a great deal of information about individuals, be they its employees (current or past), contractors, suppliers, customers or potential customers, and all of these uses will continue to be bound by the obligations of data protection laws. However, the dramatic increase in the amount of additional processing of information about individuals which will take place once the company's website is operational means that now is a good time to review whether the business's operations as a whole put it in danger of breaching data protection laws. A full data protection audit of the company's on- and offline operations should be considered.

Many of the data protection law obligations detailed in chapter 3 will require Trading Company Limited to inform fully users of its website as to what information the company uses which identifies them, and how that information will be used. Some of the obligations will also require Trading Company Limited to obtain consent from its website's users for these uses to be made. Such consents generally have to be obtained from users at the point when their information is acquired by the company, or as soon as possible after that time.

This means that it is very important that the company includes a detailed privacy policy on its website in which it comes clean about what and when user information will be obtained and how it will be used. The policy should be prominently positioned on the website and should be cross-referenced in opt-in consent wording at any point on the site where information is obtained from users (a fuller commentary on tick box wording is included in chapter 3).

The details that Trading Company Limited should include in its privacy policy will depend on what information about its users it plans to obtain and what uses it intends to make of that information. The box below illustrates some general categories of use which an online business should consider including in a website privacy policy. These are not intended to provide a definitive privacy policy.

For a list of the other steps that an online business should take before its website goes live, see chapter 3.

Issues to consider in an on-line privacy policy

1. Details of when information contained in the policy was last updated.
2. Full details of the website operator and other group companies that will be given user details – including the companies' full names and addresses.
3. Contact details of the online business for users who have enquiries about how their data is used, and to correct out of date information held by the online business.
4. A general introduction as to how user data is collected.
5. Details of whether and how cookie technology is used by the website and how it can be disabled.
6. A general description of security measures taken in connection with user details.
7. Details of how user data is used to supply products/services.
8. Details of situations in which users may be contacted .
9. Details of marketing activities for which user data will be used.
10. A description of data which may be passed to third parties and such details as are possible about likely third parties: e.g. a) data processors (e.g. call centre operators, billing system operators, hosting providers, customer support services, etc.); b) business partners; c) law enforcement agencies or other third parties authorised by law to access the data; and d) future owners of the business.
11. Details of non-European Economic Area countries to which user data will be transferred. Specific countries should be named.
12. Details of how information supplied pursuant to a job application will be used (to the extent not covered by the above points).

10. Employment

A number of employment issues arise from the decision by Trading Company Limited to provide e-mail and internet access to its employees. These issues need to be addressed at an early stage and the requisite policies and procedures put in place to minimise the risk of claims against Trading Company Limited which may be as diverse as libel, discrimination or breach of copyright. In chapter 8, we discuss the misuse of e-mail and the internet by employees and how the liability for such misuse may rest with Trading Company Limited. We consider the rights of Trading Company Limited to monitor its employees' e-mail and internet activities, taking into account the protection afforded to employees by the human rights and data protection legislation. We advise on the benefits of drafting and implementing an effective e-mail and internet policy and how to manage employees who breach the policy.

11. Tax

Trading Company Limited will need to consider the taxation implications that may arise when it sets up its website and begins to trade online. Generally, the tax rules are applied as a 'one size fits all' approach to taxing businesses.

However where businesses are complex or out of the ordinary, the rules becomes more difficult to apply with clarity. On the other hand, for businesses that make investments in technology or are smaller enterprises, there is some generous tax relief available to help develop their internet business. These areas are examined more fully in chapter 9.

Initially, it is likely that the internet business will operate as part of the existing business of Trading Company Limited. This will normally be tax-neutral from a tax point of view, so that the profits and losses of the internet operations are bundled up with the profits and losses of the existing trade, and treated as one business by the relevant tax authorities.

However, as the internet side of the business expands (perhaps into a wider range of goods and/or services unconnected with the business of Trading Company Limited), it may be desirable to transfer the internet business into a separate company. There are non-tax advantages to doing this, for example assets of the existing business are protected and liabilities of the internet business are ring fenced within Trading.com Limited. Also, it may make the internet business more attractive to potential purchasers of that business in future if it is already set up in a separate company.

A common method of separating out the internet business is to set up a new holding company to acquire the shares of Trading Company in return for an issue of shares in itself to the existing shareholders in Trading Company. The new holding company then sets up a new subsidiary company which acquires or sets up the internet business. Provided they are structured correctly, these steps can be carried out without any tax charges arising.

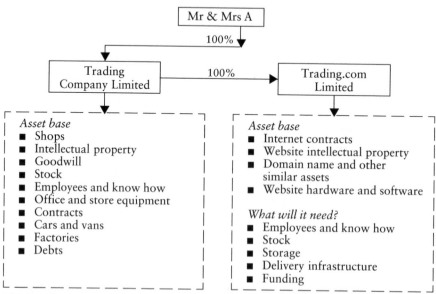

Nb: these lists are not exhaustive – they are intended for illustration purposes only.

11.1 Start-up issues

In the first year or so of internet business, perhaps one of the easier ways to provide Trading.com with the resources required to run the internet business would be to put a management agreement in place, so that Trading.com Limited can run its business immediately. There are tax issues to be considered where parent/subsidiary companies provide such services to each other. Those issues are dealt with in chapter 9. However, a simple management agreement would ensure that Trading Company Limited is able to provide know-how, other intellectual property, staff, computers and offices etc. to Trading.com as and when required. As the business develops, Trading.com Limited would probably begin to acquire its own resources and assets including domain names and other web-related assets including the customer contracts could be acquired

11.2 On-going tax obligations

In the example above, Trading Company Limited and Trading.com are in the same group for corporation tax and (if they so elect) VAT purposes. As a result, many transactions are basically ignored for tax purposes. The imposition of fees under the management agreement should be 'tax-neutral', because Trading.com is usually entitled to a deduction and Trading Company Limited must account for the receipt of that fee as income. In this way the expense and the income are offset against each other within the group. Furthermore, the assets of Trading Company can be transferred to Trading.com without any adverse tax effects. Each company will have its own profit and loss account, balance sheet, as distinct from its parent, Trading Holdings Limited.

For transactions occurring outside the group and outside the UK, such as with customers introduced over the internet, the tax position (including VAT) becomes more complicated. For general tax purposes, the existing rules apply to the internet business. For VAT purposes, specific legislation has been introduced to deal with e-commerce transactions. Although the VAT rules are supposed to be the same across the EU, different interpretations are put on the legislation by the member states. The VAT rules are considered further in chapter 9.

11.3 Tax relief

As mentioned above, most transactions within groups are ignored for tax purposes, as if the group is one single 'entity'. There is also more generous relief available to companies, which reduce the tax burden by giving a deduction against profits. More specifically, the capital allowance regime gives generous relief for expenditure on technology, e.g. computer software, especially where a company (or group of companies) is small.

11.4 Choice of funding

There are a range of ways to fund the start-up or expansion of Trading.com Limited, some of which may also involve Trading Company Limited and the shareholders. These options could be examined as the internet business expands or on start-up. An intra-group loan from Trading Company Limited may be the easiest approach at first, with third party loans, subscriptions for shares through the Enterprise Investment Scheme (EIS) or investments by Venture Capital Trusts (VCTs) being considered at a later stage. Each option has its own tax consequences, which are discussed in greater detail in chapter 9.

12. Competition law

In deciding how to conduct its business in the market place, Trading Company Limited should not overlook its duties and rights under both domestic and European competition law. The basic theme is that the company should not behave in a manner that is anti-competitive towards other competing companies or consumers. Likewise, other companies are prevented from acting in a way that is anti-competitive towards Trading Company Limited.

Broadly speaking, in order to comply with these rules, Trading Company Limited must not enter into any agreements, take any decisions or adopt any practices that may prevent, restrict or distort competition in the UK or the EC. For example, fixing prices or market sharing is strictly forbidden. If, later on, Trading Company Limited performs well and gains a significantly high market share, it may occupy a dominant position in the market and should be careful not to abuse its dominance, as this constitutes unlawful behaviour. Examples of abuse include discriminatory or excessive pricing, or refusing to supply.

Trading Company Limited should also be aware of the laws relating to merger control. If it decides to merge with another company, depending on the size of the transaction, the merger may be subject to an investigation at either domestic or European level to ensure that it will not damage competition. Competition law may, at first, seem rather draconian, but it is designed as much to protect Trading Company Limited as to control it. It is, therefore, in Trading Company Limited's interest to be able to recognise where other companies may be acting in an anti-competitive fashion or abusing a dominant position and to report such behaviour to the competition authorities for investigation.

Chapter 10 discusses these issues in more depth.

Data Protection and E-business

Introduction

Data protection laws impose obligations governing the way in which information about living individuals is processed. They also give rights to individuals in relation to how third parties use their data. This chapter is an introduction to the data protection laws most relevant to an online business and suggests the steps that should be taken to reduce the risk of an online business's operations not complying with obligations imposed by those laws.

Data protection laws have been passed in the UK since 1984, but as the internet and online trade have developed, so has the scope of the laws passed. Having initially permitted a rather *laissez-faire* approach to e-commerce privacy and encryption, the UK – along with its fellow European Union member states – is now probably the most highly regulated jurisdiction when it comes to laws governing the use of information about living individuals, in terms of both the scope of the activities regulated and the number of regulations imposed. At the time of writing, there is no sign of any respite from either the introduction of new data protection laws or from the tweaks made to existing obligations which have been a feature of this area of e-commerce law since the first of the current generation of privacy regulations was introduced in May 1999. For these reasons, anyone taking advantage of the edge which technology gives their business would be well advised to consider seriously how data protection laws impact on that business. The days of *laissez-faire* data regulation are over and the consequences of non-compliance with the rules and regulations (criminal liability, fines and bad publicity) are distinctly unattractive.

In addition to the UK's Data Protection Act 1998 (the 'Act') other key pieces of UK privacy legislation include the following:

The Privacy and Electronic Communications (EC Directive) Regulations 2003: This regulates (amongst other things):

- the use of cookies;
- unsolicited marketing e-mails, SMSs, faxes and cold calls;
- the use of automated calling systems;
- telecommunication privacy issues, such as the retention and use of traffic data, itemised billing and caller line identification information;
- restrictions on the use of location data technology; and
- the operation of the Preference Service 'do not call' lists.

The Freedom of Information Act 2000: This regulates rights of public access to information processed by and on behalf of public bodies, as well as the requirement for public bodies to publish details of the types of information that they routinely publish.

Regulation of Investigatory Powers Act 2000: Amongst other things, this incorporates regulations relevant to e-mail monitoring – The Telecommunications (Lawful Business Practice) (Interception of Communications) Regulations 2000.

The Human Rights Act 1998: This implements Article 8 of the European Convention on Human Rights – the right to respect for private and family life, home and correspondence – into UK law.

With the sole exception of the Freedom of Information Act, the Act and the above laws have all been driven by Directives of the European Parliament which the UK, like all European Union member states, is obliged to implement. This includes the ten new member states who joined the EU on 1 May 2004. Unfortunately for anyone wishing to initiate any element of electronic trade in its business today, the core European Directive which began the most recent wave of European data protection regulations was finalised in 1995 before use of the internet had developed in any meaningful way. Although it was not implemented in the UK for four and a half years, the Directive in question was not passed into law in a way which is particularly friendly to those running e-commerce services. As a result, subsequent data protection laws, while well intended, have been somewhat reactive to the rapid technology developments made since 1995 and the ways in which businesses take advantage of them. The laws have not always kept pace with these developments. Further, while European Union-led laws have ensured a degree of harmonisation of data protection laws across Europe, certain key issues are dealt with differently by different European countries. For any business, but particularly a non-European-based business, which is considering establishing operations in Europe the vast array of regulations and the subtle differences adopted by different European countries can make data protection law compliance a seemingly daunting task.

This chapter provides guidance on data protection issues by:

- explaining why compliance with data protection laws is an important issue for an online business;
- explaining which activities of an online business are likely to be regulated by data protection laws;
- summarising the major obligations which the laws impose upon an online business; and
- identifying the areas of an online business's operations that should be considered in light of the UK's data protection laws and suggesting steps which can be taken to assist compliance with them.

The laws and regulations of certain other jurisdictions are referred to below. However, this chapter should only be used as a guide to UK laws and regulations. In general terms, however, it is safe to assume that the UK's data protection laws are very similar to those passed by the other European Union member states. Similarly – and this is another generalisation – if a business complies with the European data protection laws, then it is likely to comply with the spirit of the laws of many other countries, such is the far-reaching effect of Europe's data protection laws. Should a proposed e-commerce activity appear controversial from a legal perspective, however, it is advisable to take advice on a country-by-country basis in jurisdictions that are important to a business.

1. Why compliance with data protection laws is an issue – fines, enforcement and bad publicity

The key questions a business is likely to want answered in the context of legal compliance are: What are the consequences if we get caught for non-compliance? And, what are the chances of our getting caught?

1.1 Maximum fines

A number of laws, regulations and codes of practice govern the processing of information about living individuals, but the starting point in answering these questions are the provisions of the Data Protection Act 1998 ('the Act'). Failure to comply with the Act's obligations can be punished by the imposition of fines and, in certain instances, criminal liability, both of which may be imposed on directors, managers or other officers of a company who consent to or negligently permit the non-compliance. At the time of writing, in respect of breaches of the Act, Magistrates' courts can impose fines of up to £5,000 and Crown courts unlimited fines where serious offences have been committed.

Individuals are also empowered to take action to prevent use of data that are likely to cause damage or distress. They may also obtain court orders to require inaccurate information about them to be destroyed or corrected, or to require its use to be blocked. There is also scope for private actions being taken if an individual suffers damage or distress (providing that it has led to quantifiable damage) following a breach of the Act.

1.2 Enforcement actions

The government body empowered to enforce the provisions of the Act (and certain other data protection laws) is the Office of the Information Commissioner ('OIC'). The OIC is also responsible for the enforcement of the Privacy and Electronic Communications (EC Directive) Regulations 2003 and the Freedom of Information Act 2000. Provided that an appropriate warrant is obtained, the OIC's powers include a right to enter a business's premises to seize evidence proving a breach of the Act has taken place. In 2003–2004 alone, the OIC recorded a total of 11,664 complaints or requests for assessment (compared to 54 complaints investigated and closed during the entire lifetime of the Act's predecessor, the Data Protection Act 1984). Of these, the OIC received 1,670 complaints about companies who have failed to comply with the Privacy and Electronic Communications (EC Directive) Regulations, under which complaints can be made about the sending of unsolicited direct marketing phone calls, faxes, automated calls, text, picture/video messages and emails. In the 12 months to 31 March 2004, eight individuals were prosecuted under the Act for unlawfully obtaining or disclosing information, all were convicted and the fines imposed ranged from £150 to £10,000. (Statistics taken from the OIC's Annual Report 2004, available at the OIC website).

1.3 Bad publicity and business expectations

Of more concern to any business should be the bad publicity that could result from an alleged failure to comply with data protection laws. This is particularly true for businesses whose products or services rely on the provision by its customers of sensitive information, or for businesses that are sensitive about protecting the goodwill in their brand. Most online businesses or departments consider customer trust in using technology to buy its products or services as key to their development. As certain banks and major retailers have discovered, publicity surrounding alleged breaches of Data Protection legislation relating to system security or marketing activities can be particularly unwelcome. Section 5.2 below examines the ongoing legal challenge mounted by a customer of Lloyds TSB invoking the Act in the fight against his bank's practice of transferring customers' personal data to call centres in India.

Also worth considering are public and business expectations when it comes to giving personal details to another party, particularly over the internet. It is fair to say that the growth of website privacy policies and tick box consent statements mean that many internet users expect, as a matter of course, to be told how information about them will be obtained and used, and look for an opportunity to consent or opt out of such uses. The inclusion of such policies and tick box wording are required by a number of provisions of the Act (see sections 5.3 and 5.4 below). Those not complying with the law by including them on their websites should consider whether public reaction to their sites will be affected regardless of whether they are accused of breaching data protection laws.

Similarly, most businesses tendering for suppliers to assist them by carrying out activities which involve the processing of their customers' information do so by requiring a high level of data protection law compliance. Those suppliers may not win business if they cannot show that they operate in accordance with data protection laws. They are certainly likely to be asked to give undertakings and warranties against the Data Protection Act by any well-advised customer. To turn the above points on their head, an e-business should ask itself: Can we turn data protection compliance into a selling point?

Finally, the reactions of a potential investor in, or purchaser of, an e-commerce business to risks taken by a business in relation to data protection regulation compliance should be considered. Data Protection compliance audits have become an increasingly important part of the due diligence which investors and purchasers conduct on targets before committing their money to a project.

2. Who enforces data protection laws?

The Office of the Information Commissioner
As mentioned above, the OIC is the principal enforcer of data protection laws. However, the powers of other regulators are also likely to be relevant to an e-business's activities.

The Advertising Standards Authority and the Direct Marketing Association
The Advertising Standards Authority's ('ASA') Codes of Practice which govern a large number of different forms of UK advertising and promotional activities contain obligations relevant to how personal data can be used for marketing purposes. As these rules supplement provisions included in other marketing-focused data protection legislation, it is possible that a business could be challenged by both the OIC and the ASA for the same marketing activity.

Similarly, the Direct Marketing Association (DMA) issues Codes of Practice which bind its members. These Codes are generally regarded as a good indicator of what is deemed accepted practice in the marketing services sector. It is also the DMA that operates the various Preference Service lists to which individuals and companies can enter their telephone, fax, e-mail and address details to signify that they do not consent to marketing materials being sent to those numbers/addresses. (For fuller details of this obligation see section 5.5 of this chapter.) Accordingly, even if an online business does not consider itself to be a marketing business it would be wise for it to make itself aware of the ASA's and the DMA's respective Codes of Practice. Links to the ASA's, the DMA's and the Preference Service's websites are all included in the Appendix to this book.

The Financial Services Authority

Financial Services regulators also have powers relevant to the use of personal data. For instance, the Financial Services Authority (FSA) can enforce regulations in respect of the use of personal data in marketing communications sent by financial promotions companies, under the Business Standards section of the Conduct of Business Sourcebook introduced under the Financial Services and Markets Act 2000.

The Office of Communications

Finally, the Office of Communications ('OFCOM') regulates communications-specific legislation and telecommunications licences many of which include privacy-related provisions.

3. What activities of an online business are likely to be regulated by data protection laws?

This chapter details the data protection obligations that an e-business must comply with and suggests measures that can be adopted to ensure compliance. In order effectively to identify the data privacy challenges a business may face, however, it is worth clarifying what activities are regulated by data protection laws.

The UK's data protection laws apply to *'processing'* of information conducted within the UK from which it is *'possible to identify a living individual'*. These definitions are examined in further detail below.

3.1 Server location

The obvious starting point is to ask : When is an online business likely to be deemed to be processing information *within the UK*? Where an e-business's servers or other processing equipment are located within the UK, the business will clearly be processing information within the UK. Even if its servers are located outside the UK, it is very likely that an e-business whose operations are targeted at a UK audience will involve some use of information in the UK. This is particularly the case if the business has or establishes a UK operation or if it employs staff in the UK. If that operation or those employees conduct activities such as processing online customer orders or providing customer support by viewing on-line customer information, then UK data protection laws (and the obligations and rights detailed in this chapter) will apply to those activities. Third parties may be engaged in the UK to run the business's day-to-day operations, in which case those third parties will be obliged to comply with the UK's laws although the e-business will be held ultimately responsible for their actions (see engaging third parties at section 5.6 below for further details).

If an online business is planning to house its servers or run any element of its operations from any European Union country other than the UK, then it will have to comply with local legal obligations which are likely to be broadly similar to those in force in the UK.

As European Union data protection laws are seen as onerous when compared to the laws of other jurisdictions, a global business may benefit from locating elements of its operations, such as its servers, outside the European Union. However, any decision to locate outside Europe should take into account the data privacy concerns that a lack of, or weaker, data protection laws might present for an online business. Moreover, as many other jurisdictions are following the example of the European Union by introducing stringent data protection laws, the likelihood of benefits arising in this way are likely to diminish.

3.2 'Processing personal data'

The obligations apply to the *processing* of any information from which it is *possible to identify a living individual*. These terms are defined very broadly in the Act and it is therefore inconceivable that the operations of an online business located in the UK which processes customer data will not be affected by data protection laws.

'Processing' covers just about any use of information imaginable. Everything from viewing information on a screen, storing it on a back-up server or printing the information would be deemed to be processing under the Act. Even the act of destroying data will be deemed to be processing. Likewise, it will be deemed possible to identify a living individual from information even if such an individual is not directly named in that information. The Data Protection Act says that information is regulated by its provisions if it is possible to identify someone:

(a) directly from the information in question;

(b) from the information when it is combined with other data in its possession; or

(c) from the information when it is combined with other data which is likely to come into the processor's possession.

Following the recent decision of the UK's Court of Appeal in *Durant* v. *Financial Services Authority* [2003] EWCA Civ 1746, the scope of information from which it is '*possible to identify a living individual*' appears to have been considerably narrowed. The case related to an application made to the FSA by an individual under the Act to reveal data which it had processed about him. The Court of Appeal backed the FSA's argument that it was not required to reveal large amounts of information because the data was not sufficiently personal to the applicant. It seems therefore that it is no longer likely to be the case that all documents, electronic or manual, that refer to or identify an individual constitute 'personal data' within the meaning of the Act. Information would be caught by the Act if such information affects an individual's privacy in his or her personal, business or professional life. The judgment provides that the information must be biographical in a significant sense and have the individual as its focus.

3.3 E-mail addresses, phone numbers, customer reference numbers etc

The practical effect of this is that processing information such as an e-mail address, an individual's telephone number, address, medical history, salary details or a customer reference number could be covered by the Act.

Whether an e-mail address is sufficient to identify a living individual will depend on the information contained in that address. For example, james.mullock@osborneclarke.com is more likely to identify an individual than, james@oc.com. Businesses that operate a website from which they obtain user information such as their names and addresses (for instance, via a registration page or order forms) should be aware that as a result they will be likely to be deemed to hold information sufficient to identify an individual when those details are combined with other apparently harmless information in their possession. The e-mail address james@oc.com may not be sufficient to identify James Mullock on its own, but if James Mullock is a registered user of a website and recorded this address along with his full name at any time when using the site, then, in processing his e-mail address and any information connected to it, the website owner must comply with data protection law obligations.

3.4 Paper records

It is a common misconception that data protection obligations apply only to computerised data and that manual records fall outside the ambit of the legislation. This is simply not the case. The obligations apply equally to computerised files and those paper records that form part of a *'relevant filing system'* The *Durant* case, mentioned above, clarified that for a manual filing system to be caught by data protection obligations (such as an individual's right to gain access to information a business holds about him), only those filing systems of equivalent standard or sophistication to computerised records are caught by the Act. In plain English, in addition to computerised information, data protection obligations could cover the use of information about individuals recorded on paper if that paper is stored in a structured manner or captured on film (including CCTV), audio tape, microfiche, CD-ROM or other disks. This means that use by a business of information relating to its customers, suppliers, agents or distributors, its business contacts, employees or contractors could be all regulated.

Departments of a business that will be affected are likely to include its marketing and promotions, IT, customer support, human resources, accounts and customer relations departments.

4. An overview of the major obligations imposed by data protection laws

If one major misconception made in relation to data protection laws is that they apply to computerised information only, another potentially more significant misconception is that compliance with data protection laws simply involves registering a business with the OIC.

Set out below is a brief summary of the major obligations imposed on anyone processing information about individuals and the rights which UK law gives those individuals. The table does not offer an exhaustive list of relevant obligations and rights, but it does provide a useful point of reference for a business which is considering to comply with data protection laws.

Data protection obligations and rights were originally written before the internet had taken off and the wording of the obligations is rather non-specific. As a result, the steps recommended here, which an e-business should take to seek compliance with these obligations, are intended to provide broad guidance. An online business that is serious about full compliance with data protection laws should audit its operations to ensure that the risk of not complying with the legal requirements which it faces are minimised. How such a risk assessment might be carried out is also briefly summarised in the final section of this chapter.

Summary of obligations imposed by data protection laws	Summary of rights given to individuals in respect of their data
(a) *Unsolicited junk faxes and cold calls* to companies or individuals – both are prohibited where recipients either previously notified the party contacting them that they do not wish to receive unsolicited marketing communications or have registered with the Fax or Telephone Preference Service.	(a) *Right to rectify, block, erase or destroy inaccurate information* – subject to certain exemptions, anyone who is the subject of inaccurate information can apply for a court order to enforce this right in respect of inaccurate information or any expression of opinion based upon it.
(b) *Fair and lawful processing* – an obligation that on obtaining data (or as soon as possible thereafter) individuals must have been fully informed as to how and by whom their data will be used, and an obligation which is likely to require those individuals to consent to their data being processed.	(b) *Right of information and access* – individuals can demand details of: any data held about them; the purposes for which the data are held and the source of the data. A copy of the data must also be supplied. In certain cases exemptions apply.
(c) *Adequate, relevant and non-excessive use* – following on from (b), data must be processed in a way which is adequate, relevant and not excessive given the purposes for which they were obtained.	(c) *Right to prevent processing likely to cause unwarranted damage or distress* – individuals can write to anyone processing their data to demand compliance with this right.
(d) *Data accuracy* – data must be kept accurate and, where necessary, up-to-date.	(d) *Compensation* – can be claimed for breaches of the Act which cause damage and distress.
(e) *How long data should be kept* – data should only be kept for as long as is necessary given the purposes for which they were obtained.	(e) *Right to prevent use of data for direct marketing* – individuals can write to anyone processing their data to demand compliance with this right.
(f) *Security* – data must be kept using appropriate techniques and technology to prevent unauthorised or unlawful use of the data and their accidental loss or destruction.	(f) *Automated decisions* – decisions taken about individuals without human input which significantly affect them can be challenged.

Summary of obligations imposed by data protection laws – *continued*	1. Summary of rights given to individuals in respect of their data – *continued*
(g) *Using third party data processors* – where information or access to information about individuals are given to third parties (e.g. a call centre operator or a hosting services provider) a written undertaking must be obtained from the third party that it will only use the data as instructed to do so and that it will meet the obligations of (f) above.	
(h) *Transfers abroad* – data must only be transferred from the United Kindgdom to a non-European Economic Area[a] country if that destination country offers data protection rights equivalent to those available under English law. Transfers are permitted if (amongst other situations) the individual whose data is being sent abroad consents to his or her data being sent to the specific country concerned or if the transfer is necessary for a contractual obligation to be provided to that individual.	
(i) *Notification* – details of all purposes for which data are processed must annually be notified to the OIC.	

Note:
a. The European Economic Area comprises twenty five European Union members states plus Iceland, Liechtenstein and Norway.

5. Specific data protection issues to consider

5.1 Where to locate servers, call centres, billing operations, etc.

Issues other than data protection law compliance will probably be high on the list of factors that determine how a business chooses where to locate the assets that are behind its online operations, such as its servers, call centres or billing centres. The likely cost of each different location option is likely to be top of the list. That said, the physical location of equipment and people which are used to process information about a business's customers, suppliers and employees will determine which jurisdiction's data protection laws govern those operations. Accordingly, legal factors should also be considered. If an aspect of a business's operations is likely to process a great deal of data about individuals, it makes sense to locate it in an area which will give the business fewest compliance headaches.

Basically, an online business would be well advised to assess:

- data protection laws of a country where it plans to base any business operations which will process large amounts of information about individuals; and
- data protection laws of other countries where it has subsidiaries (in order to know how easy it would be to transfer data to that country).

For instance, USA Co. is considering establishing a European operation, which will include USA Co. Ltd in the UK. It is trying to decide whether to locate its European billing processing operations in the UK, the Netherlands or India (the latter offering substantial set-up and operational cost saving advantages).

From a data protection compliance law point of view, USA Co. needs to consider the following issues:

(a) Are India's data protection laws dramatically more or less onerous than those of the UK or the Netherlands? (Those of the UK and the Netherlands are likely to be similar as both are European Union member states and so are obliged to introduce the same data protection laws.)

(b) The obligation imposed by UK law on those who transfer data from the UK to non-European Economic Area countries. If India is selected as the processing site's location, then this restriction will apply to any customer data sent to it by USA Co. Ltd, as India is not in the European Economic Area. Indeed, the local law of each of USA Co.'s other European subsidiaries will very likely impose an identical obligation.

5.2 Transferring data outside the European Economic Area

Similar to the question of where to locate overseas processing operations, the transfer of data outside the EEA will not be an issue for all online businesses. However, any UK business which has operations outside the European Economic Area (which consists of the 25 European Union Member States and Norway, Iceland and Liechtenstein) must consider obligation (h) in the table carefully, namely the general prohibition in the Act on the transfer of personal data to any country outside the EEA. It is the Eighth principle of the Act that restricts the transfer of personal data outside the EEA unless those countries 'ensure an adequate level of protection for the rights and freedoms of data subjects in relation to the processing of personal data'. The obligation is perhaps the best example of a data protection law conceived before the internet became a major force, but which nevertheless must now be complied with. This stringent requirement is designed to ensure that data protection rules cannot be weakened or even bypassed altogether in favour of countries where personal data will enjoy no legal protection, and where individuals will have no rights in respect of it.

Online businesses can meet this obligation owed to their subscribers in one of a number of ways. These include the following:

- *Fulfilling a contractual obligation*: If the transfer is made in order that a contractual obligation owed to a subscriber be fulfilled, then the obligation is deemed met (e.g. if the data is sent to enable a service to be provided to the subscriber).

- *Consent*: If the subscriber consents to his/her data being sent to a specifically named non-European Economic Area country, then the obligations will be deemed to have been complied with. Hence, listing the specific countries to which subscriber information will be sent in a website privacy policy to which subscribers then consent via opt in tick box wording, is likely to be the best means of meeting this obligation.

- *Approved destination country/Safe Harbour*: If the subscriber data is sent to a country whose data protection laws the European Commission has identified as offering adequate protection, then all transfers of data to that country will meet this obligation. To date, the countries which have been deemed adequate by the European Commission are Switzerland, Hungary, Canada, Argentina, Guernsey and Isle of Man. Twelve other countries or territories (Australia, Guernsey, Hong Kong, Isle of Man, Israel, Japan, Jersey, New Zealand, Poland, the Slovak Republic, Slovenia and Taiwan) have been identified by the OIC as having laws likely to offer adequate protection for these purposes.

India does not currently have any data protection legislation in force. However, the Indian Government announced in July 2004 that it would be amending existing legislation to address data privacy concerns voiced by the investors in India's $3.6 billion Business Process Outsourcing Industry. It is anticipated that, India's new data privacy laws will mean that it can join those countries that have been deemed 'adequate' by the European Commission.

Controversially, the US has at no stage been deemed to have laws which offer 'adequate' protection. However, in 2001, the US Department of Commerce, working alongside the European Commission, established a framework to allow US-based companies to comply with European Union data protection legislation. This solution to the export ban unique to data transfers to the US is the 'Safe Harbour' framework. The European Union recognises Safe Harbour as a legitimate way for US corporations (and European Union corporations transferring to the US) to comply with their obligations under European data protection legislation. To become Safe Harbour accredited, companies in the US must self-certify, and make a declaration that they will comply with all seven Safe Harbour principles (Notice, Choice, Transfers to Third Parties, Access, Security, Data Integrity and Enforcement), which are broadly similar to the principles set out in European data privacy law. Participation in the scheme is entirely voluntary and as at October 2004 some 600 US-based companies are on the Safe Harbour list.

In November 2004, the European Commission published its first report on the functioning of the Safe Harbour principles. The report reveals a number of serious shortcomings in the model and highlights a few concerns with the extent of US compliance. For instance, many US corporations have not published a privacy policy or have published a policy that is not compliant with the Safe Harbour principles – both key requirements of the Safe Harbour framework. The Commission is keen for the US Department of Commerce to take the initiative and produce guidelines on how to draft privacy policies, and to ensure that US companies have such a policy in place *before* being put on the Safe Harbour list. (Website privacy policies are considered in further detail at section 5.3 below.) Those US companies that are not compliant with the Safe Harbour principles may find that the European data protection authorities will use their powers to suspend overseas transfers.

- *Model contract*: If the online business which is transferring the data to a non-European Economic Area country signs a contract with the recipient of the information which incorporates model contract terms (approved by the European Commission and authorised by the UK's OIC), then adequate protection will be deemed to have been provided. The difficulty with this way of complying with the Act is that because these obligations are quite onerous, many non-European Union companies baulk at entering into a contract containing them.

Businesses which are considering outsourcing functions to India should be aware of what is (at the time of writing) an ongoing legal challenge mounted by a customer of Lloyds TSB against his bank's practice of transferring customers' sensitive personal data to Indian call centres, a challenge which could threaten the future of such offshoring practices. Given that India lies beyond the reach of the European data protection rules, the customer (backed by the 45,000 member Lloyds TSB Group Union) has demanded that no sensitive personal data relating to him be transferred without his express consent. The case, currently before the OIC, underlines that protests in the UK against out-sourcing jobs to low cost destinations abroad is turning into a highly charged debate about security and privacy concerns

5.3 Website privacy policies

Informing individuals of the uses that will be made of their data, and obtaining their consent for these uses to be made, are common features of the obligations included in column 1 of the table (pp. 78–9) (in particular, they are relevant to obligations (a), (b), (c) and (h)). For this reason a clearly worded privacy policy should be included on any website from which information about individuals is either overtly or covertly obtained. The policy should detail what infor-mation is obtained by the online business about those who use its website, and what uses will be made of those data or any other data relating to those individuals which come into the business's possession. Some suggested uses that might be included in a privacy policy are set out in chapter 2.

Of key importance is for the policy to detail as many future purposes for which user data may be used as possible. An online business that uses its sub-scriber's data for a new purpose for which it has not obtained the subscriber's consent will have to re-contact its users to obtain their permission before it can proceed with a new use. The policy should also be linked to 'opt-in' consent wording so that users have an opportunity to give their approval for their data to be used in the manner set out in the website's privacy policy. Points to note in relation to such consent wording are set out in the next section.

Regulations introduced in the UK in 2003 also now require websites to clearly bring to their users' attention details of any use of cookies or other similar technologies which may be made by the site. Users must be told what informa-tion will be obtained from them, how it will be used and given the option to disable the cookie. As a result many sites include a separate cookie policy which sets out this information and explains the consequences of a user disabling a cookie, as this may affect the effectiveness of the website's performance.

5.4 Consent boxes – opt in or opt out consent

To explain to end users how their data will be used and to obtain users' consent necessary to comply with the obligations set out in the table above, websites should ideally link their privacy policy to a tick box statement. The question which we are asked most frequently about website tick boxes is: Do they have to be worded so that a user gives 'opt-in' consent as opposed to 'opt out' consent? In other words, does the user have to give a positive indication that he/she consents by clicking a tick into a box?

Sensitive data

In certain scenarios opt in consent is an absolute requirement. For instance if any 'sensitive personal data', as defined in the Act, is gathered from end users then their explicit consent must be obtained before processing commences or as soon as possible thereafter.

'Sensitive personal data' is any information about an individual's:

- racial or ethnic origin;
- political opinions;
- religious or other similar beliefs;
- membership of a trade union;
- physical or mental health or condition;
- sexual life; and
- criminal record or offences committed or alleged to have been committed.

Thus, websites that obtain or deal in any of these types of information should definitely include opt-in consent wording linked to their privacy policies.

Spam, SMS, fax, telephone marketing and opt-in consent

Since the introduction of the Act, European and UK laws have attached an express requirement to obtain opt-in consent to certain uses of data, most notably unsolicited marketing activities.

The law in this area is still developing and certain exemptions from the requirement to obtain opt-in consent do exist, most notably where unsolicited mail is sent to existing customers who have bought similar goods or services to those being marketed. However, sales and marketing departments would be well advised to regularly review their databases and planned campaigns against current legal obligations.

As a guide to UK law at the time of writing, the table below details whether opt in consent is required in respect of unsolicited marketing sent via any of the channels detailed in the table's left-hand column. The table also indicates where a so-called 'do not contact' registry is run by the Preference Service.

Note that UK law takes a different approach to corporate and non-corporate recipients of unsolicited marketing. Confusingly, the definition of non-corporate is such that some partnerships and sole traders are covered with the result that any unsolicited marketing sent to these types of business will have to meet different consent criteria than materials sent to PLC or Limited companies.

		Opt In Consent?	Opt Out Consent?	Pref. Service Check?
Automated calling system	*Corporate*	✓		
	Non-corporate	✓		
Fax	*Corporate*		✓	✓
	Non-corporate	✓		✓
Phone	*Corporate*		✓	✓
	Non-corporate		✓	✓
E-mail	*Corporate*		✓	
	Non-corporate	✓		
SMS	*Corporate*		✓	
	Non-corporate	✓		

Marketing faxes, telephone calls, e-mails and SMS messages should also include details of how a recipient can terminate its receipt of such marketing. Also, E-commerce laws require that the subject line of any unsolicited marketing e-mails clearly indicate that the mail contains marketing material thus enabling the recipient to delete the mail without reading it.

Tick box statements

Relying on a pre-ticked opt in box as an indication of an end-user's consent to receiving unsolicited marketing is unlikely to succeed. Indeed the OIC's guidance regarding the obtaining of all end-user consent is that it should always be freely given and fully informed.

The OIC has also indicated that it prefers to see websites break down tick boxes by reference to different activities. For instance, including two tick boxes on a registration page:

■ one of which refers specifically to the possible receipt of marketing materials by e-mail (set up as a box which requires to be ticked by a user); and
■ the other which refers to other uses which will be made of the user's data (which could be set up with a link to a privacy policy)

would enable an end user to reject the first but accept other uses of data outlined via the second.

In preparing tick boxes to be included on a website or in marketing materials the following checklist of issues to consider may assist:

- *Privacy policy* – Has a full description of all current and future activities been prepared? Are all group and third party businesses mentioned to whom end user data will be sent? Have all overseas transfers of data been mentioned?

- *Opt in or opt out?* – Is fax, e-mail or SMS marketing to be sent to non-corporate recipients? Will sensitive data be collected from end-users? If yes then opt-in consent will be required. See below for example wording.

- *Location of tick box* – A site's registration page is likely to be the best location, but this should be considered on a site-by-site basis.

- *Cookie policy* – Does the website utilise cookies? If yes, does the site's privacy policy provide sufficient information about how information obtained via cookies will be used and how the cookies can be disabled?

An opt-in consent tick box like the following should be included on any part of a website from which user information is obtained:

> *By ticking this box I confirm that I have read and understood your Privacy Policy* [include link to policy] *and that I consent to the activities detailed in it.*

An alternative approach would be to link the submitting of a registration form with the giving of consent, for example, by prominently including the following wording on a registration page's submit button:

> *By submitting this form I confirm that I have read and understood your Privacy Policy* [include link to policy] *and that I consent to the activities detailed in it.*

A golden rule in respect of tick box wording – whether opt-in or opt-out – is that they should always be clearly visible.

5.5 Security

As one might expect, data protection laws include obligations that require anyone processing information about living individuals to do so in a secure way. The wording of the relevant obligation is not specific. It refers to a requirement to use *'appropriate techniques and technology'* to prevent unauthorised or unlawful use or accidental loss of that data (see obligation (f) in the table). The OIC has stated in its guidance notes to the Act that compliance with this requirement will be judged against the technology available at the time and the costs involved in taking advantage of that security. The reliability of staff who have access to data is also a relevant factor to take into consideration.

Given this obligation, it is difficult to generalise about the steps an online business should take to ensure that its data processing activities are deemed to be secure. Common sense will provide a useful guide and the opinion of expert security consultants should be sought where specific knowledge is lacking within a business's internal technology departments. Businesses should bear in mind that, as with other data protection law obligations, security obligations will potentially apply to its use of paper information as well as to its processing of machine-readable data. As already highlighted at section 3 above, the Act regulates any structured collection of information that identifies a living individual. Therefore, the security under which files of customer records and accounts information are held should be reviewed just as carefully as the firewall and virus alert technology used by the business's technology systems.

5.6 Engaging third parties – call centre providers, billing processors, hosting services technical support

With the security requirements detailed above in mind, an online business should also consider the circumstances under which it engages third parties to process data about its customers, suppliers, distributors, contractors, employees or any other individuals involved in its operations. The Act contains specific requirements that oblige anyone who shares such information with a data processor to take responsibility for the processor's actions by requiring them to:

- Choose a data processor which gives sufficient guarantees in respect of the security measures which it will use in processing data; and
- Enter a written contract with the processor obliging it to:
  - use their data as instructed to do so; and
  - process the data at all times using appropriate techniques and technology to prevent unauthorised or unlawful use or accidental loss of that data.

The OIC has provided further important guidance on the issue of data security. Businesses should check whether third party data processors have in place appropriate security measures both in terms of the technology they use and how it is managed. For example, an e-business should enquire whether any potential data processor is certified to ISO 1 7799, a widely used but very stringent global information security standard. It is interesting to note that 16 Indian companies have already adopted BS7799 (the pre-cursor to the ISO standard) with many more Indian companies planning to do so in an effort to win valuable outsourcing contracts (according to India's main trade association for the IT industry, NASSCOM).

A business whose data processors cause a security breach can be held liable for that breach. Therefore, the contractual terms agreed by an online business with any third parties to whom it outsources certain operations should be revised carefully. Such operations might include, its call centre, its invoice processing, its hosting operations or the technical support of its equipment. In each of these scenarios the third party outsourcer is likely to be given personal data about the online business's customers. Accordingly, the online business needs to enter into a written agreement with each third party under which strict security undertakings are given to the business.

5.7 Notification (or registering under the Data Protection Act)

Subject to certain exemptions, all businesses that process information about individuals are required to have undergone a notification process with the OIC. A standard form needs to be completed, on which the online business sets out details of the types of data it will process and the purposes for which processing will take place. Notifications must be updated and renewed annually and a fee (currently £35) must be paid to the OIC for it to process the notification. Some data does not need to be notified, for example uses made of most non-computerised data, and details of data used for staff administration, advertising and marketing or accounting purposes are also exempted from notification. Notifications can be made online at the OIC's website (details are included in the Appendix to this book). It is not possible to make a group-wide notification with the OIC. Individual company details are required to be submitted separately.

Businesses should be wary of bogus notification agencies that send official-looking notices demanding between £95 and £135 to register under the Act. Specific industries which have been targeted include the IT sector, HR sector and the childcare sector. Nearly 43,000 of the 131,605 calls to the OIC's Notification Helpline in 2004 related to these bogus agencies (one such agency being the 'Data Processing Protection Corporation Limited'). In an effort to raise awareness of such bogus agencies and to prevent more businesses being duped, the OIC has issued a number of press releases throughout 2004 on this matter and has worked closely with the Office of Fair Trading (OFT). The OFT has obtained undertakings from numerous individuals that they will not be involved in misleading advertising for data protection notification services. The OIC also writes to businesses that have previously paid exorbitant fees to notify via a bogus agency to advise businesses that they can now renew directly with the OIC for £35.

Further information is detailed in the OIC's Annual Report 2004, available at the OIC website.

It would be wise (and is an OIC recommendation) for an online business to appoint an individual within its organisation to take responsibility for ensuring that its data protection notification is up-to-date and accurate. This individual could also take responsibility for dealing with other data protection issues, such as ensuring that a prompt response is given to requests from individuals to gain access to information which is processed about them by the e-business.

5.8 Privacy audits

The list of issues relevant to online businesses set out in this chapter demonstrates the sheer volume of legislation that potentially could affect a business's e-commerce activities – and it is important that businesses acknowledge that compliance with such data protection regulations is non-negotiable. As we have outlined in this chapter, failure by businesses to take such obligations seriously can result in a variety of legal problems and sanctions – the most serious of which is the potential imposition of criminal liability and unlimited fines on companies and their directors.

Any business concerned about the bad publicity or the fines that could result from a breach of data protection laws being uncovered should audit its activities to assess:

■ where risks arise;
■ where those risks are business critical; and
■ what changes can be made to reduce those risks.

It is not possible to draw up a definitive list of actions for every type of business, but the following points may be of assistance:

1. The business activities which should be audited for compliance with the obligations of data protection laws are those that involve the use of any information from which it is possible to identify a living individual. Departments whose activities are therefore likely to be relevant are: personnel, marketing, customer relations, IT/technology support and accounts/billing.

2. In introducing the audit to staff, involve senior management. If changes to procedures need to be made to reduce the risk of non-compliance with data protection laws, these changes will then be easier to implement. Senior management have a vested interested in ensuring data protection compliance as they potentially can be held personally liable for certain breaches of the Act.

3. Bring together the heads of the departments most likely to be audited to explain why the audit is necessary (emphasising the consequences of serious non-compliance), what areas of their activities are regulated and how they will be audited.

4. Prepare a questionnaire to circulate within the departments to assess what information about individuals is processed by that department and the

purposes for which it is used or could be used in the future. This information-gathering process could be supplemented with a round of interviews with staff in relevant departments. In particular consider:

- how information is obtained;
- how information is used;
- what individuals are told when their data are obtained;
- what consents are obtained from individuals;
- whether the information is sent abroad and if so where;
- how long information is kept and how it is kept accurate and up-to-date;
- security measures taken to safeguard the information;
- whether third parties are engaged to process the information and if they are what contracts have been entered with those third parties;
- the business's ability to retrieve information if requested to do so; and
- the business's notification to the OIC – i.e. does it include all information processed and all purposes for which processing is taking place?

5. Assess the results for compliance with the obligations of data protection laws detailed above and the extent to which it is desirable to change current policies and procedures to reduce the risk of non-compliance.

Those e-commerce businesses that decide to carry out data protection compliance audits can reap significant rewards. For instance, an audit can allow the market reputation of an online business to remain untarnished by any bad publicity. Data protection compliance can also be a critical selling tool to any prospective purchaser. Equally as critical to a company's bottom line, a data privacy compliance audit of its activities and online operations should allow that business to identify and crucially, avoid areas of potential financial risk.

Website Content – Whose Responsibility?

Introduction

A business operating online will necessarily publish large amounts of content on its website. To a large degree, the business will be able to exercise control over this content (for example, the business's own content relating to its services); however, there may be content on the site which a business could have difficulty controlling. Such instances usually occur where a business allows a user to post material on its site, such as by operating a bulletin board, where users can post comments or exchange information with other users.

Who is responsible for this content if an aggrieved person presents a legal claim? Can the business point the aggrieved person in the direction of the user making the posting? Or can the internet services provider hosting the business's website be held responsible?

This chapter highlights some of the claims that can arise from website content. In particular, it seeks to show how far an internet services provider ('ISP') can be held responsible for content on websites that they either operate or host.

Businesses that are aware of the potential liability attached to content will be better placed to judge the content that they intend to display on their websites. Where material has been posted by a third party, businesses that are aware of the potential liability attached to content will be better placed to determine what practices should be implemented to minimise the risk of claims.

1. The Internet Service Provider – publisher or carrier?

A business operating online or a website operator, which allows unknown third party material to be posted on its site, faces similar considerations, in terms of legal liability, to ISPs on account of its reduced ability to control what might end up being displayed. Some might argue that an ISP should receive greater immunity from liability because of the sheer volume of content in which it must deal, in contrast to a website operator, who would be responsible for vetting its own site only. Such argument is beyond the scope of this chapter, which focuses generally on ISP liability.

Central to the debate on the extent of ISP liability at both civil and criminal law has been the issue as to whether an ISP is a 'publisher' like a newspaper, or a 'carrier' such as a telecommunications service provider. If an ISP is a publisher, then it is more likely to be found liable for content 'published'. Alternatively, where it is viewed as a carrier (or mere conduit), it is less likely to be held liable for the content it permits users to access. The E-commerce Directive (Directive on Legal Aspects of Information Society Services (2000/31/EC) which was implemented into English law in August 2002 in the form of the Electronic Commerce (EC Directive) Regulations 2002 ('Regulations')) aims to rectify the uncertainty. (See section 4 below.) Regulations 17–19 create a defence for intermediary service providers, including ISPs, for claims arising due to content. Under these Regulations it seems that an ISP who is merely providing access to this content as a 'mere conduit', (namely that the ISP did not initiate the transmission, did not select the receiver of the transmission and did not select or modify the content contained in the transmission), will not be liable for any civil or criminal sanction as a result of that transmission. The ISP must show that it is only giving access to a communication network for the purpose of making the transmission more effective and that the activity is of a mere technical, automatic and passive nature which implies that the ISP has neither knowledge or control over the content that is transmitted or stored. This defence also covers an ISP's acts of transient storage of information and hosting providing that the ISP does not have actual knowledge of the unlawful activity and, if it obtains such knowledge, that it acts expeditiously to remove or to disable access to the content. However, although we can look to the Regulations, as well as the definition of 'publisher' under section 1 of the Defamation Act 1996, the actual fact of whether an ISP is publisher or carrier, or indeed neither, is decided by reference to each specific piece of legislation under which the potential liability falls. It may also be decided on the facts of the case. Therefore, in order to assess fully the risks associated with website content it is still necessary to consider separately actions under English law, both civil and criminal, commonly perceived to give rise to ISP liability, some of which are set out below.

2. Civil liability

2.1 Defamation

Defamation claims have, perhaps, attracted more publicity than any other civil right of action. This section concentrates on what constitutes defamation under English law and whether or not an ISP or website operator might become liable under English defamation legislation.

What is defamation?

An action in defamation requires a statement to have been published that harms a person's reputation. Written or other 'tangible' defamatory statements are known as libel, whereas spoken defamatory statements are known as slander. A defamatory statement must be a false statement, so that a defence to a defamation claim is truth. In other words, even if a statement harms another's reputation, it is not defamatory if it is true. Other defences include 'absolute' or 'qualified' privilege and 'fair comment'. However, the defences that are likely to be relevant to an ISP which is not the maker of a statement are not so much to do with the content of the statement and the motivations for making it, but the manner in which such statement was made available to the public.

It is worth noting that the internet has greatly increased defamation claims as one individual can post a statement which can be seen worldwide in seconds. This raises the issue of where is the applicable jurisdiction for a claim when the posting is on the internet. In the recent case of *King* v. *Lewis* [2004] EWHC 168, the publication of defamatory material was discussed by reference to territory and place of claims. It was stated that the common law regards the publication of an internet posting as taking place where it was downloaded. This means that you can have multiple publications. In addition, a cause of action will accrue in ANY jurisdiction as a result of such publication unless the defendant is able to demonstrate that the claimant really has nothing to protect by way of reputation in that jurisdiction. As such, although Mr King was based in the US, the downloading of the statement in the UK was sufficient for a claim in England as Mr King was sufficiently well known in England to enjoy a reputation there.

When is an ISP liable?

Whether an ISP is liable for defamatory statement on its servers or its website, or whether it is the author who is solely liable, will depend on whether the ISP can be classed as a 'publisher' under the Defamation Act 1996. Under the Defamation Act a person will not be classed as an author, editor or publisher if he is involved only:

- in printing, producing, distributing or selling printed material containing the statement; or
- in (i) processing, making copies of, distributing or selling any electronic medium in or on which the statement is recorded, or (ii) operating or providing any equipment, system or service from which the statement is retrieved, copied, distributed or made available in electronic form; or
- as the operator of or provider of access to a communications system by means of which the statement is transmitted, or made available, by a person over whom he has no effective control.

The courts have indicated expressly or impliedly that the third category set out above can exempt ISPs from being classed as publishers. Logically one would also expect a website operator to be exempt under the second category. *Totalise plc* v. *Motley Fool Ltd* (2001) EMLR 29, appears to confirm such expectation by finding that the website operator, Motley Fool, was not a responsible for publication under section 10 of the Contempt of Court Act 1981 as there was no editorial control. (However, it is worth noting that, in this case, the Court did consider that disclosure was necessary in the interests of justice and adduced other arguments justifying the making of such an order against the website operator).

Another case confirming this approach with respect to ISPs concerned an injunction preventing the publication of the identities of the two young men convicted of murdering James Bulger (*Thompson and Venables* v. *Newsgroup Newspapers* [2001] Fam 430). Certain campaigners intended to publish recent photographs of one of them on the internet. Although not a defamation case, the High Court agreed to grant special dispensation to ISPs. It was decided that, unlike the general press, for the lifespan of this injunction, ISPs will be liable only if they know that prohibited material has been or is likely to be placed on their servers or accessed via their services and they have failed to take *all reasonable steps* to prevent this publication or to block access to it.

The proviso that ISPs must take all reasonable steps to prevent publication or to block access is important, as the same is expressly set out under the Defamation Act. For the Act states that where a person is not the author, editor or publisher of a defamatory statement, in order to avoid liability, he must also show that:

- he took reasonable care in relation to the statement's publication; and
- he did not know, and had no reason to believe, that what he did caused or contributed to the publication of a defamatory statement.

In the case of *Godfrey* v. *Demon Internet Ltd* [2001] QB 201, Demon Internet faced liability for defamation for material posted by an unidentified third party about Dr Godfrey, but did not take any action to remove the offending posting for ten days following a complaint by Dr Godfrey. The judge concluded that, although an ISP may not be a publisher within the meaning of the Defamation Act, because it (i) chose to store postings, and (ii) could edit or delete the postings, it could none the less be held responsible for causing or contributing to that publication. The court was of the view that Demon Internet could not show that it had taken 'reasonable care' in relation to the publication needed under the Act to exempt it from liability.

The conclusion to be drawn is that providing an ISP does not exercise any 'editorial control' over the information published, and takes reasonable steps to remove any defamatory material brought to its attention, then it is unlikely to be held responsible for that defamatory material. Therefore, an ISP needs to have procedures in place to react quickly to any complaint about material posted to a site. Ways in which an ISP might best avoid liability are discussed at the end of this chapter. However, there is still much scope for debate on how ISPs can minimise risks since, as in the *Bulger* case, the courts have so far declined to give guidance on what are the reasonable steps an ISP must take to prevent publication of, or block access to, offending material.

Likewise, the E-commerce Directive (and UK Regulations) do not set out to impose specific 'notice and takedown' procedures following a complaint to an ISP but rather seek to encourage self-regulatory systems. However the UK Regulations do state that an ISP is required to 'act expeditiously to remove or to disable access to the information' once it has the requisite degree of 'knowledge or awareness' of the illegal posting. Although many ISP organisations in the UK have contacted the European Commission to ask for guidance in relation to a) how they should judge whether a posting is illegal, and hence how to know the circumstances when it should be taken down and b) what sort of timescales are required in relation to acting 'expeditiously', the Commission has made it clear that it favours voluntary self-regulation in the industry, with self-regulatory bodies devising their own codes of practice (rather than the UK imposing formal legislation, although the Directive does not prevent other member states doing this).

2.2 Intellectual property

Intellectual property rights are rights that subsist in intangible property. The scope of intangible property protected is very broad and could take the form of a song, a play, a computer program, a compilation or some form of distinctive branding. Intellectual property rights most relevant to the content of websites are copyright, database rights, trade marks and passing off. Some intellectual property rights, namely trade marks and passing off, are also relevant to the subject of domain names (not themselves intellectual property rights). Trade marks and passing off in the context of domain name disputes are discussed in detail in chapter 7.

Copyright infringement

Copyright is the term given to certain legal rights that protect the *expression* of ideas (but not the ideas themselves). Copyright arises automatically when a work is created without the need for registration and can take many forms: literary, musical or dramatic works. In addition, the fixation of works into other mediums can themselves attract copyright such as sound recordings, films or broadcasts. Text, images, music and video footage therefore are all usually 'works' for the purposes of copyright, as are computer programs which are considered to be 'literary works'.

The Copyright Designs and Patents Act 1988 (CDPA) gives the owner of copyright the right to control the manner or extent to which a work is exploited and covers, for example:

- copying – such as simply reproducing a literary work onto a website ('copying' under the CDPA includes storing material in electronic form);
- issuing copies to the public – such as allowing an unpublished work to be downloaded via a website;
- performing, showing or playing in public – such as making concerts or films available to the public via a website;
- broadcasting – such as live concerts broadcasted over the internet; and
- adapting – extracts of a work used or manipulated for use in some way, such as song lyrics modified for the purposes of an advertising campaign.

When displaying another's content (which usually amounts to copying or issuing copies to the public) an ISP must take care not to infringe another's copyright. No knowledge element is required for copyright infringement, thus it is irrelevant whether an ISP is ignorant as to whether or not a third party's copyright exists in a work. Furthermore, copyright infringement can occur even if just part of a work is used, if that part is a substantial part. Whether that particular part used is a substantial part of the work is judged qualitatively and is not solely based on how much of a work has been reproduced, so that, for example, the reproduction of a few distinctive bars of a song could sustain a claim for copyright infringement. Hence, an ISP may not avoid copyright infringement by simply using small extracts of another's work.

An ISP should therefore attempt to limit the risk of copyright infringement by ensuring it has the consent of the copyright owner to its material for the activities for which it intends to use it. Alternatively, the CDPA does permit certain activities and it is possible an ISP may be able to bring itself within the permitted exceptions. The exceptions include use of the material for research, education, the reporting of current events and for the purposes of criticism or review. However, in all cases where there is a risk of infringement, ISPs should err on the side of caution and obtain a licence from the copyright owner which permits the ISP to make the content available via its site to users.

Databases

Some databases will be protected by copyright as original compilations, however most databases will be protected by the Copyright and Rights in Databases Regulations 1997 (SI 1997 No. 3032). Under the regulations, a database is defined as a collection of independent data arranged in a systematic and methodical way individually accessible by electronic or other means. Due to the way in which websites are constructed, a website will generally fall within the definition of a database, as it is a collection of data files stored in a systematic way which allows for the formation of individual web pages.

The 'database right' is granted to a person who takes the initiative or invests in the obtaining, verifying or presenting of the contents of the database. The owner of a database right can prevent the extraction of all or a substantial part of the database, or the repeated systematic extraction of insubstantial parts if such repeated extraction in itself amounts to an extraction of a substantial part. Reproducing the content of another's website (a database in itself) could give rise to a claim for infringement of database rights. The full extent of the database right has recently been considered by the ECJ judgment in *British Horseracing Board Limited* ('BHB') v. *William Hill Organisation Limited* [2005] 1 CMLR 15. A claim was bought against William Hill by the BHB for the reproduction of various lists of race runners and riders. The court reviewed the following issues: (a) Had there been relevant investment by BHB in creating the reproduced material in order for database rights to exist? and (b) What criteria is required to establish infringement (i.e. what amounts to extraction and re-use for the purposes of infringement; how should a court assess whether a substantial or insubstantial part has been extracted and re-used; and in what circumstances can the repeated use of insubstantial parts be an infringement?) The court reviewed these issues and found in favour of William Hill (although the BHB may take this case to the Court of Appeal). This was because the court found that the material extracted did not amount to a 'substantial part' and that there was not sufficient investment by BHB in the creation of the database. The implications of this decision are that database rights will be of more limited application than first thought. However if a party can show sufficient investment in the creation of the database then it will still be a powerful tool.

Trade marks

A trade mark is some form of graphical representation which is capable of distinguishing the source of a product or service. Trade marks can therefore be words, images, shapes and, in some cases, a mere combination of letters, numbers or colours. They are valuable tools used by businesses to differentiate their brand or product line to generate repeat business. The Trade Marks Act 1994 gives certain monopoly rights to use a trade mark to the owner of that mark where it has been registered with the UK Trade Marks Agency (or the European Union trade marks registry, the Office for Harmonisation in the Internal Market or OHIM).

Furthermore, a trade mark owner can sue for damages for loss sustained through any unauthorised use of his or her mark, or for use of a mark which is similar to his or her registered mark and is being used in association with the same or similar goods or services, providing customers are likely to be confused by the use of the similar mark.

An ISP might find itself infringing the trade mark rights of another person if it displays a trade mark on a website without that person's consent to do so. Thus, using the trade mark to advertise or offer goods or services for sale under that mark will infringe a trade mark owner's rights if it done without his or her consent. This fact is important to bear in mind where an ISP is offering second-hand goods for sale on its site, or operating an online auction for the sale of goods between users, where it is unlikely that there is a reseller arrangement in place between the ISP and the trade mark owner under which one would ordinarily expect the re-seller to have been given the right to use the mark.

One exception under the Trade Marks Act to the restriction on usage is the permission to use another's mark for the purposes of comparative advertising. An ISP may wish to refer to the products or services of others in its advertisements in order to show its own goods or services in a favourable light. Providing it is done in accordance with honest commercial practices and providing use does not take 'unfair advantage' of the mark or is detrimental to its distinctive character or reputation, such advertising may involve the use of the other parties' trade marks.

What constitutes the 'unfair advantage' of a mark has been much debated with no firm conclusions, as by its very nature, comparative advertising shows another's goods or services to be inferior, which could take unfair advantage of a mark or be detrimental to its reputation. The Control of Misleading Advertisements (Amendment) Regulations 2000 attempts to address the problem by setting out certain conditions that a comparative advertisement should meet. By adhering to these Regulations, the ISP at least limits the risk that it will be infringing trade marks or acting illegally in advertising campaigns that compare the goods or services of another to its own.

Passing off

Passing off is an area of law that protects the goodwill of business and seeks to restrain one business from passing off its goods or services as being those of another. Although much of a business's goodwill is concerned with its name, so that a claim for passing off will often overlap with trade mark infringement actions, passing off is wide in scope and is capable of protecting names, logos, materials, advertising themes and any other part of a business's general 'get-up' that distinguishes its goods or services from those of others. There is no requirement for registration in order to invoke the law of passing off, but a business must first have a reputation, in other words some goodwill, to protect.

Essentially, a claim for passing off will be made out if a misrepresentation is made by a business to potential customers which causes confusion as to the origin or association of its goods/services, and it is reasonably foreseeable that the goodwill of another business will be injured by this confusion and is likely to suffer loss as a result. A fraudulent motive is not necessary for a claim of passing off and relief may be granted even where the passing off was unintentional. ISPs may find that passing off is particularly relevant in cases of 'deep linking' and 'framing'.

Deep linking and framing

'Deep linking' is the linking of a user from one website to another in such a way so as to bypass the homepage of the second site. Bypassing a homepage can be objectionable as it may enable a user to bypass registration or log in procedures, terms and conditions of use, or revenue generating advertising.

'Framing' is the linking of one website with another in a manner that presents the content of one or more pages from a linked website within the frame of the original website, sometimes even removing all distinguishing features of the linked site so that the user is deceived into believing that that he or she is still viewing content from the original site.

Potentially, copying (by downloading or storing) text as a result of a link could give rise to a claim for infringement of copyright or database rights. Framing another's text or otherwise embellishing material taken from a third party's site could lead to a claim for passing off. Using a trade mark as a link button could give rise to a claim of passing off or for trade mark infringement. However, the status of deep linking and framing and to what extent such practices will be caught by copyright, database and trade mark legislation or the law of passing off is still untested in the UK and it thus remains unclear whether the consent of the owner of a website is required before a link can be provided to his or her site. In view of the uncertainty, some practical guidance is given at the end of this chapter to assist with minimising the risks of infringing another's intellectual property rights by linking or framing.

Metatags

Metatags are words or a series of words embedded in a website's HMTL (Hypertext Mark Up Language, the language used to create internet documents) which are descriptive of the site and enable search engines to pick out relevant sites in response to a user request. Some website operators have used another's trade marks as metatags as a means of diverting users to their sites. Use of another's trade marks in this way may amount to trade mark infringement (*Roadtech Computer System Ltd* v. *Mandata (Management and Data Services) Ltd* [2000] ETMR 970, where Mandata admitted trade mark infringement and the Court awarded damages to Roadtech).

2.3 Confidential information

The law of confidence protects confidential information from disclosure to parties to whom the owner of that information has not authorised disclosure. Information protected can be personal, commercial, industrial, state – in fact information of almost any character, providing:

■ it is specific;
■ is of limited availability;
■ has a quality of confidence;
■ has been disclosed to another in circumstances containing an obligation of confidence; and
■ unauthorised use of that information has caused harm to the person who imparted it.

Specific

For material to be protected as confidential it must be possible to point to a piece or collection of material that is not so entwined with publicly available material that it is impossible to isolate and identify.

Limited availability

In the context of confidential information, limited availability does not necessarily mean that the authorised user group is narrow, but could include any material that is communicated to recipients on the understanding that it is for their use alone. In fact, the action could be made out if all the individual items of information constituting the material were publicly available, but if others would need to expend effort or money collating the information in the form in which it was communicated deems the material of limited availability.

Quality of confidence

Material having the quality of confidence is material that is not a matter of general public knowledge.

Obligation of confidence

Examples of relationships that confer an obligation of confidence include an employment relationship, or a customer's relationship with its bank, confidence imposed under a contract, or any information that is disclosed to another marked 'confidential'.

Unauthorised use has caused harm

Material that has no value is not protected. The value need not be commercial, but trivial information such as gossip is not protected.

Breach of confidence

A breach of confidence is committed when a recipient:

- discloses or uses information; or
- receives information

when he or she knows, or ought to know, that its disclosure, use or receipt is unauthorised. Even if the material was initially obtained innocently, a breach of confidence can be committed if the recipient realises or ought to realise that the material is confidential and retains or uses the material improperly.

The case of *Sir Elton John* v. *Countess Joulebine* [2001] Masons CLR 91, demonstrates how the law of confidence is relevant to ISPs. Countess Joulebine failed to defend an action brought by Elton John and his solicitors for breach of confidence, in respect of the display on the Countess's website of a legal opinion of Elton John's legal counsel concerning Elton John's ongoing legal action against his accountants. It was accepted that she was not initially aware that the information had been posted, however she was deemed to have 'received' the information once she became aware that it was on the site. Although the Countess also claimed that she did not realise that the legal opinion was confidential, the court found that she *should* have realised that the information was confidential and consequently ensured its removal from her site.

It is perhaps noteworthy that Countess Joulebine claimed not to have received (and on this point was not challenged) any complaints about the posting of counsel's legal opinion on the site and yet remained liable. Thus, it is clear that ISPs will need to exercise their own judgment as to the confidential nature of any material posted and take appropriate action of their own accord in order to escape liability.

3. Criminal liability

Certain website content can lead to prosecution for a criminal offence. Some of the most topical forms of criminal liability that can arise are discussed below.

Offences can be committed by individuals and by companies. Usually, if a company acts upon a decision made by its board and thereby commits an offence, then the company is prosecuted. Penalty on conviction is a fine. However, in certain circumstances, and notably for the offences of obscene publications, indecent child photographs and racial hatred set out below, the legislation permits officers of a company to be charged for the offences personally in addition to the company. When charged personally with some of the offences described below, officers of a company could face imprisonment on conviction.

ISPs should also bear in mind that, providing a magistrate agrees that there are reasonable grounds, the police possess powers of entry and seizure to confiscate hardware and other equipment on which offending material is suspected to be stored. Powers of search and seizure can be exercised prior to the commencement of any prosecution and regardless as to whether or not a prosecution is subsequently launched. Quite apart from any damage that might result from seizure of equipment, the police may remove documents and other information relating to the trade carried out by the ISP, which can exacerbate the disruption to a business.

As the law in this area develops, certain cases have demonstrated that courts may take a broad view of what constitutes legal jurisdiction. The country where material is uploaded or hosted is not necessarily that which determines jurisdiction, but the place in which it is downloaded. Holocaust denials, Nazi memorabilia, defamation and pornography have all spelled trouble for those who thought that they were protected by the law of the country in which uploading took place. However, if material can be accessed in another jurisdiction where it is regarded as illegal, then native courts may well take the view that the suppliers of such material are subject to their laws. Instances of this have already occurred in Germany, Australia, France and the United Kingdom.

In addition to the provisions of criminal law, ISPs also need to be aware of potential regulatory developments. One example of this is the common labelling system proposed by Ofcom in its media literacy strategy. Under the Communications Act 2003, Ofcom is obliged to 'bring about a better public understanding of the nature and characteristics of material published by means of electronic media'. Following consultation on this matter, Ofcom has stated its support for the development of a common labelling system which would provide 'greater consistency in presenting information related to possible harm and offence and to protect young and vulnerable people from inappropriate material'. To achieve this end, Ofcom has proposed the creation of a cross-platform working group which includes major ISPs, broadcasters and mobile phone operators.

3.1 Obscene publications

Under the Obscene Publications Act 1959 it is an offence for any person either: to publish an obscene article (regardless of whether or not this is done for gain) or to have an obscene article for publication for gain (regardless of whether that gain is his, or another person's). In the latter case, someone is judged to have an article if it is within their ownership, possession or control. In either case, the maximum penalty is three years' imprisonment and/or a fine. There are three elements to the offence that must be fulfilled. An ISP must have:

- published;
- an article*;
- which is obscene.

*The definition of 'article' is broad. It covers material that can be read or looked at, and includes, within its ambit, sound recordings, films or any other records of a picture or pictures.

Publishing

By making material available to be downloaded from a website an ISP will, on the face of it, 'publish' that material under this legislation. Further, the Act itself expressly states that publishing includes transmitting electronically stored data and, in this context, the courts have interpreted 'publication' as meaning both the uploading and downloading of material. Clearly, ISPs could find themselves liable as a publisher for material they make available to the public.

Article

An article under the Obscene Publications Act can be in the form of text, an image or even information on a computer disc. Material found on a website hosted on ISP servers is likely to be construed as an 'article'.

Obscene

An article is considered obscene if it tends to 'deprave and corrupt' persons likely to read, see, or hear it. The material covered includes not just porno-graphic materials as are commonly associated with the concept of obscene materials, but also material relating to explosives, violence or perhaps even illicit drugs. For instance, following the broadcast over the internet of hostage executions in Iraq, it was suggested in some quarters that those publishing this material might also be acting in breach of the Act. Although this theory has not yet been tested in court, such discussion underlines an important fact: the definition of 'obscene' is neither fixed nor narrowly confined. It may well alter over time according to social circumstances and perception.

Defences

It is a defence to offences under this Act for a person to show that they had not examined the article in question, and they had no reasonable cause to suspect that their publication of the article would lead to liability for such an offence.

Since, on the face of it, by making obscene material available via a website an ISP is likely to be guilty of the offence, it must therefore ensure that it is in a position to be able to rely on one of the defences available and that its business practice facilitates such reliance. For example, an ISP may decide not to monitor the content hosted on its servers or posted to its website so that it can prove that it had not examined the obscene article. (Admittedly a refusal to monitor is perhaps more difficult to justify when a website operator is merely operating a single site.) Or, if the material concerned is only available on a section of the ISP's site, such as a subscription or password-protected section that is not accessible to children, then it may be more difficult for the prosecution to prove that material has a tendency to deprave and corrupt those likely to view it. However, as demonstrated by *R v. Perrin* [2002] EWCA Crim 747, all hope of such a defence would evaporate if samples of the obscene material contained in restricted sections were to be displayed on a web-page accessible to the public.

3.2 Indecent images of children

The Protection of Children Act 1978 contains a variety of offences relating to indecent images of children. The offence most relevant to ISPs concerns: (a) making such images; and (b) distributing or showing such images. The maximum penalty is ten years' imprisonment and/or a fine.

For an ISP to be convicted, the elements therefore are as follows:

- an image;
- must have been made, distributed or shown;
- of a child;
- which is indecent.

Image

An image includes a photograph and a pseudo-photograph (such as a computer-generated graphic image) and any material stored on a computer, disk or other electronic means that can be converted into a photograph.

Making, distributing or showing

In theory, ISPs can actually be convicted of 'making' an indecent image as the technological process of a user uploading such an image onto its servers involves the copying of the image by the ISP's server. Easier to prove is the distribution and/or displaying of such images. An ISP can be deemed to 'distribute' images by the fact they are stored on its servers and then made accessible to internet users with or without the use of a password.

Child
A child is defined as a person under the age of eighteen.

Indecent
Whether a photograph is indecent is a matter for a jury or magistrate trying the case to decide.

Defence
Falling within a defence is clearly important for an ISP. The legislation provides a defence to the acts of displaying an indecent image for those that can show that they had had not seen the image and therefore did not know or have any cause to suspect that such an image would be indecent. If the presence of an indecent photograph is brought to the attention of ISP staff, such as through a user complaint, then the ISP must ensure that the material is deleted or handed over to a law enforcement agency immediately, or the ISP runs the risk of not being able to rely on the defence.

3.3 Racial hatred

The Public Order Act 1986 prohibits:

(a) the display of written material;
(b) the publishing or distributing of written material;
(c) the distribution, showing or playing of visual images or sounds; and
(d) including, in a programme service, a programme which has visual images or sounds, which are threatening, abusive or insulting and where there is either an intent to encourage racial hatred or such racial hatred is likely to result. The maximum penalty is seven years' imprisonment and/or a fine.

Therefore, to be convicted of an offence, an ISP must have:

- committed any of the acts listed in (a) to (d) above;
- which were threatening, abusive or insulting; and
- where the material was intended to encourage racial hatred or such racial hatred was likely to result.

Displaying, publishing or distributing
What constitutes the display, publication or distribution of offending material under this Act is likely to entail the same analysis as discussed for previous criminal offences. An ISP can be deemed to fulfil one or more activities by the

fact that images are either displayed on a website, or stored on its servers and made accessible to internet users.

Written material
Written material includes any sign or visual representation.

Programme and programme service
A 'programme' does not have to be lengthy – it may simply be an advertisement. A programme service consists of sending, by means of an electronic network sounds and/or images for reception at two or more places in the UK, or for reception at a location in the UK for presentation to members of the public or to any group of persons.

Threatening, abusive or insulting
Whether the material is 'threatening, abusive or insulting' must be determined by reference to the ordinary dictionary meanings of such words.

Intended or likely to encourage racial hatred
This aspect makes plain that even if an ISP did not intend to stir up racial hatred by any such display or publication or distribution, it can still be convicted of the offence if a jury or magistrate considers that racial hatred would be likely to result from the material. (Racial hatred under the Act is hatred against a group of persons in Great Britain defined by reference to colour, race, nationality, or ethnic or national origins – examples of ethnic groups that are not a race or nationality are Sikhs and Jews.)

Defence
The Act provides a defence to ISPs that can prove that they were unaware of the content of the material and that they did not suspect and had no reason to suspect that the material concerned was threatening, abusive or insulting. Again, as with other offences under the Act, the ISP could argue that in not vetting content on its servers prior to to that content becoming available to the public, it acted as a 'mere conduit' without any reason to know of or suspect the nature of the content. But the ISP must be aware that such a defence will be lost if it fails to act expeditiously once offending material has been brought to its attention by means of a complaint from a user or member of the public. Once again, therefore, careful attention to the ISP's internal procedures dealing with complaints is critical.

The Public Order Act 1986 contains a number of additional offences that could apply to ISPs, such as the the possession of racially inflammatory material with a view to it being displayed, published, distributed, shown or played. Each offence contains a defence in similar terms to that already outlined above.

3.4 Financial services

The Financial Services and Markets Act 2000 (FSMA) places a restriction on financial promotion: it prohibits a person, in the course of business, from communicating an invitation or inducement to engage in investment activity unless either the person communicating the inducement is authorised under the Act to do so, or the content of the communication is approved by an authorised person. The defence for those accused of committing this offence consists of showing that:

(a) they had reasonable grounds for believing that the content of the communication was prepared or approved by an authorised person; and
(b) they took all reasonable precautions to avoid committing the offence.

However, failure to comply with the provisions of the Act, or to present a viable defence, may result in a maximum penalty of two years' imprisonment and/or a fine.

The Financial Services Authority Handbook says that a financial promotion may be communicated, amongst other things, by means of general advertising on websites or mailshots by e-mail. It further states that an inducement or invitation may consist of a link to a website or a banner advertisement on a website. It is therefore advisable for ISPs to give careful consideration to the type of information they are providing, as well as the means of communicating it. While exemptions are provided under the FSMA 2000 (Financial Promotion) Order 2001 for hosting, caching and acting as a 'mere conduit', these are dependent on a number of conditions being satisfied. ISPs who are unsure whether or not their activities constitute financial promotions would be well-advised to seek relevant professional advice to ensure that they are operating within the parameters of the law.

3.5 Regulation of Investigatory Powers Act 2000

In some circumstances and notwithstanding that an ISP itself might have no liability at either civil or criminal law for the content of a website, an ISP can become liable to disclose information about the user who is responsible.

The Regulation of Investigatory Powers Act 2000 (RIPA) came into force on 28 July 2000. The basic premise of the Act is that it is a criminal offence for a person (including an ISP) to intercept, at any place in the UK, any communication in the course of its transmission.

Exceptions are permitted primarily related to law enforcement and, therefore, a business sending data over the internet or via e-mail, whether or not this is part of its operation of a website, should be aware that it is forbidden to intercept third-party data (unless consent has been obtained), although that data (including its own data and not just third-party data) is liable to interception by enforcement agencies and other government bodies.

Under RIPA, disclosure of traffic data (such as to whom and from whom the communication is being transmitted) or the disclosure of the contents of the communication, can be ordered even where additional methods of confidentiality have been used, such as a password, access code or form of encryption needed to unlock the data into a readable form. In all cases it is a criminal offence not to comply, and can result in a maximum penalty of two years' imprisonment and/or a fine.

Data intercepted under this Act which is encrypted will need to be decrypted. Any person reasonably believed to be in possession of the key, or in possession of information which might facilitate the discovery of the encryption key, can be required to disclose the facilitating information or use the key to produce the intercepted data in intelligible form. Sometimes disclosure of the encryption key itself can be ordered. Failure to comply can result in a criminal prosecution for an offence carrying a maximum penalty of two years' imprisonment and/or a fine. It is also a criminal offence for a person to tip off any party that disclosure relating to the encryption key has taken place. The maximum penalty in such circumstances is five years' imprisonment and/or a fine.

Human rights implications

Where the interception relates to traffic data, the Act permits, for example, the police or Customs and Excise to require an ISP to intercept data for a number of reasons including: the economic well-being of the UK, public safety, preventing or detecting crime or preventing disorder, collecting any tax, duty or levy. It has, therefore, been argued that the government will invariably be able to justify almost all cases of interception when RIPA has been drafted in such wide terms.

Interception of data inevitably makes the government vulnerable to claims of unlawful interference with human rights and rights to privacy in particular the right to respect for private and family life, home and correspondence enshrined in Article 8 of the European Convention on Human Rights and implemented into UK law in the Human Rights Act 1998. The Convention imposes a positive obligation on the UK government to take measures which actively promote and safeguard the rights enshrined within it and makes it unlawful for a public authority to act in a way incompatible with a Convention right.

3.6 Anti-Terrorism, Crime and Security Act 2001

Most ISPs claim to delete data once it is no longer needed for billing purposes – on average, this is said to be three months. Any enforced retention period beyond the standard business practice is likely to have cost consequences for internet services providers in terms of (i) archive burdens in that vast amounts of data might have to be stored; and (ii) retrieval, which is likely to be expensive and difficult to manage. Any costs consequences for an ISP are likely to be passed down to the operators of the websites it hosts or to other users of its services.

Data retention has become a major concern and rumours of the introduction of lengthy data retention periods (some sources originally hinted at seven years) circulated for a considerable time before any guidance was given by the government in the form of the Voluntary Code of Practice (see below). With strong pressure exerted by law enforcement agencies following the attacks on the World Trade Centre on 11 September 2001, many ISPs feared that the UK government would implement excessive retention requirements, ostensibly for the purposes of national security and the prevention and detection of criminal offences. The resulting Anti-Terrorism Crime and Security Act 2001 (ATCSA) did little to alleviate concerns. Although the Act gives the Secretary of State the power to make a contribution towards the costs of data retention, it need only be provided in such cases '*as he thinks fit*'. Hence payments are entirely at the government's discretion and may not cover the full costs incurred.

But costs aren't the only concern, for the ATCSA merely provides a structure for compelling data retention without the detail. It permits the Secretary of State to issue, and revise, a code of practice 'relating to the retention by communications providers of communications data obtained or held by them'. Following a consultation process, in which respondents expressed concerns over likely cost, proposed timescales for retention of data, and the disparity between the suggested retention and access regimes, the Home Office produced a Voluntary Code of Practice ('the Code') which was brought into effect on 5 December 2003 by The Retention of Communications Data (Code of Practice) Order 2003.

The basic tenet of the Code is to extend the period beyond which communications providers normally retain communications data for business purposes. Although the Code was made and issued in accordance with the provisions of the ATCSA, like that Act, it relies on the definition of 'communications data' set out in Chapter 2, Part 1 of RIPA. According to this, communications data is separated into three types: traffic data (by which the movement and destination of the communication may be tracked); use made of service data (which shows what services were used without revealing the content of the communication); client data (information which does not fall into either of the other two categories but which may be held or obtained by the communications provider and which provides information about a subscriber).

In the foreword to the Code, the government states that its intention in seeking to extend the retention period for communications data beyond that normally employed for business purposes is 'to ensure that the UK security, intelligence and law enforcement agencies have sufficient information available to them to assist them in protecting the UK's national security and to investigate terrorism'. More specifically, section 102(3) of the ATCSA is quoted as the underlying purpose of the Code, that is, to serve: (a) the purposes of safeguarding national security (b) the purposes of prevention or detection of crime or the prosecution of offenders which may relate directly or indirectly to national security.

The Code applies to 'all communication service providers who provide a public telecommunications service in the United Kingdom ... and who retain communications data in line with the provisions of the Act'. Appendix A to the Code sets out various types of data together with relevant retention periods. The types of data include: subscriber information; telephony data SMS, EMS and MMS data; e-mail data, ISP data, and web activity logs. The maximum retention period is 12 months (subscriber and telephony data), while the minimum period specified is four days for web activity logs. Two other categories of data, which consist of Other Services and Collateral Data, have an unspecified retention period. This is dependent on the data involved.

A subject about which the Code is less specific is that relating to costs. Where the retention period for national security purposes is not substantially larger than that for business purposes, the communications provider is expected to bear the burden of any additional costs; and, even where the retention periods for national security purposes are significantly longer, the government undertakes only to 'contribute a reasonable proportion of the marginal cost as appropriate'. These are hardly words of comfort for those within the industry who, for a long time, have feared the pecuniary impact of such extended retention periods on their businesses. Perhaps it is for this reason that commentators on the subject have reported a less than enthusiastic response to the Code from communications providers who do not appear to have been in any rush to sign up to it.

The ATCSA stipulates that failure to comply with a code of practice will not, of itself, result in criminal or civil proceedings. Thus, the government is not able to force a communications provider to comply with the Voluntary Code of Practice. However, another of the Act's provisions confers a power on the Secretary of State to authorise directions about retention of communications data if 'it appears ... that it is necessary to do so'. In this case, compliance with the directions would be mandatory and legally enforceable.

In the event that the Code proves unsuccessful, the Secretary of State might, therefore, be expected to make legally binding directions under the Act. However, the necessity for such action may well be pre-empted by developments in Europe.

In March 2004, the European Council issued a Declaration on combating terrorism in which it issued instructions requiring the consideration of 'proposals for establishing rules on the retention of communications traffic data by service providers'. The result was a Draft Framework Decision ('DFD'), submitted by the United Kingdom, France, Sweden and Ireland which aims to harmonise rules governing data retention throughout member states. Potentially, its impact could be far more sweeping than the provisions of the Code. For instance, the DFD proposes a minimum retention period of 12 months, with 36 months as the maximum. However, it goes on to state that 'Member states may have longer periods for retention of data dependent upon national criteria when such retention constitutes a necessary, appropriate and proportionate measure within a democratic society'. The reasons which the DFD proposes for retaining data are also more specific than those set out in the Code, whose main aim is, rather vaguely, stated to consist of protecting national security and preventing/detecting crime. The DFD states that 'it is necessary to retain data in order to trace the source of illegal content such as child pornography and racist and xenophobic material; the source of attacks against information systems; and to identify those involved in using electronic communications networks for the purpose of organised crime and terrorism'. In reality, this may not represent an extension of scope, so much as a clarification of the basis on which any relevant EU law is to be made. While the elements listed may fall within the criminal legislation of several member states, this may not be true of all. However, only time will tell.

When it issued its initial instructions regarding the retention of communications data, the European Council proposed that priority should be given to examination of relevant proposals with a view to their adoption by June 2005. The DFD suggests that implementation of its provisions by all member states should take place within two years of adoption and it is feasible, therefore, that new EU-wide rules could be in place by 2007.

Businesses should bear in mind that ISPs may, at some point, be compelled to disclose *and* store data transmitted by them over the internet or via e-mail. Where a business is a website operator, the obligations on an ISP will extend to data transmitted by users of that business's website. Businesses should also be aware that ISPs are likely to exclude in their terms of service with website operators any liability for the accuracy or consequences of such data stored and disclosed in this way.

3.7 Liability of a website operator to disclose a user's identity

RIPA and the Anti-Terrorism Crime and Security Act set out the statutory requirements on ISPs to reveal to *government bodies* traffic data or the content of communications of users. In addition, there is an obligation under UK civil law on website operators to disclose the identity of a user of its site to *private persons* where a person is contemplating bringing a claim against that user for content he or she has posted to a site (e.g. for defamation or for intellectual property infringement).

However, some key cases demonstrate the courts' awareness of the competing claims on an innocent intermediary (e.g. an ISP or a website operator) who is required to disclose the identity of a third party who would otherwise have remained anonymous.

The first of these cases was that of *Norwich Pharmacal Company and Others* v. *Commissioners of Customs and Excise* [1974] AC 133. In this case, patent owner Norwich Pharmacal required Customs and Excise to reveal the identity of persons who had imported its patented products without licence. Customs and Excise justified their non-disclosure of the information on the grounds that such disclosure would: (a) obstruct them in the performance of their statutory duties; and (b) be prejudicial to those whose identity was disclosed. While alluding to the difficulty of ordering disclosure against an innocent intermediary, the Court nevertheless allowed Norwich Pharmacal's application. Lord Cross of Chelsea enumerated a set of principles that have been much quoted in subsequent cases. He said that, in order to decide whether or not to grant such an application, the Court needed to decide whether, in all the circumstances it was right to make an order. To reach that decision, it should consider the following:

(a) the strength of the applicant's case against the unknown alleged wrong-doer;

(b) the relation subsisting between the alleged wrongdoer and the respondent; whether the information could be obtained from another source; whether the giving of information would put the respondent to trouble which could not be compensated by the payment of all expenses by the applicant.

The principles established in *Norwich Pharmacal* resulted in what is referred to now as a *Norwich Pharmacal* application. This has proved a useful means of obtaining disclosure of identity in a number of instances, including a recent case of alleged copyright piracy (see the *BPI* case below).

Website operators who run discussion rooms, may find themselves in an invidious position when subscribers use that facility to post defamatory remarks. This was the situation in *Totalise Plc* v. *The Motley Fool Ltd and Interactive Investor Ltd* (2001) EMLR 29. Totalise sought a court order to obtain information concerning the identity of an anonymous contributor, called Z Dust, from the defendants. In this case, the Court held that the material posted by Z Dust was clearly defamatory and that disclosure was necessary in the interests of justice. Other elements influencing the Court's decision to grant an order for disclosure were:

(a) a strong *prima facie* case against Z Dust;

(b) the seriousness of the defamatory material;

(c) the serious threat of damage to the claimant posed by Z Dust's campaign;

(d) Z Dust was taking advantage of the anonymity afforded by the discussion boards;

(e) the claimant had no other means of identifying Z Dust.

The Court subsequently granted an order for disclosure on the grounds that '*to find otherwise would be to give the clearest indication to those who wish to defame that they can do so with impunity behind the screen of anonymity made possible by the use of websites on the internet*'. The Court also awarded costs against the defendants.

A subsequent appeal from this judgment by one of the defendants, highlights the dilemma in which website operators and ISPs may find themselves when caught between protecting the identity of a subscriber and satisfying requests for disclosure from an outraged third party.

While not questioning the Court's initial decision on disclosure, defendant Interactive *did* challenge its award of costs against it. (In *Norwich Pharmacal* applications, it is usual for the applicant to pay the costs). Interactive argued that it had not disclosed the identity of Z Dust on its own initiative due to its fear of breaching: (a) the provisions of the Data Protection Act; and (b) the terms of its own privacy policy under which it was contractually obliged not to reveal the identity of its users. Interactive had therefore opted to play it safe, preferring to wait for the Court's decision in a matter where it was unsure of its legal position.

In this instance, Interactive's 'wait-and-see' strategy paid off and the award of costs, initially made against it, was reversed. In this latter case, the Court of Appeal said that '*it is for the applicant to satisfy the Court that the order should be made, not for the defendant to take a view which could be wrong*'. The Court also stated its belief that it was '*legitimate for a party, such as Interactive, who reasonably agrees to keep information confidential and private to refuse to voluntarily hand over such information*'. These words echo those of Lord Cross of Chelsea in the *Norwich Pharmacal* case, who said that: '*in any case in which there was the least doubt as to whether disclosure should be made the person to whom the request was made would be fully justified in saying that he would only make it under an order of the Court*'.

Two key points seem to emerge from the cases referred to above: (a) in the interests of doing justice to a claimant, courts may waive an intermediary's statutory or contractual duties and order disclosure of a third party's identity; and (b) when requested by an aggrieved party to disclose the identity of a third party, intermediaries who are uncertain of their legal position (and potential liability under statutory or contractual law) may be better advised to await a decision from the Court rather than acting on their own initiative. While such an intermediary should put all the facts before the Court (for example, notifying the Court of the existence of any relevant confidentiality agreements) in most cases, it would be well-advised not to oppose the other party's application for disclosure because of cost implications.

It seems likely that, in the future, ISPs may experience further use of *Norwich Pharmacal* applications in relation to cases of illegal file sharing. The British Phonographic Institute (BPI) recently succeeded in obtaining an order requiring a number of ISPs to reveal the names of account-holders who the BPI believes to be guilty of illegally sharing copyrighted sound recordings.

Finally, when an intermediary is required to make a disclosure of the kind discussed in this section, how much information needs to be given? Earlier case law on disclosure of a wrongdoer's identity (dealing in circumstances unrelated to the internet) suggests that the information to be supplied is not limited to a name and address, but is *'all information necessary to enable a party to decide whether it is worth suing the wrongdoer'* (*Société Romanaise de la Chaussure SA v. British Shoe Corp Ltd* [1991] FSR 1). Such interpretation could mean the disclosure of all information that the ISP holds for that user and, taken to the extreme, could extend to data relating to financial status such as assets or income, which almost always is a consideration when deciding whether or not to sue. (*Note*: Although not covered in this chapter, it may be useful to note in this context that CPR 31.17 provides for discovery of *documents* (as opposed to 'information').)

4. Recent legislation affecting ISPs

4.1 The E-commerce Directive (implemented in the UK in August 2002 as the Electronic Commerce (EC Directive) Regulations 2002)

The E-commerce Directive (2000/31/EC) makes certain pronouncements on the treatment of an ISP. In order to encourage the setting up of e-businesses within the European Union, the Directive attempts to limit the liability of an ISP by ensuring that it is regarded across all member states as a carrier or mere conduit.

Important provisions of the Directive are set out below. Provisions relating to mere conduits and monitoring are likely to be relevant to both internet service providers and website operators, whereas the provisions relating to caching and hosting are likely to affect ISPs only. The Directive has been implemented in the UK as the Electronic Commerce (EC Directive) Regulations 2002 and came into effect in August 2002.

No obligation to monitor

The Directive sets out that no general obligation should be imposed by member states on ISPs to screen or actively monitor third-party content, including obligations to filter content for evidence of illegal activity.

Mere conduit

The Directive provides an exemption from liability for ISPs where they play a *passive* role as a conduit of information for users by the transmission of information via a communications network.

Therefore, provided that an ISP does not:

■ transmit its own information but only that of its users;
■ initiate the transmission;
■ select the receivers of the transmission; or
■ select or modify the information during the course of transmission

then the ISP's role is considered to be passive or that of a 'mere conduit', and it should escape liability for third-party content either as the primary wrongdoer as or as an accessory.

Storage/Caching

Caching is the process whereby a web browser stores a set of web page images temporarily either on the hard disk of the user or the server of the ISP, in order to avoid having to download the same material repeatedly. Most browsers keep copies of the pages viewed by a user so they may be redisplayed quickly when the user returns to them, thus speeding up the time it takes to access information on the internet.

Liability will be avoided if the ISP:

■ does not modify the information;
■ complies with access conditions and any industry standards on updating the information;
■ does not interfere with technology used to obtain traffic data; and
■ acts expeditiously to remove or disable access to information once it is made aware that access has been removed or disabled at source, or that its removal or disablement has been ordered by a governing authority.

Hosting

In the case of hosting, protection is available providing the ISP does not:

■ have 'actual knowledge' of the illegality of the information;
■ delay in removing or disabling access to the information once it is made aware of any illegality by a 'qualified notice';
■ initiate the transmission;

- choose the recipient; or
- modify the information.

What constitutes 'actual knowledge' or a 'qualified notice' has not been set out in the Directive, and this has led ISPs and commentators to express the view that the implementation of the Directive in any uniform or practical way will result in difficulty. Furthermore, it must be borne in mind that, whilst the Directive attempts to set out the sort of legislation one can expect in the UK and across the EU, implementation by member states can often reveal differing interpretations. In the UK, there are no specific legal definitions for knowledge, notice or takedown as a system of self-regulation is preferred. However the UK Regulations do state that an ISP is required to 'act expeditiously to remove or to disable access to the information' once it has the requisite degree of knowledge or awareness of the illegal posting. This is an ongoing issue for the UK ISPs as they are keen for further guidance on this issue to ensure that they are not unnecessarily removing material that is in fact legal, nor are they ignoring illegal material.

4.2 The Tobacco Advertising and Promotion Act 2002

This Act has been a cause of concern to ISPs because it provides that a person who publishes a tobacco advertisement in the course of their business, or who causes such an advertisement to be published, is guilty of an offence. The Act also specifically states that it is an offence to 'distribute' any such advertisements. 'Distributing' includes transmitting an advertisement in an electronic form, or providing the means for such a transmission. Clearly, the activities of an ISP will be caught by one or both prohibited activities.

The Act does contain a defence targeted at ISPs, in that an ISP charged with the offence of publishing advertisements by electronic means may escape conviction if it can show that it was unaware that the material was, or contained, a tobacco advertisement. However, despite the availability of a defence the Internet Services Providers Association expressed concern that the Act treated ISPs as potential 'publishers' (as opposed to neutral channels of communication). Such an approach, it is argued, conflicts with the neutral status given to ISPs as 'mere conduits' under the E-commerce Directive.

Due to slow progress and its controversial nature within the tobacco industry, enactment of this legislation initially looked dubious, however it finally received Royal Assent on 7 November 2002 and came into force on 14 February 2003.

The timetable for implementation was as follows:

- *14 February 2003*: From this date it was an offence to advertise tobacco products on billboards, newspapers, magazines, direct mail etc.
- *Point of Sale (POS) advertising*: The draft regulations governing advertising and promotional material at POS were laid on 18 March 2004. They entered into force on 21 December 2004.
- *Transitional phase-out for sponsorship*: 30 July 2003 for domestic sponsorships: 31 July 2005 for 'global events' such as Formula One and World Snooker.
- *Brandsharing*: Regulations on brandsharing were laid on 20 May 2004. These are due to enter into force on 31 July 2005.

4.3 Cybercrime Convention (entered into force on 1 July 2004)

Some of the crimes set out earlier are covered by the Council of Europe's Convention on Cybercrime, which was adopted by the Committee of Ministers on 8 November 2001 and has been open for signature by member states since 23 November 2001. Although, members of the Council are from Europe, non-members may also ratify the treaty. To date, 34 Council of Europe member states have signed the Convention as well as four non-member countries, namely the US, Canada, South Africa and Japan.

The Convention is the first international treaty on crimes committed via the internet and aims to provide a common international policy for, in particular, computer-related fraud, copyright infringement, child pornography and hacking. It also sets out search and seizure procedures, measures for international cooperation between law enforcement agencies, interception of communications data and it is supplemented by an additional Protocol making any publication of racist and xenophobic propaganda via computer networks a criminal offence. The latter provision was omitted from the Convention itself on the basis of arguments from the US that such an offence would represent a violation of freedom of expression as guaranteed by the first amendment to the US Constitution.

Controversially, the Convention also contains provisions that compel the storage and processing of data about users for authorities investigating cybercrimes, which includes the collecting and storage of real-time traffic and content data related to specified internet communications or users. Information collected and stored by an ISP would then be liable to disclosure to a domestic or trans-border law enforcement agency. These proposals go a step further than RIPA, which deals with interception of data which is in the possession of an ISP only and does not impose any obligation upon an internet service provider to actively collect and store the data transmitted. To date, the UK has signed but not yet ratified the Cybercrime Convention. However, UK laws such as the Data Protection Act 1998, the Copyright, Designs and Patents

Act 1988, the Communications Act 2003, the Computer Misuse Act 1990 and the Protection of Children Act 1978 already deal with the Convention's requirements.

5. Minimising the risks associated with content

This chapter has discussed a number of ways in which an ISP might be liable for the content on a website. Where an ISP has itself placed content on a site, then it will be responsible for that content. However, sometimes an ISP (be it an internet service provider or website operator) might find itself liable for content placed by a third party, since in this latter respect, the law is not always clear where to lay the blame. Amidst the legal confusion however, some suggestions on how to minimise the risk of claims can still be made.

5.1 Monitoring

Where the offending material originates from a third party, the best way to reduce the chances of complaint and minimise risk of legal action is by exercising thorough control over postings to remove offending material. Yet the difficulty is that such editorial control needs to be rigorous and generally speaking, either an ISP will not have sufficient resources for foolproof editorial control to be workable or will not wish to incur the costs of providing it. Where editorial control is not foolproof, the courts have indicated that an ISP may be penalised and yet, had the ISP not carried out monitoring in the first place, it might have escaped liability, for example, in a defamation action (see above). With these factors in mind, and the fact that the UK Electronic Commerce (EC Directive) Regulations 2002 does not impose an obligation on ISPs to monitor content, an ISP may feel it appropriate not to monitor third party material.

On the other hand, an ISP could consider exercising some monitoring by using automated systems (e.g. word triggering). There is support in US case law that unintelligent automated word exclusion does not equate with editorial control. (*Lunney* v. *Prodigy Services Co* 723 NE 2d 539, order dated 1 May 2000. Although the Supreme Court did not discuss the type of instances where an electronic bulletin board operator might qualify as publisher, the courts below did. Key considerations were the exercise of responsibility for the publication and editorial control: 94 NY 2d 242 (2nd Cir. 1999) and [1998] WL 999836 (NYAD 2 Dept).)

The position has not yet been considered in the UK, however automated word triggering could be regarded as part of exercising reasonable care with respect to material posted, as required by, for example financial services legislation, or it could assist an ISP in fulfilling some of the defences against criminal liability, where it is a requirement that an ISP show that it had no reason to suspect the material being displayed by it was illegal (see above).

5.2 Notice and takedown

Even where an ISP chooses not to monitor third party content, an ISP can still be liable for illegal material if it is made aware of such material via another means. It is therefore important that an ISP should have procedures in place to remove such material once it becomes aware of any suspected illegality. This is usually referred to as a 'notice and takedown procedure'. A rapid takedown procedure should be put in place so that any material that an ISP suspects may be in some way illegal or offensive, or for which there is a complaint, can be quickly removed from a website. ISPs may reserve the right to shut down or block access to sites carrying such material. (In *Sir Elton John* v. *Countess Joulebine* the website's ISP had already shut down the site against the will of the Countess before the matter had reached the court.)

How does an ISP assess whether the complaints it receives from a third party about content are genuine or not? Acting on a claim that has no reasonable basis can lead to undesirable publicity or even claims of a breach of human rights, particularly freedom of expression. This is a difficult area because, as discussed above, the courts have declined to give legal guidance as to what would constitute an acceptable notice and takedown procedure preferring to leave the industry to form a system of self-regulation.

Any notice and takedown procedure adopted should have a means of weeding out frivolous claims. For example, the complainant and person responsible for the material in question could be required to do one or more of the following:

- prove its identity;
- make a statutory declaration (if a company) or sworn statement setting out why a posting should or should not be removed within a defined period of time;
- agree to indemnify the ISP against any loss it incurs arising out of the takedown or reinstatement of material; and/or
- prove its solvency.

None of the above suggestions goes to the merits of a claim, but strict procedures may deter those who might otherwise be tempted to act vexatiously.

Next, the foundations for a good notice and takedown procedure are good internal procedures. These procedures must be sufficient to ensure that any complaints received from users regarding content are dealt with quickly adequately and that no complaint is accidentally overlooked. Practical suggestions that an ISP could implement to ensure the sufficiency of its internal procedures include:

- users should be provided with an obvious and accessible method to communicate complaints (e.g. a dedicated e-mail address for complaints regarding content, which may be accessed via a link on the ISP's website);
- clear channels for complaints and predetermined procedures for providing quick, reactive measures irrespective of the merits of the complaint;
- training to ensure staff are aware of complaints procedures and the importance of adherence to the complaints procedures;
- training to ensure that decision-makers are aware of matters affecting an ISP's liability; and
- since any decision *not* to remove the material could affect use of a defence by an ISP both under civil and criminal law, it is prudent to ensure that such decision is taken by a senior identified member of staff who makes the risk assessment of the decision.

An ISP should assess whether creating a separate 'walled garden' for certain content on the server is advisable, for example, in respect of pornographic material or content not suitable for children. Certainly, if the material alleged to make out an offence under the Obscene Publications Act remains accessible to children, it might be easier for the prosecution to prove that material has a tendency to deprave and corrupt those likely to view it.

5.3 Relationships with law enforcement agencies

At the same time, dialogue should be facilitated between an ISP and one or more law enforcement agencies. A cooperative relationship could:

- serve to persuade law enforcement agencies that the ISP is actively seeking to limit the presence of dangerous content on its site, which could result in an ISP receiving the benefit of the doubt in decisions to prosecute;
- enable law enforcement agencies to better understand the difficulties faced by an ISP attempting to control third-party content;
- agencies could assist with the development of a cost-effective strategy for retaining/retrieving data by ISPs for law enforcement purposes; and
- assist in demonstrating that the ISP has taken all reasonable action to eliminate dangerous content in the event of a prosecution.

An ISP could also consider whether it will actively report and hand over any illicit material discovered on a site to a law enforcement agency or to simply delete it. It should be remembered that deleting material might amount to a destruction of evidence. ISPs should therefore consider handing over data or alternative actions to deletion, such as merely disabling access, providing appropriate care is taken to prevent committing an offence, such as in the case of the 'making' of indecent photographs of children merely by loading the images (see above).

5.4 Terms and conditions

Terms and conditions represent the contract between an ISP and a user for the provision of the ISP's service. Terms and conditions should be prepared and be clearly posted on the ISP's website so as to protect an ISP in its relationship with its user as far as possible. Where users are able to post content to a site, it is advisable that the terms and conditions include the following:

- a prohibition on a user posting any illegal material or material which infringes a third party's rights or is in any way defamatory or offensive;
- express permission for the ISP to remove any data posted by a user at its sole discretion, without the need for complaint, or a need to establish whether any complaint is justified;
- a prohibition on replacing data that an ISP has removed;
- a clear statement that any postings are not to be treated as statements of fact and are expressions of opinions only (certain defences against a defamation claim only apply to statements objectively classed as opinions);
- a clear statement that all postings in no way represent the opinions of, or are endorsed by, the ISP;
- reservation of the right for the ISP to monitor postings (without imposing an obligation on the ISP to monitor); and
- the user's agreement to indemnify the ISP against all claims brought against the ISP for material which the user has posted (although the indemnity will be undermined by incorrect user information and user impecuniosity).

5.5 Disclosure of a user's identity

As an ISP may be obliged to disclose information that they hold on users to authorised third parties, that disclosure might put an ISP in conflict with its user terms and conditions or any separate privacy statement. To help minimise this risk, it is advisable that a ISP considers carrying the following:

- obtain assurances from a party requesting disclosure of a user's identity that it isgenuinely investigating its legal remedies and that the information is not available from another source;
- obtain assurances from a party requesting disclosure of a user's identity that the degree of disclosure requested is necessary having regard to its relevance to the proceedings contemplated;

- obtain from a party requesting disclosure of a user's identity its agreement to indemnify the ISP against loss should any assurances prove false;
- reserve the right in any privacy statement for the ISP to disclose personal information to a third party where wrongdoing is alleged, without the necessity for any claim to be commenced or proved; and
- when there is any doubt about the legitimacy of disclosure of a user's identity to a third party, it is perhaps best to leave the decision to the courts.

5.6 Relationships with third party website operators or business partners

This chapter has shown how claims for intellectual property infringement could arise out by the use of third party content on a website, either by that content being posted by the ISP itself or posted by a third party.

An ISP should obtain a licence to display content which is not its own and should ensure that it obtains assurances, sometimes referred to as contractual warranties, from any person providing material that it too has obtained licences from third parties where necessary. It would be also prudent to obtain an indemnity against any loss sustained through an infringement claim. Similar warranties and indemnities should be obtained from users as part of the user terms and conditions, where users are able to post material to the website.

In addition to the use of third party content, linking and framing practices pose risks for an ISP. In these circumstances it is always advisable to obtain the consent of owner of the linked site to such practices. Where it is not practically feasible to obtain consent, an ISP should carry out the following:

- avoid using another's trade mark or logo as a link button, but rather use the website's domain name;
- avoid linking in a manner which reproduces the original text as this could give rise to claims for database or copyright infringement, instead an ISP should create a pathway to a page which has been put on the site by the site owner;
- avoid surrounding the text from another website with the ISP's own trade marks or distinctive content as this might confuse users about whose content they are viewing;
- set up frames so that there is a clear distinction between the ISP's content and the content of the linked site; and
- check the terms and conditions of the linked site to ensure that linking to that site or framing it is not prohibited or restricted by those terms and conditions.

5.7 Insurance

It is advisable for an ISP to seek and maintain sufficient insurance against the risk that it might incur damages and costs arising out of the potential areas of civil liability and fines or compensation arising out of the potential areas of criminal liability that have been discussed.

5.8 Regularly review the law and the business's internal procedures

As the laws relating to content liability are constantly evolving, an ISP's legal position and standard industry practices should change accordingly. Therefore, an ISP is advised to keep its position under regular review and ensure it is up-to-date with legal and industry developments.

Contracting for Services and Agreeing Service Levels

Introduction

Online businesses (or e-businesses) can be peculiarly reliant on third-party service providers in order to function, so getting the relationship with such providers right is a critical task. The reliance arises because companies embarking on e-commerce rarely have the skills and services in-house to support their operations, either because:

- they are new ventures themselves (without the wish or the finance to create a large infrastructure);
- they are traditional businesses which maintain e-commerce operations but see such operations as 'non-core' and have elected to outsource to access the relevant experience they themselves are lacking; or
- sometimes they have elected to leverage the vast talent pools, low costs and technical capabilities of an offshore supply.

The criticality is enhanced because the services contracted for are often fundamental to the business itself – for example, the provision of billing or customer relationship management (CRM) services and fulfilment (i.e. the delivery of their goods and services). And, for a new 'virtual' e-commerce company, there may be the additional complication that the contractor will be a much larger and more experienced organisation, giving limited scope for negotiation.

Thus the contractor often has two principal characteristics:

- the provision of business-critical services which can directly affect the functioning and profitabilityof the online business; and
- involvement, often directly, in the relationship with the customers of the online business.

This chapter considers the contracts that an online business will enter into with such contractors, considering in particular:

- the types and structure of contracts, especially where there are multiple contractors;
- key issues in negotiating contracts; and
- the key issues in the contracts themselves.

1. Types of contracts and structuring the deal(s)

The typical online business can find itself at the centre of a web of contracts:

A number of these contracts, and the issues of branding and intellectual property rights, are dealt with elsewhere in this book. However, the multiplicity of agreements, and their nature and interdependence, can make negotiating and entering into them a daunting prospect. Some guidance on negotiation is set out below.

One answer to the complications of this scenario is to appoint a Systems Integrator (SI) whose role is to find and bring together the disparate service providers. This removes what may otherwise be an almost intolerable burden on the online business, but can raise its own problems.

There are two main models, illustrated below with pros and cons.

Model 1: True SI

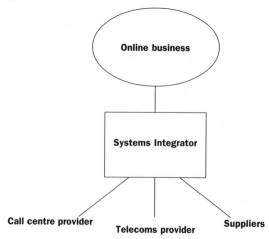

Characteristics: the SI enters into subcontracts directly with the various third parties; the online business has one contract, with the SI.

Pros	Cons
A single point of management contact for the online business	No direct contact with the various service providers, so they are less aware of the online business's business needs
Single point of billing	An extra business extracting profit from the grid of relationships. A cost which is passed on to the online business
SI takes legal responsibility for the performance of the service providers	This assumes that that SI will actually enforce the subcontracts and that the SI is substantial enough to meet the legal obligations of all of the subcontractors
SI manages changes of service providers	No direct control over the identity of what may be key subcontractors

Model 2: Systems manager

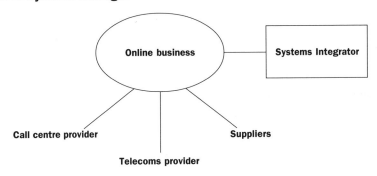

Characteristics: the SI does not directly contract with the various service providers but manages them on behalf of the online business.

Pros	Cons
Online business ultimately controls all the relationships but does not have the burden of day-to-day management	There are opportunities for finger-pointing when there are service failures – was there a failure in management or not? Although the systems can manage bill payment, there is no true single integrated invoice
The SI can be replaced without major impact on the other continuing relationships	Some management is still required to manage the managers

The traditional objection to the true SI Model 1 is that there is no direct right of action by the e-commerce organisation against the subcontractors, which could leave it vulnerable if the SI is not good for the money or has commercial objections to enforcing the subcontracts. The problem is as set out below:

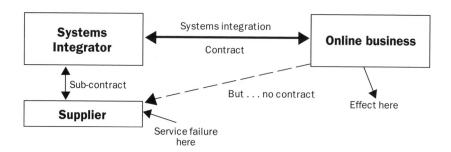

However, a relatively recent (but often ignored) statute, the Contracts (Rights of Third Parties) Act 1999 does allow the online business to enforce the subcontract directly, provided that the Systems Integration contract makes it clear that such a right is to be specified in the subcontract. This Act removes the concept of privity of contract (that only a party to a contract could in fact enforce rights under such contract) in a variety of circumstances. Now, if the provisions of the Act are not excluded, third parties on whom a contractual benefit is conferred have the benefit of enforcing these rights (even if they are not a party to the original contract). This can be very useful to confer rights on other stakeholders under a contractual services relationship, e.g. other companies within a group or as the diagram above conferring a direct right of action where there is no contract.

2. Structuring the contracts

Naturally there will be business concerns to settle the right price in return for the best attainable services. Of course these and other parameters agreed need to be recorded and the contracts which embody the services have two complementary roles here:

- *passively*, they record the commercial agreement between the parties; and
- *actively*, the act of negotiating the contracts can help to highlight potential misunderstandings and to make it less likely that they will arise in practice. The contracts also act as a checklist of issues to be addressed in the negotiation process. The process of negotiation is looked at in more detail below.

The resulting agreement is a legally enforceable contract which places obligations on the parties, the basic principles of which are discussed in more detail in

Chapter 1. Typically, the services agreement is likely to be in place for as long as five years and it has two main functions:

- to set out clearly the parties' obligations to each other at day one; and
- to allow the parties to evolve service provision over time and to end the relationship rationally.

These may appear to be competing ambitions: the aim must be to prepare a contract which balances them so as best to serve the commercial needs of both the parties. The contents of the agreement are examined at section 4 below.

Before considering the process of tendering for and negotiating the services contract, it is important to bear in mind the typical structure of the document. It is common to hear the term 'Service Level Agreement' (SLA) applied to these contracts; however this term is misleading. The SLA is typically a description of the services and the standard to which they are to be provided, but does not contain the basic terms and conditions, nor the charging provisions. In fact, the technical aspects of the SLA need to be seen in the context of the document as whole:

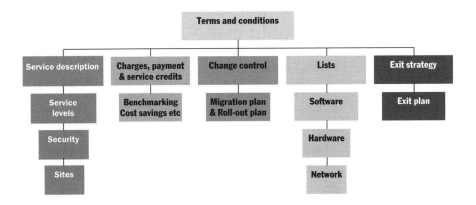

The elements are examined in more detail below, but to summarise:

Contractual element	Contents and purpose
Terms and conditions (T&Cs)	Typically, the 'legal' aspects of the agreement are set out at the start of the document, with the schedules, which deal with more technical or procedural issues being annexed to them. This should not conceal the fact that the T&Cs and the schedules form an integrated whole (it is important to remember this during negotiation to ensure all elements fit together and there are no contradictions, e.g. because different elements are prepared by different teams).

Contractual element *continued*	Contents and purpose *continued*
Terms and conditions (T&Cs) *continued*	The T&Cs typically begin with the defined terms which will be used throughout the document – these are really just shorthand to avoid setting out a complex description each time. For example, it is easier to refer to the 'Index' and only define it up front as 'the percentage change in the xyz index published by abc. . .'. Getting the definitions right is often the key to the rest of the contract as they force the draftsperson to think clearly at the outset. The clauses then follow in as close to a logical order as possible. For example, you would expect the statement about the commencement date to be early on in the contract dispute resolution and the termination and exit clauses to be near the end. Conventionally, the last few clauses are 'boilerplate', i.e. clauses that always tend to be included. These include a clause on the service of notices and on other housekeeping matters. Just because they are standard doesn't mean they are automatically suitable for that particular deal and they need careful review and often specific tailoring. The last clause usually sets out the legal system which will govern the contract and any litigation. It is tempting to skip through these clauses, but it is important to review them every time. One clause which will be of great importance is that relating to assignment and subcontracting.
Services schedule	The first schedule is usually where the services are described, together with the levels to which the services are provided and any associated standards to be met and the consequences of failure. Sometimes important elements will be split out into sections or schedules (e.g. to discuss security levels or disaster recovery procedures or to set out particular sites or locations that will be maintained or rolled-out).
Charges	Although the agreement will refer to the charges, usually the amount of the charges and the timing and means of payment are set out in a schedule.
Value for money	Linked to the charges is the question of how these are to vary over the period of the contract – assuming that there is not a fixed price (e.g. will the price changes be linked to a certain published index, or can the customer take the services and price it pays and compare these like with like to benchmark against other providers, services or prices in the market and then perhaps change the existing parameters accordingly?).

Contractual element *continued*	Contents and purpose *continued*
Change control	Assuming that the services are to be provided for a number of years, the services will change over time (because of technical innovation or changes in the customer's business and requirements) and the contract should set out a procedure for managing and implementing the changes.
Exit	The contract will inevitably come to an end (whether amicably or because of an irreconcilable failure) and, if the services are complex or critical, the online business will want to ensure that there is an orderly transition to a new service provider. It's prudent to document what is to happen at the point of exit, what cooperation and assistance the service provider should assist with and at whose cost.

The holistic nature of the service agreement can be illustrated by a pie chart:

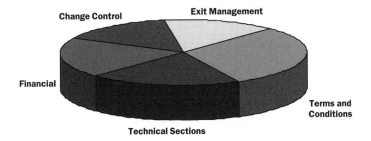

3. Procurement of services and negotiating the contract

Assuming that the online business is intending to negotiate the service contracts itself, rather than via an SI, it will not only need to go through a disciplined procedure to ensure that it gets value for money, but also to manage the process of negotiating. As noted above, a new online business may have limited leverage and experience of negotiating, so imposing the proper process is even more critical.

Some organisations, such as government bodies and regulated industries (such as utilities), are bound by public procurement rules which impose obligations to advertise the services and to follow prescribed procedures.

3.1 Requests for proposals and invitations to tender

Assuming the services are of sufficient value and criticality to warrant the effort, best practice is to go through a competitive tendering procedure. This enables the online business to maximise its commercial strength at the initial stages so as to obtain the best deal by asking companies to compete to provide services. It is important to bear in mind some key principles in preparing the documents to be sent out.

Although there are no hard-and-fast definitions, there are two kinds of documents used for competitive tendering: a Request for Proposals and a subsequent Invitation to Tender. The characteristics of these are:

Request for Proposals (RFP)	Invitation to Tender (ITT)
A speculative document sent to a large number of potential tenderers, to elicit expressions of interest	A focused document sent to a manageable number (say, 5) potential tenderers, identified from the responses to the RFP
Contains a general statement of the online business's business requirements	Contains specific requirements as to the services to be provided
	Contains a draft contract – see comment below

It is important for the online business to bear four points in mind when creating these documents, and the ITT in particular:

- that it can be expensive for a tenderer to go through and manage a formal tendering process, so the RFP and ITT should be seen as documents selling the services to potential service providers as well as seeking bids to provide those services;
- the online business needs to make its requirements clear without specifying too prescriptively how the services are to be provided – it does not want to prevent innovative solutions being proposed;
- that any information sent out by the online business should be marked as being confidential and the tenderers should be asked to sign up to a non-disclosure agreement (NDA) prior to disclosure. The NDA will generally need to be reciprocal: the tenderers will not wish to disclose sensitive information (such as pricing or technical solutions) without the online business having agreed to keep it confidential; and
- the ITT should make it clear that it is not an offer and that the online business is not obliged to accept the lowest or any proposal.

It is good practice for the online business to include a form of services contract with the ITT and require potential service providers to bid on these terms. The aim is not so much to wrong-foot the bidders as to create a level contractual playing field. The online business can concentrate on reviewing the bids' relative technical and commercial merits without having to compare the small print of several sets of standard terms and conditions. Standard terms and conditions are unlikely to be helpful in any event. Again, from the online business's perspective, they are likely to be unfavourable in a number of respects, including the remedies for failure to provide the services and the level of liability the service providers are prepared to accept.

If the online business does include draft terms and conditions with the ITT, it must bear in mind a number of points:

- there is no value in proposing unreasonable terms, which will not elicit sensible bids;
- certain terms will not be able to be tied down at this stage and only the principles to be adopted can be set out. As with describing the required services in the ITT, the online business must tread a careful line between giving too little information for the service providers to go on and being so precise that initiative and alternative views are stifled;
- the ITT must make it clear that the bidders must respond to the draft terms by either accepting them or raising all major issues in the response. The online business should use the element of competition to its advantage. It should also examine the detailed promises made at the 'sell' phase and make sure these offers are matched and documented when the contract is drafted.

It is usually recommended that an online business should carry out parallel negotiations with at least two bidders, with a third in reserve. In practice, this is a counsel of perfection: rarely will an online business have the time or the resources required to manage such a process. Experience suggests that the process works only if the same negotiation team carries out both sets of negotiation, which is both tiring and apt to lead to confusion. A more pragmatic solution is to rely on the process set out above to elicit all the major commercial, technical and legal issues while there is maximum competition and then to proceed with one favoured potential service provider while keeping another one 'warm'.

Clearly, this does not give the online business the same commercial leverage as a true parallel negotiation, but it has the advantage of allowing resources to be concentrated; further, it may be possible to set some assumptions out at the outset. This raises the question of interim agreements, heads of agreement and the like.

3.2 Heads of Agreement, etc.

Various terms are used for documents signed prior to the formal contract – these include: Heads of Agreement, Memoranda of Understanding (MoU), Letters of Intent (LOI) and Interim Agreements. None of these has any specific legal meaning and the key is to identify what the intention of the document is and whether the effort of negotiating one will be worth it. What is key is whether or not the contents of such documents are legally binding or, as some of the names suggest, merely statements of future intent.

It is usually not in the online business's interest to sign a substantive contract before the commercial and technical details are fully worked out. However, there may be reasons why one or both of the parties want to sign an agreement prior to the completion of the formal contract:

Supplier's reasons

(i) **Lead times**: if, in order to fulfil its obligations under the final contract, the service provider has to place orders with third party service providers, it could be left exposed if the contract is not completed. The service provider may want to agree with the online business that if the contract is not signed, the online business will still pay towards the third party order. Usually, this would depend on the reason for the failure to sign the substantive agreement.

(ii) **Exclusivity**: the service provider may offer price concessions on the basis that it is the 'preferred service provider' – i.e. that there is a period during which the online business will negotiate exclusively with it. As noted above, this flies in the face of the use of competitive tendering so it is rarely in the online business's interests to agree.

(iii) **Assumptions**: if the service provider has quoted prices on the basis of certain assumptions it may want these to be acknowledged in case it wishes to revisit the prices during negotiation.

(iv) **Confidentiality**: the service provider may want to require the online business to refrain from disclosing to other potential service providers in the bid process the financial and technical basis of its bid.

(v) **Internal management**: it may be important to the sales team that it has some acknowledgement from the online business that it is serious about proceeding, so as to gain internal authorisation to commit resources to the negotiation process.

Online business's reasons

(i) **Assumptions**: the online business may want to formalise certain assumptions, particularly over price, which it has made in deciding to proceed in the negotiations with a particular service provider. The aim

---

would be to prevent the service provider reopening these points at a later date when it feels in a stronger bargaining position.

(ii) **Confidentiality**: the online business may wish to establish that the contents of the ITT and other information gleaned by the potential service providers in the course of negotiations should be treated as confidential.

(iii) **Wasted expenditure**: the online business may want to recover its wasted fees and expenses if the negotiations abort for reasons connected with the service provider.

(iv) **Internal management**: the online business may require some commitment from the service provider in order to gain board or other clearance to proceed with the negotiations.

In approaching the question of a pre-contract agreement, the online business should consider two questions:

1. Will the effort of negotiating such an agreement detract from the resources available for settling the terms of the substantive contract?
2. Does it need the pre-contract agreement to be legally binding or simply to be a statement of its position so that it has some moral authority in the negotiations?

Experience shows that negotiating an interim agreement can often be an expensive distraction from the real business of getting the substantive transaction done.

3.3 Principles of negotiation

How the deal is negotiated is as much dictated by the circumstances and time available as principles, however there are some basic rules of thumb:

- There is a great temptation to plunge straight into meetings. The parties should be wary of this – meetings are enormously time-consuming and should only take place if there is an agenda and clear deliverables.
- Generally, assuming that the potential service provider has made a formal response to the contract in the ITT, the online business can issue a fresh draft, taking into account the points it accepts and noting the others.
- The potential service provider should then be asked to respond in writing to this draft and this can form the agenda for an initial meeting.

Set out below are some basic principles for negotiation, which could be tabled at the beginning of the process or as a part of the ITT to outline the intended negotiation process.

PRINCIPLES OF NEGOTIATION

Introduction

The aim of negotiation is, self-evidently, to reach agreement. However, experience shows that an unstructured approach to the process can lead to misunderstandings, delay and frustration. This document summarises some basic principles which the provider is required to adhere to. They are drawn from experience of many transactions and reflect also the Best Practice Guidelines drawn up for the National Outsourcing Association (NOA) and a number of consultancies.

The principles are:

- *the negotiations will take place on the basis of the documents submitted by the online business and not the provider's standard terms and conditions;*

- *the parties should agree who has authority on each side to make binding decisions in meetings and commit to having that person in each meeting;*

- *while complying with the principle above, the people attending each meeting should be kept to a minimum commensurate with having the right skills/decision makers present;*

- *generally, there should be as few lawyer-only meetings as possible;*

- *the parties should agree a timetable for meetings, for example two days of meetings per week with time in between for new drafts to be produced and considered;*

- *however, the parties should not have any particular meeting for the sake of it or if either party is not ready to comment on the most recent draft;*

- *the online business's lawyers shall have control over the documents and shall exercise strict version control and control over electronic copies. Although the provider may, for convenience, submit electronic mark-ups of the documents, any agreed amendments will be made to the control documents held by the online business's lawyers;*

- *amendments to documents should be clearly marked and if possible annotated to give context where a commercial reason or deal point key to the nature of the amendment is made; and*

- *when points are conceded/agreed, a note should be taken and neither party should re-open a point unless there is a real and imperative commercial reason.*

4. Types of contract

4.1 Standard terms

As noted above, a service provider's standard terms and conditions are unlikely to be an ideal starting point for the online business. By their very nature they have not been drafted and edited specifically for the deal in question and their generic nature probably leaves more questions than answers. In any event they will be drafted in favour of the service provider that produced them and will usually put the online business on the back foot before negotiations have even begun. Though the standardisation can offer the prospect of saving time and expense the real benefit usually rests with the service provider whose standard terms offer them deal consistency and watered down risk and levels of commitment. An online business should always think twice before standard terms are adopted.

4.2 A unique contract

Many service relationships are complex and in trying to mould and straight-jacket a deal to pre-existing prescribed terms essential deal principles and parameters can sometimes be lost. It's far more advisable to start afresh documenting the services relationship carefully and using this process to ensure important commercial and service issues are highlighted and that there is a meeting of the minds for the final resulting service relationship. Clearly documenting the relationship is key because over time:

- the people that reach the an agreement may change;
- services and service needs change and the contract needs the solid foundation to be able to flex for this; and
- disputes arise where there is a mismatch of expectations – negotiation should highlight and resolve these within the contract before it is signed.

4.3 What if there's no contract?

A recent case in the English courts has highlighted the importance of having an agreed contract, setting out the obligations and understanding of both parties. In *Co-operative Group (CWS) Limited (formerly Co-operative Wholesale Society Limited)* v. *International Computers Limited* [2003] EWCA Civ 1955, the Co-operative Society (CWS) brought a claim against International Computers Limited (ICL) for damages of almost £11 million for allegedly breaching the contract under which ICL had agreed to develop software for use in CWS's food stores. CWS claimed that a contract had been created by correspondence and that the main clauses of the contract had been agreed except the consequences of non-delivery of software within a particular timescale, and the penalties for late delivery. While the legal teams of both parties continued to negotiate the contract, ICL built and began to deliver software but before the software had been delivered in its final form, CWS purported to terminate the contract by reason of ICL failing to deliver the software on time.

The court found that there was in fact no contract, (and also found that had there been a contract, ICL would not have been in breach of it) and stated that it was entirely for the parties to decide whether they wish to be bound by the contract and, if so, for the parties to decide which terms were important or unimportant and remained to be agreed – it is not up to the court to decide what terms are important in a potential contract. In this case the court found that, despite ICL having commenced work on the software, both parties regarded the presence or absence of a penalty clause relating to late delivery of the product as fundamental and neither party would have entered into the agreement unless the clause, as they wanted to see it, was present in the final version. CWS appealed the decision and the Court of Appeal has ordered a re-trial. At the time of writing, it is not clear whether the parties will continue this re-trial.

The risks for any online business not having a full signed contract are obvious and it should be wary of allowing a service provider to commence its obligations under a service contract without what it considers to be key clauses in place.

5. Key issues in a services contract

5.1 Describing the services

Set out in schedules to the agreement there should be clear, detailed descriptions of the services and the levels to which such services are to be provided. These should be practical and workable, but it must be appreciated that the schedules are an integral part of the contract and that therefore they should be treated as legal as well as technical documents. The key test is: Can they be read and understood by someone new to the relationship, the services and the parties? The following box sets out some basic principles for agreeing the service levels:

PRINCIPLES FOR DRAFTING THE SERVICE LEVELS

There shall be a clear list of the services to be provided to the online business by the provider with associated obligations to provide the services to an agreed quality and standard.

Services will be clearly defined, i.e.:

- *stating what services are to be provided and how quality is to be measured (e.g. quality control);*

- *what time scales are allowed for service delivery and availability of service (in terms of quality and quantity of services – i.e. usability);*

- *stating the period over which the services are to be available (taking account of agreed unavailability);*

- *stating actual quality and permitted deviation from a standard as a percentage of the total (and provide a means to quantify this);*

- *stating responsibility for monitoring and reporting;*

- *stating a maximum permitted tolerance of service level quality and targets for re-performing inadequate services and time to re-perform the affected service; and*

- *stating service boundaries and responsibilities for all network services and including detail as to network responsibility.*

For each element of each of the services there shall be a specific and/or a general response time or other measure of quality, reflecting the speed of each service and the throughput of that service. The service levels should set out the overall quality of the service deliverable using concepts such as availability, reliability, serviceability, response and productivity to set the targets for delivery.

Where appropriate, for each element of each of the services there shall be a specific and/or a general response time or other measure of quality, reflecting the speed of each service and the performance of that service.

For all services, there will be a procedure for reporting, logging and escalating problems. Problems will be categorised (e.g. into critical, major, minor or cosmetic) and there will be obligations to respond within appropriate time scales.

5.2 Controlling quality

Failure to provide the services to the standards set out in the descriptions will be a breach of contract entitling the online business to sue for damages. However, unless the online business is also prepared to terminate the agreement, it will not wish to damage the relationship by resorting to the courts. The contract should therefore set out less contentious alternatives to make sure that there is recourse for the online business should service provision be inadequate. The usual method is to link service levels to predetermined credits against charges. The aim is for service credits to be an automatic remedy which apply without dispute. The contract therefore has to set out clearly how services levels will be measured and credits calculated.

Beyond service credits there may be other levels of remedies, including the payment of more substantial damages, ending with total or partial termination (see below). When setting such compensatory credits or rebates the online business needs to be mindful of the incentive factor to ensure the measure has the desired effect on service quality (is it cheaper to pay the credits than implement a service fix to meet the service levels?), but also it should ensure the measure is not penal. Under English contract law a penalty is unenforceable and the online business should ensure the credit, rebate or liquidated damage is a 'genuine pre-estimate of the loss that would otherwise be suffered'. The issue of risk allocation is considered in more depth at section 6 below.

5.3 Controlling change

It is inconceivable that the online business's requirements will remain static and therefore the agreement must incorporate a mechanism for managing change. The aim of the process must be to ensure that the online business has confidence that it is receiving the right services at the right price. This breaks down into a number of steps:

1. *Identifying the changes*: It is important that an organisation contracting out business critical service realises that it is not abdicating responsibility for its CRM, billing, fulfilment or other strategy. It is never wise to leave a service provider in the roles of both specifying a requirement and then fulfilling it. Instead, the contract should allow for a review process that enables both parties to agree the online business's future requirements but with ultimate control residing in the online business.
2. *Providing changed services*: These generally are of three kinds:
   - Volume changes to existing services – including taking more processing or storage resources or taking additional bandwidth. In such cases the

agreement would normally specify a formula for varying the existing unit charges to reflect increases, or potentially decreases, in volumes. Whether the unit price is increased to reflect decreases in usage depends on whether the parties have agreed volume discounts for the initial services and whether the service provider is permitted to protect its revenue stream under the contract irrespective of actual volumes.

- Other changes to existing services. The contract should contain a more formal process for the service provider to quote to provide such changes and for the online business to be provided with information justifying such charges. This should reflect the fact that the service provider has a built-in advantage when it comes to tendering for such work over alternative service providers.
- New services. Here, there should be a formal market testing procedure where the online business can require the service provider to quote against other potential service providers.

5.4 Intellectual property rights (IPRs)

Where the service provider is creating IPRs – whether in graphics, documents or software – the online business needs to work out whether these rights are significant enough to be identified and, if so, whether it needs to own those rights. It is easy for an online business to get hung up over ownership of copyright and other IPR. Often, a better question is to consider who should be able to use such rights and on what basis? For example, if the service provider owns the rights, does the online business need a licence to use them, and, if so, should this be on an exclusive basis or should the service provider be able to use the rights for other customers? Should the licence only be in relation to the receipt of the services or should it extend in time beyond the contract – for example, so that a future service provider can use the IPR to provide the services.

5.5 Controlling prices

The online business will also expect to see a mechanism for controlling price increases over the life of the agreement. Given that the costs of certain components of the prices – such as bandwidth in a telecoms contract – are likely to come down over time, this should be reflected in the charges. The parties may agree an indexation mechanism, akin to that in telecommunications licences, such as the application of an 'RPI minus x' formula. A more sophisticated approach is benchmarking (or 'comparative analysis'), where the service provider's charges are compared against those of comparable alternative service providers providing comparable services and adjusted to reflect market trends. The problem with this kind of approach is drafting a mechanism which allows for the identification of comparable service providers and services so as to produce a meaningful benchmarking process. Most favoured nation (MFN) clauses are sometimes sought with bland statements along the lines that if the service provider ever supplies another customer offering better pricing or service standards to that customer then the service provider will match these terms in the existing relationship. Commercial teams and procurement groups like these kinds of provisions but in reality how is the beneficiary of such a clause ever going to know (as confidentiality clauses usually prevent such a disclosure)? Also, in any other circumstance is the comparison really like with like? In practice such MFN clauses are rarely enforced or successful.

5.6 Dispute management

This breaks down into two areas:

1. *Preventing disputes*: In addition to the strategic reviews mentioned above, the agreement should provide for regular liaison meetings and exchange of information. It should also set out which office holders at the online business and service provider are authorised to agree changes to the services or to make other decisions relating to the supply of the services; and
2. *Resolving disputes*: the contract should set out the basic mechanisms for internal escalation of disputes and their reference to an independent expert, alternative dispute resolution or the courts. As a breakdown in the user/ service provider relationship is likely to be very damaging to both parties, serious thought should be given to the merits of alternative dispute resolution. Fall out badly in year one and the parties may have another four years of a contract to muddle through. Better to resolve properly, resurrect the relationship and continue.

5.7 Termination

Both parties, but particularly the online business, should give some thought to the circumstances in which the contract can be brought to an end. The most obvious time is at the expiry of a fixed-term arrangement. However it is usually difficult (and inadvisable) for a complex services arrangement to 'drop dead' on a particular date so fixed-term contracts are rare. More usually, the parties can bring the contract to an end on the service of notice after the initial term, otherwise the contract rolls on. Where there is a long-term contract (e.g. ten years), the online business may wish to have the option to terminate earlier, albeit on payment of a termination fee.

The typical triggers for termination are considered later in this chapter.

6. Risk allocation

As noted above, the online business is unlikely to wish to terminate the contract for poor service provision unless it has no option. Instead, it will look to other remedies, such as service credits. However, typically a service provider will look to set these at a very low level (often a few per cent of the relevant charges, measured over a month) that leaves the online business with difficulties should its actual losses exceed this but should it not wish to terminate and sue for damages.

In fact, some service providers use service credits as a kind of limit of liability and try to specify that the online business may not recover any other kind of financial remedy without terminating the agreement. The online business should resist this kind of provision, which benefits only the service provider, and should also consider what other remedies it may want to recover during the term of the agreement.

This involves the online business making an appraisal of the business impact to its own business and operations of a failure to provide the services and a judgment as to what level of loss it is reasonable to expect the service provider to accept. The service provider will not accept unlimited liability, and will take the view that it is not there to underwrite the online business. It will look at its potential exposure in the light of the value of the contract (often in terms of profit rather than revenue).

While being mindful of this approach by the service provider, the online business should not accept a level of liability that does not provide some protection for its business. The contact generally has to address two scenarios when it comes to the liability of the service provider: liability prior to termination and liability on termination for breach by the service provider. Set out below are the basic principles governing remedies and liability.

6.1 Remedies

Any failure by a service provider to provide the services in accordance with the contract is a breach of contract, which would entitle the online business to sue for damages or to terminate the contract. A court order either compelling performance of an obligation or restraining a breach could also be sought, but would generally be more appropriate in the context of, say, an exit strategy.

In practice, of course, no online business would wish to sue an incumbent service provider and therefore the recovery of damages by way of court action is generally unpalatable as an option unless the contract is terminated. It is necessary to have other remedies within the contract, otherwise, the online business risks having no effective control over the performance of the service provider (the service provider, of course, being aware that termination would be a risky and extreme option).

This section on remedies concentrates on those that should appear in a prudently drafted services agreement to come into effect prior to termination.

Assuming that there are clear service levels and a mechanism for discerning and measuring compliance or failure, the contract must address the consequences of any failure. A number of mechanisms are used, and their advantages and disadvantages are set out below.

Remedy	Pros	Cons
Escalation (referral of issue up the management chain) – could include generating a service review or a formal correction plan.	Simple – focuses the attention of the correct levels of management on a particular issue. Less contentious and more 'positive' than money-based remedies.	Unless linked to another remedy, such as service credits, has no teeth and can be used as a stalling tactic by the service provider.
Service credits, liquidated damages and rebates of charges.	Simple (can be linked mechanically to service failures). Avoids the need to sue for damages. Scalable: can increase to reflect severity and/or persistence of problem. Hit the service provider in the pocket.	If set too low, can allow the service provider to avoid rectifying a problem if it is cheaper to pay service credits. Often are more of a management tool than a true representation of loss.
Re-performance of failed services.	May be more attractive to the service provider than paying out money. Focus on fixing the problem rather than getting money back.	Only relevant where it makes sense to re-perform: more applicable to discrete jobs or batch work (e.g. printing).
Services in kind (e.g. free consultancy).	May be more attractive to the service provider than paying out money.	Online business has to be sure that there will be real benefit in the services.

Remedy	Pros	Cons
Specific costs or losses – must link to the facts of the deal, but examples could be: – recovering the costs of wasted advertising; – recovering the costs of obtaining fill-in services from a third party; or – lost cost of money.	Can be a very useful bridge between service credits and termination – avoiding some of the cons of service credits. A way of getting damages, linked to service failure, without suing or terminating.	Service providers do not like them!
Partial termination.	Allows the failing service to be cut out of the agreement without having to terminate the entire agreement.	Service providers resist. There must be a mechanism for exit and for reducing the remaining charges. May not be technically or commercially feasible.
Loss of some other benefit, e.g. exclusivity or inclusion in a re-tender or cancellation of a related contract (e.g. maintenance or support).	More palatable than a money-based remedy, but does focus the mind of the service provider.	May have little direct meaning if there is only one service provider in the market.
Intellectual property rights: where the online business has the IPR, this could involve terminating a licence to the service provider or removing exclusivity; or where the service provider has the IPR, this could involve a licence coming into effect or material which is in escrow being released.	May enhance the ability of the online business elsewhere without actually having to terminate.	Only relevant where there is specific IPR which is not generally available. May involve a process of going to a third party (e.g. source code escrow agent) or be expensive to set up.
Others specific to the circumstances?		

In practice, a number of these types of remedies may be used in an agreement, but it is almost invariable practice to have escalation and service credits.

Another legal concept is built into most services relationships – the concept of *force majeure*. Essentially service providers will wish to reserve a right to suspend their performance of the services and related obligations if events which are outside of their reasonable control take place.

Commonly included in the *force majeure* clause are acts of God, fire, flood and terrorism and sometimes even strikes and lockouts. The online business needs to be careful it doesn't allow the service provider a get out of jail free card in circumstances where it is actually most reliant on the service provider to perform the services. If the contract is for disaster recovery and the reinstatement of essential customer transaction data the online business may want stringent obligations on the service provider just at the point the *force majeure* clause cuts in to relieve the service provider of any obligations under the services contract. *Force majeure* clauses need to be considered contextually.

6.2 Liability and damages

The overriding principles governing what the online business can recover in damages for service failure are complex but can be summed up in two deceptively simple statements:

- the aim of contractual damages is to put the innocent party in the same position as if the contract had been performed. The obvious example of this would be the incremental costs incurred in receiving the relevant services from an alternative service provider; and
- damages must flow directly from the breach.

In practice, it is the second statement which causes most debate – what are 'direct' (as opposed to 'indirect' or 'consequential') losses? Are lost profits recoverable as direct losses?

There are also some basic rules, which govern the way that the courts will award damages. Essentially, the innocent party has the onus to prove:

- that there was a breach of contract;
- that losses were suffered and how much these losses were; and
- that those losses were of a kind which can be recovered – i.e. are direct.

There is also a duty on the innocent party to 'mitigate' its loss – in other words, to be reasonable in its conduct so as to minimise its exposure.

In theory, the contract could be silent as to these issues and allow the courts to make the decisions. In practice, no service provider will accept this position and will seek to limit its liability in two parameters: the kinds of loss it will accept as being recoverable and the absolute financial amount of exposure it will bear.

146

There are rules governing the enforceability of limitation of liability clauses, however, where the parties have negotiated the clause fully, it is wise to assume that it will be enforceable. It is therefore important that the online business is happy with the clause and is not intending to rely on legal technicalities.

It is for the parties to agree the parameters as regards types of loss and the financial cap. There are some rules of thumb, however:

- most service providers will accept as a matter of course that the reasonable incremental costs of going to another service provider are recoverable;
- at the other extreme, it is no longer tenable for service providers of services to have a blanket exclusion of liability for business losses such as loss of profit – whether these losses are accepted are a matter for negotiation, rather than principle. Where a service is business-critical and particularly where it is intrinsic to the online business's ability to generate money, it would be perfectly appropriate to seek to recover lost profit where a service failure impedes that money generation. Clearly, the ability to prove and quantify the loss needs to be considered;
- one option would be to be silent in the contract as to whether business losses are recoverable and leave it to the courts to determine whether loss of profit (for example) is a direct loss. In some instances, it is preferable to set out expressly in the contract a list of losses which are pre-agreed to be direct;
- sometimes liquidated damages may be more palatable to the service provider than referring to loss of profit expressly;
- other losses which could be listed include those set out in the note on remedies above;
- the financial cap generally bears some relationship to the contract value – for a services contract, for example, a multiple of the annual value would be a good starting point, a cap of less than one year's charges would be on the low side;
- a distinction is often made between a per event cap and an aggregate cap. A pragmatic view might be to regard these as being the same, given that the online business is unlikely to sue unless the contract is terminated and that termination is likely to stem from one event.

Where services are intrinsic to the success of an online business's business, it would be perfectly reasonable for the online business to insist both on recovering business losses and that such losses could be considerable in amount.

Recent English case law has emphasised the importance of carefully agreeing and documenting limitation of liability clauses and ensuring that the clauses are reasonable under the guidelines set out in Schedule 2 of the Unfair Contract Terms Act 1977 (see chapter 1 for a further description of these guidelines). This point was emphasised by the court in *SAM Business Systems Limited* v. *Hedley & Co.* [2002] EWHC 2733. Hedley commissioned SAM to supply and install a software system, which would ensure that Hedley would be Y2K compliant. The system was riddled with problems from its first use and although SAM tried to solve these problems, after 17 months, Hedley changed to an alternative system. SAM then issued proceedings against Hedley for outstanding payment in respect of the initial implementation of the software and for the time spent by SAM in attempting to resolve the problems with the software, claiming over £310,000. Hedley then counterclaimed for over £780,000 in respect of damages suffered as a result of the failure of the software. The High Court ordered Hedley to pay SAM less than £10,000 and the case cannot be seen as a victory for either party.

The parties had to rely on the three sheets of A4 paper that contained the agreement for the supply of software, hardware, software licences and bespoke modifications to the packaged products. These 'contracts' contained an entire agreement clause, a money back guarantee if the software was rejected and a broad blanket exclusion of liability clause, which excluded liability for direct damages, incidental and consequential losses, and loss of profit and potentially excluded damages for misrepresentation. In finding for SAM, the court noted that it was necessary to consider the reasonableness of the combined effect of the exclusion and limitation of liability clauses under the Unfair Contract Terms Act 1977. It was held that these clauses were only made reasonable by SAM's inclusion of a money back guarantee, entitling a customer to claim back the purchase price if the software was rejected. This was an adequate remedy for the customer and had this clause not been included the exclusion of liability clause would have been unenforceable.

Limitation of liability clauses were also considered in the case of *University of Keele* v. *PriceWaterHouse* [2004] EWCA Civ 583 where PriceWaterHouse (PW) offered to establish a profit-related pay scheme (PRP) for Keele University (Keele), which PW advised would make significant savings for Keele. Based on PW's advice Keele began to operate the PRP scheme. However, it failed to operate correctly. Keele did not make the anticipated savings and PW subsequently admitted that its advice had been negligent. Keele brought an action for damages suffered as a result of PW's negligent advice but PW argued that it was not liable for damages and loss of savings as they were specifically excluded in an exemption clause under its terms of engagement.

This exclusion clause contained a two-limb limitation on liability; the first limb stated that PW '. . . accepts liability to pay damages in respect of loss or damage suffered by [the client] as a direct result of [PW] providing the services . . .'. The second limb expressly excluded '. . . all other liability, in particular consequential loss and failure to realise anticipated savings or benefits'. The Court of Appeal held that the correct approach to the construction of the contractual clause was to consider both limbs as a whole and to consider whether the two were capable of reconciliation. On the face of it, under the first limb of the clause PW could be interpreted as accepting liability for the loss of anticipated savings, however under the second limb this was expressly referred to as an excluded liability. The Court of Appeal held that the use of the word 'other' at the start of the second limb reconciled the apparently conflicting clauses: the first limb took precedence, and the second limb formed a residual category of liability and so PW was liable for Keele's loss.

7. Re-tendering, termination and exit

No one likes to enter into a service relationship thinking about what would happen if the deal collapsed or the online business simply wanted to change to a cheaper or better service provider. However, the consequences of not addressing at the outset how the parties are to manage these situations can be dire. From the online business's point of view, it can find itself trapped with an unsatisfactory service provider with no real ability to do anything except renew the contract. Without provisions for a smooth transfer of operations an interruption in business continuity is likely and this may hit the bottom line. From the service provider's perspective, a messy 'divorce' could mean bad publicity so handling the end of a contract smoothly and professionally should be a high priority.

There are three main scenarios that the parties to an existing services relationship can find themselves in:

1. The contract is approaching its end and the online business wants to re-tender to decide whether to renew the contract or change service providers.
2. The contract is being terminated at its end with a change of service providers or the taking of services in-house.
3. The contract is being terminated for breach, with a consequent change of service providers or the taking of services in-house.

In each case, either the contract will set out adequately what the parties' rights and obligations are or it will not. This section considers how to assess the true situation and suggests how to deal with the all too usual situation where the contract is inadequate.

7.1 Re-tendering

Assuming that neither party is in breach, and even if the online business is satisfied with the services, it is likely that the online business will want to go through a re-tendering process even if the aim is only to renegotiate the existing contract. If the online business allows an existing contract to roll on, it is unlikely to benefit from the competitive edge offered by other potential service providers, in terms of quality and range of service and price.

To do this, the online business first has to make sure that it allows itself sufficient time. Given that from start to finish the original contracting out is likely to have taken a number of months, the online business should ideally start thinking about the re-tendering 12 months before the contract expires or can be brought to an end by notice.

If there is to be a meaningful re-tendering exercise, the online business will want to issue an invitation to tender to a number of potential service providers. In order to elicit sensible bids, this ITT will need to contain basic information about the assets and services that the potential new service providers will inherit.

7.2 What does the online business need to know?

The online business will need to be able to give any potential new service provider information about:

- *Physical assets*: as these are needed for service provision, potential new service providers may need to know what equipment is being used in the provision of services, what state it is in and what can be transferred at what cost.
- *Contracts with third party service providers, especially of software, maintenance or other critical services*: again, the new service provider will want to know what these are and whether they can be transferred to it, and, if so, at what cost in terms of consent fees.
- *Staff*: The Transfer of Undertakings (Protection of Employment) Regulations 1981 (TUPE) can apply on the change of service providers and the effect can be to transfer the relevant employees of the sitting service provider to the new one. Potential new service providers need to know whether TUPE will apply and, if so, exactly who will transfer and on what terms. The issues here include:
  – the existing service provider faces the possible loss of skilled employees to a competitor. On the other hand, if those employees would have been made redundant on the ending of the contract, the existing service provider avoids having to pay any redundancy costs and can end up with a windfall situation. Subject to its overriding obligation to provide the services in accordance with the contract up to the point of termination, it could also judiciously redeploy the best employees and move less valuable staff to the undertaking which will transfer to the new service provider; and
  – the new service provider faces taking on a group of employees whom it does not know and who have been trained by another service provider.

This may or may not suit the new service provider, particularly if it inherits outstanding liabilities, the old service provider's less valuable staff and the possibility of a redundancy bill.

- *Services*: in order to set out in the ITT what the online business wants, it needs to know what it currently receives. This means that the online business must have information to hand both as to the nature of the current services and also the levels to which they have been provided and any problems with that service provision.
- *Access to information and general cooperation*: potential new service providers will also want to know what general level of access to information, key personnel, premises and other material it will have and what obligations the sitting service provider will have to cooperate in the handover of services.

If the contract sets out rights for the online business to obtain and disclose this kind of information and deals with the process of hand-over of service provision, then the existing parties merely need to comply with their obligations.

7.3 Termination and transfer of suppliers

There are two scenarios here: the contract is being terminated for breach or one party has exercised a right to terminate at the end of the agreed term. The latter is relatively straightforward; it is termination for other reasons which requires further consideration.

7.4 Termination for breach, etc.

The first issue is to assess what rights of termination the contract contains. From the online business's point of view, the triggers for termination could include:

- breach of a material obligation of the service provider. What is 'material' may not always be clear and the contract may include a non-exhaustive list of breaches which would be treated as being material. Where a breach is capable of being put right, it is normal to specify a reasonable period during which the service provider must remedy the breach;
- if the service provider is in financial difficulties;
- convenience: if the contract is for a long fixed duration, then the contract may allow the online business the right to break it at certain points, on the payment of a fee;
- change of control: if the ownership of the service provider is of importance to the online business, the contract may specify that the online business has a right to terminate the contract if the ownership changes;

- change of nature: similarly, if the service provider disposes of business interests or assets such that the online business loses confidence in its long-term commitment to servicing clients in the area of the contract, the online business may have a right to terminate; and

- loss of external accreditation/licensing: if the service provider loses, for example, ISO accreditation or a licence or accreditation key to providing the services, the online business may also be able to terminate.

In respect of the last three options, it may be that the online business would not exercise the right to terminate, but would use the possibility as a lever to ensure that the service provider provided suitable reassurance about its long-term ability to provide the services.

The service provider will also want the right to terminate for the online business's breach or insolvency. Given that the only serious breach an online business can commit is to fail to pay, it is unlikely that it would concede an immediate right to terminate and the contract would usually instead provide for the payment of interest on outstanding amounts.

7.5 Rights on termination

Irrespective of the cause of termination, whether by expiry or on breach by either party, both the online business and the service provider will want to see an orderly transfer of service provision. The species of rights which should be considered are:

- information: as noted in connection with re-tendering, the online business will need information about how the current services are being provided, who is providing them and using what assets and contracts;

- contracts: the online business will want to be able to compel the service provider to assign relevant third party contracts either to the online business or to a new service provider, including any important software licences;

- hardware and other physical assets: the online business may need the option to purchase necessary equipment being used by the service provider and will want to set out also the basis of valuing that equipment; and

- intellectual property: where the service provider uses its own software in the provision of the services and this cannot be obtained in the market place, the online business may require a licence for it or the new service provider to use the software, at least on a temporary basis. Where this is the existing service provider's proprietary software, this may be a sensitive point.

The online business may also want the right to solicit key staff members, irrespective of the TUPE situation, and, in extreme circumstances, a right to enter the service provider's premises to take back relevant equipment and information.

Although the exit strategy which the parties agree will be similar whatever the circumstances of termination, it must of course take account of who, if anyone, is at fault. If the online business is at fault, it can expect to have less stringent rights and to pay for all cooperation provided. If the service provider is at fault, some assistance should be provided free of charge as a kind of self-help remedy for the online business.

8. Offshore outsourcing

Much has been made of leveraging cheaper, highly skilled technical resources offshore. Areas such as Bangalore, India, Shanghai, China and Sofia in Bulgaria have attracted incessant technical interest because of the skill sets and quality services they offer. Many online businesses consider offshoring to:

- reduce cost and increase shareholder value;
- increase the margin on revenues because development or service costs are substantially lower;
- improve service and consequently customer satisfaction; and
- achieve great business flexibility.

Offshoring clearly has its advantages in certain sectors and for certain services offshoring is now a real choice. Most of the principles and discussions in this chapter equally apply to such a relationship (though the online business should be aware of legal differences arising from local law, including employment laws, company laws and mandatory laws).

8.1 The offshoring services agreement

Documenting and agreeing a contract for services with an overseas element is all the more important because, once signed, daily communication and management may be affected. The online business should consider some of the structuring points discussed in the first section of this chapter (e.g. Model 1 or Model 2) to see if relying on a third party to take away some of the management pain is right for them.

With an offshore provider it is highly recommended that the online business enters into any relationship with its eyes open and careful due diligence into the service provider, its service promises, substance and the experience of other customers is time well spent.

The online business must proactively manage the offshore operations ensuring it has access to the information and service managers it needs in order to do so. As well as building in adequate service measurement, reporting and project management and service controls the online business should pay particular attention to:

- retaining essential service delivery knowledge (if it all goes wrong does the online business have the expertise in-house to take control and implement a revised delivery solution?);
- the risk management practices of the service provider and the added risk of offshoring (this involves a process of risk identification, analysis and then planning to ensure solutions have been pre-planned where appropriate so that failures don't completely derail the services);
- taking extra care to protect intellectual property (could the fancy service solution the online business paid for upfront be quickly rolled out to a competitor or does it even know what has been developed so it can reuse or protect the intellectual creations and effort?);
- having resilient solutions for security and continuity (to formulate an effective plan the online business needs to ensure it understands the environment which is difficult at a long distance); and
- culture and language (the online business needs to understand negotiation behaviour and expectations both to settle upon a deal but also to ensure it deals with the most relevant officers within the service provider organisation).

8.2 Additional hurdles – data protection

Data protection laws and issues are discussed more fully in Chapter 3. It is important to note that offshoring can cause additional data protection compliance issues when the service provider is based outside of the European Economic Area (EEA). Therefore outsourcing services to countries like China and India can pose particular problems. Currently, there is no specific data protection legislation in either China or India and consequently both are deemed to have inadequate data protection regimes by the EU. Therefore an online business needs to ensure that it implements a compliant international data transfer regime before sending a data subject's personal details to these countries.

Following increasing pressure from the European Union, and more particularly Indian business groups finding the EU data protection laws a barrier to their business, the Indian government has stated that it intends to introduce new legislation on data protection shortly (possibly due mid-2005). Although draft legislation has not yet been released, the legislation is expected to be similar to the data protection rights in Europe and will prescribe how data is collected and used. Whether this is sufficient for the EU to recognise the resulting regime as offering adequate data protection remains to be seen. Until such time the online business needs to protect all international data transfers accordingly.

6 The Legal Risks of Webvertising

> *Who was it that said existing, analogue advertising law controls were well able to cope with digital media marketing? Whoever it was, and it may have been me, has been proved very wrong.*
>
> Stephen Groom
> Head of Br@ndlegal Osborne Clarke

Introduction

At the height of the internet boom, webvertising was seen as a golden opportunity to bring marketing messages to customers via this far-reaching media.

The recent growth of the internet means that more advertising and marketing messages are read worldwide and that compliance with (worldwide) advertising laws has become more complex.

This chapter deals with the principal legal issues that arise under UK law when advertising online.

1. Netiquette for advertisers

Before launching into the legal and regulatory issues of webvertising in the UK, advertisers should always bear in mind the unofficial code of practice for online users, otherwise known as 'netiquette'. Sending unsolicited advertisements or marketing materials will be considered unacceptable by many recipients and may lead to complaints or direct action (e.g. so-called 'flaming') from users or the ISP carrying the ad.

The internet is a great way of reaching a large audience for your products, but it is also a place in which it is very easy to cause great inconvenience and annoyance to a very large number of people.

An advertiser can minimise the risk of problems by following a few simple rules of netiquette which mainly come down to understanding the internet before using it as a marketing medium.

A few rules of netiquette to bear in mind are:

1. Targeted advertisements for products that actually meet a need of the recipient will generally be more acceptable than generic material sent out on a blanket basis.
2. Do not unnecessarily upset, offend or anger people by the content of an advertisement.
3. Do not send out unsolicited emails or marketing messages.
4. Include a prominent 'unsubscribe' mechanism.

2. Regulation of webvertising in the UK

2.1 The CAP Code

In the UK, a self-regulatory system has been developed by the advertising industry, which is represented by the British Code of Advertising, Sales Promotion and Direct Marketing (the CAP Code). The CAP Code contains a comprehensive set of rules for advertisements and sales promotions.

The basic principles of the CAP Code are that advertisements should be:

(a) legal, decent, honest and truthful;
(b) prepared with a sense of responsibility to consumers and to society;
(c) in line with the principles of fair competition generally accepted in business.

The CAP Code complements statute and common law, but does not have effect as law itself.

2.2 The Committee of Advertising Practice

The CAP Code is written by the advertising industry through the Committee of Advertising Practice (the CAP). All the main trade and professional bodies representing advertisers, agencies, service suppliers and media owners are members of CAP. In addition to writing the CAP Code, CAP also has some powers of enforcement. It can for instance recommend to its media owner members that they refuse to accept particular ads. Even if an advertiser is not a member of CAP (or one of the other trade bodies), it will be required to observe the CAP Code.

2.3 Online advertising

All advertisements and promotions in non-broadcast media are covered by the CAP Code. This includes certain internet advertisements and promotions.

2.4 Ofcom

Ofcom was set up by statute as the super-regulator for the UK communications industries at the end of 2003, replacing the five previous regulators ITC, Radio Authority, BSC, Oftel and Radiocommunications Agency. As such Ofcom is responsible for writing and enforcing the Advertising Standards Codes applicable to advertisements and promotions in broadcast media (i.e. radio and television, but not internet), although since 1 November 2004 it has sub-contracted these responsibilities out to the ASA (see below) and the CAP. Despite this connection with the CAP and the ASA, OFCOM has no direct role in relation to the regulation of webvertising.

3. ASA

3.1 Regulated webvertising

The CAP Code is regulated by the Advertising Standards Authority (ASA). In addition, as mentioned above, the ASA (since November 2004) is now also responsible for regulating the television and radio Advertising Standards Codes (in respect of advertisements and promotions in broadcast media).

The CAP Code regulates the following types of internet advertising and promotion:

- online advertisements in paid for space including banners, pop-up and other advertisements, but excluding any generic product information on an advertiser's home pages; and
- sales promotions anywhere online.

The ambit of ASA regulation is restricted as the ASA does not have the resources to regulate all types of advertising that appear on the internet.

3.2 Complaints

If a consumer feels (s)he has been misled or offended by an internet advertisement regulated by the ASA, (s)he can complain to the ASA, who will investigate the complaint. A company or organisation can also complain to the ASA against another company or competitor. It is also possible for the ASA to investigate advertisements even in the absence of any complaint.

The ASA council (consisting of twelve independent and advertising members) will adjudicate in respect of the complaint. Both the complainant and the advertiser are notified of the ASA adjudication. If the complaint is not upheld, no further action is taken. Upheld complaints may result in the advertisement being withdrawn or amended (see section 3.3 below).

3.3 What sanctions can the ASA impose?

The ASA has a number of sanctions it can use to ensure that advertisements that breach the CAP Code are amended or withdrawn. Media owners play an important part in ensuring compliance with an ASA adjudication (see section 3.5 below).

If an online advertisement has been held to be in breach of the CAP Code, the advertisers can change or withdraw it. In the vast majority of cases, advertisers act quickly to make any changes necessary to bring their ads in line with the CAP Code. If the ad is not changed or withdrawn, the CAP can ask publishers and media owners to refuse more space online for an advertisement until it has been changed.

Furthermore, any incentives available through membership of some of the advertising trade bodies may be withdrawn from advertisers who do not comply with ASA decisions.

In the case of persistent or deliberate offenders, the ASA can refer an advertiser, its agency or publisher to the Office of Fair Trading which in turn can seek an injunction to prevent the same or similar claims being made in future ads under the Control of Misleading Advertisements Regulations 1988 (see section 4.2 below).

3.4 Adverse publicity

In addition to the sanctions available to the ASA, the ASA's adjudications are published online (www.asa.org.uk), with a hard copy summary of all the decisions being made available to interested parties on a regular basis. The adjudications of the ASA are read by the media, government departments, the advertising industry and consumer bodies. They are often the subject of intense media interest especially if complaints are upheld arising from well-known organisations or their brands. Most advertisers would want to avoid any such adverse publicity.

3.5 Traditional vs. internet adjudications

The self-regulation system relies on the participation of media owners to enforce the adjudications of the ASA. Trade associations of traditional media owners require that their members must refuse bookings for advertisements that have been the subject of upheld complaints by the ASA. This requirement has been agreed between the Trade Associations and CAP. As a result, virtually all media owners comply with ASA adjudications in the traditional media.

The Interactive Advertising Bureau UK (www.iabuk.net), the trade association for interactive advertising, electronic commerce and online marketing, is a member of CAP and may require its members to comply with the CAP Code. The IAB supports e-commerce, interactive advertising and online marketing by establishing standards for the industry, developing innovative research projects and keeping members informed of developments in the sector.

However, the IAB (or any other existing trade body for online advertisers) cannot enforce the adjudications of the ASA. Webvertisers may therefore choose to ignore adverse adjudications by the ASA.

As a result, ASA adjudications in respect of online advertisement may have less bite in practice than adjudications in respect of advertising on traditional media. Nevertheless, the online advertisers will still suffer the bad publicity from an adverse ASA ruling.

3.6 Is self-regulation effective for online advertising?

As generic product information of a company on its home page falls outside the regulatory ambit of the ASA, advertisements which may breach the CAP Code if advertised in traditional media, may be accessible on the internet via the advertiser's home page. This gap in the regulatory system is illustrated by a controversial campaign of the retail chain French Connection in the summer of 2001.

French Connection's advertising campaign 'Kinky Bugger' was deemed to contain an unacceptable level of sexual innuendo for broadcast on UK television. A subsequent poster campaign with the caption 'Sorry' directed the public to French Connection's website to see the 'Kinky Bugger' advertisement (www.fcukinkybugger.com). The public complained that the poster was offensive and the ASA held that the poster should be withdrawn.

Meanwhile, the 'Kinky Bugger' advertisement could be viewed online without regulatory consequences.

3.7 Admark

To increase consumer confidence in online advertising, CAP launched the 'Admark' scheme for internet advertising on 17 May 2001. Admark is an opt-in scheme that allows member advertisers and publishers to indicate that their online advertisements are 'legal, decent, honest and truthful', by displaying the Admark icon on their 'paid for' adverts and providing information about the scheme on their websites.

The benefit for consumers is that they can recognise that the advertiser has agreed to comply with the CAP Code and ASA adjudications by the Admark icon displayed on the advertiser's website. Consumers can also search for members on the Admark website (www.admark.org.uk) and see which of the online brands have opted in to the admark scheme.

Admark does not cover advertisers' own claims on their websites (apart from sales promotions) as these are not regulated by the CAP Code or the ASA. Advertisers will benefit from consumer reassurance by joining the scheme for an annual fee. In addition to payment of a fee, membership will impose additional obligations on the advertiser under Admark's terms and conditions.

4. Statutory provisions

Companies that advertise online should consider a number of statutory provisions applicable to webvertising. This chapter deals with the most relevant statutes.

4.1 Trade Descriptions Act 1968

The Trade Descriptions Act 1968 makes it an offence to apply a false trade description to any goods or services. A trade description includes an indication of quantity or size, method of manufacture, descriptions for purpose or place or date of manufacture, or any other history of the goods and/or services.

As all goods sold online are sold by description, particular care is required. A trade description can only be false if it is false to a material degree. Therefore some minor inconsequential mis-description of goods may not necessarily be unlawful.

When considering whether an advertisement includes a false trade description the whole advertisement must be considered as well as the reaction of a reasonable customer to it. For example, a poster advertisement showing 'Ribena Tooth Kind' bottles as bristles on a toothbrush were held to be a misleading description of the 'Ribena Tooth Kind' drink as it implied that the product actively benefited oral health. A claim made by the advertisers in a trade press advertisement that 'Ribena Tooth Kind does not encourage tooth decay' was also found to be misleading as being an absolute rather than a comparative claim. The ASA adjudication was upheld in the High Court.

The offence is one of strict liability and the advertiser may not rely on a disclaimer. However there is a special defence for publishers of advertisements which is referred to as the 'advertiser's defence'. Where a person is in the business of publishing advertisements and receives an advertisement in the ordinary course of business and did not know, or had no reason to suspect, that the publication would amount to an offence, they will be able to claim advertiser's defence.

The regulatory codes discussed earlier on in this chapter also contain a prohibition on making misleading claims in advertisements.

4.2 Control of Misleading Advertisements Regulations 1988

The Control of Misleading Advertisements Regulations 1988 (as amended) provide a legal backstop in cases where an advertiser ignores an adverse ASA decision under the CAP Code. In such cases the ASA can refer the matter to the Office of Fair Trading (the OFT) and the OFT can seek an undertaking that the advertising in question will be stopped from anyone responsible for commissioning, preparing or disseminating it. If that is not given or is not honoured, the OFT can seek an injunction from the court to prevent its further appearance. In addition under the Enterprise Act 2002 certain other organisations representing consumers, such as Trading Standards, may now also apply to the court directly to enforce the Regulations using 'Enforcement Orders' (previously known as 'Stop Now Orders').

4.3 Trade Marks Act 1994

The Trade Marks Act is another relevant statute to keep in mind when advertising online.

What is a trade mark?

A trade mark is a sign that distinguishes goods or services of one business from those of another. Marks that may be registered as a trade mark include names, shapes, letters, numerals, signatures and designs.

Trade mark owners will often draw attention to their registered trade mark rights by use of the ® symbol following the mark. Alternatively, a search on the Patent Office's website (www.patent.gov.uk) can help reveal whether a mark is registered (or has been applied for).

Use of a registered trade mark

Marketing or advertising goods can require the consent of the trade mark owner if for example the logo, name or shape of the product is registered as a trade mark.

Some recent court cases have looked particularly at a situation where a vendor, without the consent of a trade mark proprietor, is marketing goods within the European Economic Area (EEA) which were placed on the market outside the EEA.

Tesco and Levi's case

The court case brought (*inter alia*) by Levi Strauss against Tesco and Costco for selling Levi's jeans (amongst other designer goods) in their shops at a much lower price than the official Levi's distributors in the UK, illustrates the issue of obtaining a trade mark owner's consent before marketing their imported goods.

Consent of a trade mark proprietor to the marketing within the EEA of products bearing their mark which have previously been placed on the market outside the EEA by that proprietor, is required before such goods may be marketed in the EEA.

A judgment from the European Court of Justice followed a referral from the High Court in proceedings pending between the same parties. The European Court of Justice held that a person who markets the products of a trade mark proprietor has to demonstrate that the proprietor has renounced his right to oppose the placing of his goods on the market within the EEA.

Use of competitor's trade mark

Furthermore, using a competitor's trade mark online – for example, as a comparison between products or services available on the advertiser's website and those of the competitor – will be allowed under the Trade Marks Act 1994 only as long as use of the competitor's trade mark does not take unfair advantage of the mark and is in accordance with honest practices in commercial matters. Comparative advertising is more fully addressed in section 5 below.

Use of unregistered marks

If dealing with unregistered trade marks, the advertiser may still risk a claim for passing off (see chapter 1).

Exceptions

Subject to certain provisions, the Trade Marks Act 1994 allows use of a registered trade mark by any person for the purpose of identifying goods or services as those of the owner or licensee of the mark.

For example, an online car dealer may refer to the fact that it sells a particular type of car and use that car's trade mark to denote that it sells that particular type of car.

Use of someone's registered trade mark is also allowed to indicate the kind, quality, intended purpose or other characteristics of the goods or services. For example, it is not an infringement under the Trade Marks Act 1994 to state that the goods and services sold on the website are suitable for use with a particular type of product.

Remedies

Where trade mark infringement takes place, the trade mark owner has various remedies. These include an injunction to stop the infringer from using his trade mark, delivery up of all infringing goods or erasure of the mark or destruction of all infringing goods. The trade mark owner may also sue for damages or for an account of profits resulting from the infringement. In addition to any claim for damages, it may be costly for an advertiser if it has to change or withdraw an advertisement as a result of infringing someone's trade mark.

4.4 Passing off

In addition to any statutory liability, online advertising may also risk liability under common law, most notably for defamation or passing off claims.

The law of passing off aims to prevent people being misled as to the nature, quality or origin of advertised goods and services.

Advertisers need to be aware of the law of passing off as it places restrictions on the content of descriptions for goods and services so that they do not take unfair advantage of other traders' reputations and goodwill.

Examples of how a misrepresentation may lead to a claim in passing off include claiming a connection with another well-established business, imputing the authority or consent of the holder of the goodwill, and using the name or mark of another trader.

Advertisers accused of passing off may have certain defences available to them. Depending on the details of the claim, the advertiser may be able to use as a defence the fact that a mark is not distinctive, that consent was obtained, or that the traders have concurrent rights.

4.5 Defamation

Advertising that makes statements which are derogatory about other companies or individuals may give rise to liability for defamation.

Every person who is responsible for a defamatory publication is a potential defendant. Therefore the advertiser and the owner and/or operator of a website may be potentially liable for a defamatory advertisement.

Defences to claims for defamation are available. These include justification – where it can be shown that the statement and its defamatory meaning are true and fair comment – broadly speaking, where the statement complained of is an honest expression of a reasonably held opinion.

The principal remedies for defamation claims are the payment of damages and obtaining an injunction to prevent publication of the advertisement. In certain cases, corrective advertising can also be ordered.

To minimise potential liability for defamation an advertiser should:

- check that all statements of fact contained in the advertisement are true and can be proved to be true;
- if a statement is a comment rather than a statement of fact, make it clear that it is an opinion;
- ensure opinions expressed are fair; and
- ensure that indemnity insurance is in place.

5. Comparative Advertising Regulations

The Control of Misleading Advertising (Amendment) Regulations 2000 allow product owners to compare their products with those of competitors either directly or indirectly, subject to certain requirements being fulfilled which are set out in the Regulations.

5.1 Requirements for comparative advertisements

Comparative advertising is defined as any ad which '*in any way, either explicitly or by implication, identifies a competitor or goods or services offered by a competitor*'. If an advertisement comes within this definition it will automatically be illegal unless it satisfies the seven requirements set out in the Regulations.

The most important of these seven requirements are:

(a) advertisers must compare like with like, which means that an advertisement must compare goods or services meeting the same needs or intended for the same purpose;
(b) the advertisement must objectively compare one or more material, relevant, verifiable and representative features of the goods and services (which may include price); and
(c) the advertisement must not discredit or denigrate the trade marks of the competitor.

A comparative advertisement will only be lawful if all seven requirements are met.

5.2 Special offers

The Regulations include an eighth rule for special offers. In respect of an advertisement for a special offer, any comparison must indicate the date on which the offer ends, whether it is subject to availability, or whether specific conditions apply, and must state a date when the special offer starts.

5.3 Enforcement of the Regulations

Product owners can complain to the Office of Fair Trading or the ASA if they have been subject to comparative advertising which they think breaches these rules.

Under the Enterprise Act 2002, certain other organisations representing consumers, such as Trading Standards, may now also apply to the court directly to enforce the Regulations using 'Enforcement Orders' (previously known as 'Stop Now Orders').

6. Copyright and other intellectual property rights

All materials used in webvertising must be cleared for copyright and other intellectual property rights to ensure that they do not infringe the rights of a third party.

6.1 Obtaining a licence

The advertiser and/or the website owner must ensure that it obtains a licence from all third parties who may own intellectual property rights in the advertisement. The licence must cover use on the internet and must be for the whole period that the advertisement is available online.

7. Distance Selling and Marketing

The Distance Selling Regulations 2000 give the consumer various rights where the supplier and consumer do not meet face to face. Online sales are an obvious example of distance sales.

7.1 When do the Regulations apply?

The Regulations apply only in a business-to-consumer relationship, whereby the consumer is defined as any person not acting in the course of business. If a company acts outside its business (for example, the purchase of computers by a flower shop), then the Regulations will apply.

7.2 Exclusions

Various goods and services are excluded from the Regulations such as contracts for a regular delivery of newspapers, financial services (but see section 7.6 below) and contracts for the provision of accommodation, transport, catering or leisure services.

7.3 Rights of information

The online supplier of goods and services must give the consumer various pieces of information set out in the Regulations.

In respect of online advertising, the most relevant information includes:

165

- informing the consumer of the full costs of the goods and services including all taxes and charges; and
- the period for which an offer or the price remains valid.

7.4 Right to cancel

The consumer has a right to cancel a contract concluded online within seven working days following either delivery of the goods or conclusion of the contract if it is for services.

If the consumer exercises his right of cancellation, he has a right to return the goods at the supplier's expense and has the right to be reimbursed for the purchase price within thirty days of rejecting the goods.

7.5 Non-cancellable contracts

In respect of some distance contracts the consumer is not given the right to cancel.

Non-cancellable contracts include: contracts for the supply of audio or computer software if they are unsealed by the customer, magazines, personalised goods and gaming, betting or lottery services.

7.6 Distance marketing of consumer financial products

The Distance Marketing Directive, which aims to protect retail consumers who deal with a financial services firm or acquire a financial services product without face to face contact, was implemented in the UK on 31 October 2004 by virtue of the Distance Marketing Directive Instrument 2004 (amending the FSA Handbook, in respect of first mortgages, general insurance policies, life assurance and pensions) and the Financial Services (Distance Marketing) Regulations 2004 (in respect of second mortgages, debt management services and credit cards).

Both the Instrument and the Regulations set out two categories of compulsory disclosures that must be made in respect of distance sales of consumer financial products, and provide the consumer with a right to cancel (within a period of either fourteen or thirty days).

8. Foreign laws of webvertising

8.1 US advertising laws

The Federal Trade Commission's guidelines for internet advertising give an overview of how US consumer protection laws apply to commercial activities online.

The guidelines state the basic principles of US advertising law that apply to online advertising:

- advertising must be truthful and not misleading;
- advertisers must have evidence to back up their claims;
- advertisements cannot be unfair.

The Guidelines further provide that disclosures that are required to prevent deception or to provide consumers with material information about a transaction must be presented clearly and conspicuously. The US also has additional rules such as the Children's Online Privacy Protection Act (COPPA), which applies to the online collection of personal information from children under 13 years of age, and the CAN-SPAM Act, which imposes a series of requirements on the use of e-mail messages to combat commercial e-mail that is unwanted by the recipient and/or deceptive.

8.2 European advertising rules

Even though legislation of the member states of the European Union will be similar to a great extent on issues governed by European legislation, local legal advice should always be taken. In some countries alcohol advertising is banned. In others, advertising directed at children is heavily regulated. It is also worth noting that non-sensitive issues in one country, e.g. lingerie advertisements, may lead to massive public outcry in others.

Different views that may exist on nudity in advertisements throughout Europe are illustrated by claims brought in Brussels and France in respect of advertisements containing an element of nudity.

An Adecco television spot featuring an unattractive and overweight employer in his fifties doing a striptease in front of a young woman, and ending up wearing nothing but an employment contract, was withdrawn by commercial broadcaster RTBF after various complaints. Adecco wanted a court order requiring the broadcaster to carry the spot. RTBF argued that the advertisement was immoral and encouraged sexual harassment in the work place. The court rejected RTBF's arguments and upheld Adecco's 'right to be humorous'.

In France the self-regulatory ad watchdog BVP ordered that a poster advertising French clothing which featured a near naked woman squatting doggy style opposite a sheep (but not revealing too much) with the ad captions 'I need a sweater' was ordered to be taken down.

Cultural differences in areas such as sex and gender in advertising may differ substantially, even between neighbouring European countries, and care should be taken when putting such advertisements online.

9. Pricing

Misleading consumers as to the price of goods or services is unlawful. The Consumer Protection Act 1987 provides a prohibition on misleading price indications of goods or services. It is also an offence, if the price indication contained in advertisements becomes misleading, for the advertiser not to take reasonable steps to prevent consumers from relying on the price indication. In addition the Price Marking Order 2004 (in force since July 2004) requires that an unambiguous, easily identifiable and clearly legible indication of the selling price must, in a distance sales context, be given in proximity to a visual or written description of the product.

9.1 Online pricing

Case law in the UK generally suggests that prices identified on a website are an invitation to treat and that the consumer offers to buy the particular product for that price. The offer may or may not be accepted by the advertiser.

Companies selling products online outside the UK should ensure that the method of pricing and currency conversion is not misleading to consumers, for example by stating the equivalent of the price in pounds sterling.

Areas of particular caution are where prices of goods fluctuate or when prices vary depending on when the product is ordered.

9.2 What amounts to misleading pricing?

Customers may be misled as to the price if:

- the price indicated is less than the actual price;
- the applicability of the price does not depend on the fact or circumstances on which its applicability does in fact depend; or
- the price includes any hidden charges (such as taxes, delivery costs etc).

The method of determining a price may also be misleading.

9.3 Specific rules

In some circumstances specific rules apply to price indications, for example when a price does not apply to all methods of payment.

9.4 Pricing

The checklist below may help to ensure the provisions on price indications are met:

✓ CHECKLIST

→ is the price the consumer will have to pay for the product clearly stated?
→ is the price indication accurate and does it cover the total charge payable?
→ if a price only applies to a limited number of goods or services or not to the goods or services as advertised, is this made clear?
→ are there any hidden charges such as postage, packaging and delivery?
→ if VAT is payable, is VAT included in the price?
→ is any price comparison accurate and valid?
→ if prices are liable to change is this stated?
→ if the goods and or services available outside the UK, are the prices for each country where the goods and services are available stated?
→ do any specific pricing rules apply?

---

10. Particular products and their rules

The advertising and marketing of particular products may attract specific legislation which should be particularly considered. The following sub-paragraphs deal with some particular products although this is not an exhaustive list.

10.1 Tobacco

Advertising tobacco products is subject to strict rules across Europe, and in some countries (including the UK) such advertising is more or less banned altogether.

The position in the UK is that as a result of the Tobacco Advertising and Promotion Act 2002 all forms of tobacco advertising are banned, including transmitting a tobacco advert in electronic form, participating in doing so, or providing the means of transmission. However the Act does not cover advertisements for rolling papers or filters and does permit certain tobacco advertising at point of sale.

The CAP Code contains specific rules concerning advertisements for rolling papers and filters.

10.2 Alcoholic products

The CAP Code and other non-legal regulatory codes impose important restrictions on the advertisement of alcoholic products. The Food Labelling Regulations 1996, for example, restrict the use of various terms indicating a specific product as a 'wine', 'non-alcoholic wine' etc in the advertising of alcoholic products.

For the purposes of the CAP Code, alcoholic drinks are those that exceed 1.2 per cent alcohol by volume.

The main aim of the CAP Code is that advertising should not encourage excessive drinking and should not be aimed at people under 18 (or likely to appeal to people under 18).

The CAP Code also restricts the medium on which alcoholic products may be advertised. No medium should be used to advertise alcoholic drinks if more than 25 per cent of its audience is under 18 years of age.

Low alcohol drinks (those that contain between 0.5 per cent and 1.2 per cent alcohol by volume) are also covered in the CAP Code. Advertisers should ensure that low alcohol drinks are not promoted in a way that encourages their inappropriate consumption and should not depict activities that require complete sobriety.

10.3 Children

The restrictions relating to advertising and children fall into three main categories:

- restricting advertisements with children as the subject matter;
- prohibitions on material which puts children's welfare at risk (for example, selling indecent photographs of children online); and
- restrictions on advertisements aimed at children.

Various statutory and regulatory restrictions apply to advertisements with children as its subject matter. The Adoption Act 1976 for example forbids any advertisement for any person (not being an adoption agency) to indicate its willingness to arrange the adoption of a child.

The Protection of Children Act 1978 places restrictions under the second category set out above and provides a prohibition on advertising the sale or display of indecent photographs of children.

The CAP Code also sets out specific rules concerning advertising aimed at children, for example it states that advertisements and promotions addressed to or featuring children should not exploit their loyalty, vulnerability or lack of experience.

10.4 Other particular products

Special restrictions apply to a variety of other particular products that are outside the scope of this chapter, for example medicinal products, weapons, organic products and fireworks.

11. Gaming, betting and lotteries advertisements

There are various legal and regulatory provisions relating to betting, lotteries and gaming advertisements. Generally speaking advertisements that invite people to make bets are heavily restricted and advertisements which encourage youngsters to bet are unlawful.

11.1 Statutory provisions

Under the Gaming Act 1968 advertising that publicises gaming is prohibited, subject to certain exceptions, for example advertising of bingo, which is allowed.

The advertising of lotteries is also unlawful, subject to certain exceptions (most importantly in respect of the National Lottery). However the existing legal provisions are due to be replaced by a new Gambling Bill which is expected to be enacted sometime in 2005.

11.2 The CAP Code

The CAP Code also incorporates specific rules for betting and gaming ads, aimed primarily at discouraging excessive gambling. Care should also be taken so as not to exploit the young or socially vulnerable. An advertisement should not be directed at people under 18 and people shown gambling should not look under 25.

11.3 The *Victor Chandler* case

In *Victor Chandler* v. *Customs and Excise Commissioners* [2000] 1 WLR 1296, the Court of Appeal held that Victor Chandler, a bookmaker, whose business was located abroad was entitled to solicit custom within the United Kingdom by broadcasting advertisements on Teletext.

Victor Chandler's argument was that advertisements under the Betting and Gaming Duties Act 1981 were limited to advertisements in document form and that the means by which the advertisements broadcast on Teletext were made available for viewing did not involve the issue, circulation or distribution of any document.

As the Betting and Gaming Duties Act was enacted in 1972, Parliament would not have contemplated the means by which advertisements can now be created circulated and distributed electronically. However this case shows that even Acts enacted in the 'brick age' may cause problems for internet advertisers.

12. Advertising holidays on the internet

Advertising holidays online may attract specific problems and complaints. The most common types of problems are:

- the advertised flight price is not inclusive of all airport or other taxes; or
- the flight price advertised is subject to limited availability or other restrictions.

Misleading advertisements for holidays and other travel can cause great irritation and upset to travellers.

Advertisers should ensure that their ads for holidays and travel do not mislead consumers about anything likely to influence their decision to purchase the holiday or travel.

12.1 What does the CAP Code say?

The CAP Code contains a number of requirements for holiday and travel advertisements. As a general rule, no advertisement should mislead consumers in any way and the CAP Code requires the following:

- all prices should be stated inclusive of all taxes and charges and any extras should be specifically mentioned;
- any terms and conditions or limitations on the holiday or travel must be clearly stated, for example, if the price is calculated on two people sharing a room;
- all amenities advertised should be available and any restrictions (for example non-availability during off-peak season) should be clearly stated;
- illustrations and photographs used in the advertisements must be up to date and accurate;
- sales promotions which offer free holidays must not incorporate any hidden costs for the winner (for example compulsory insurance, airport taxes and other fees).

12.2 Other rules

Advertisers are also bound by the codes of practice of other regulatory bodies such as ABTA and IATA. The general statutory laws relating to misleading advertisements also apply.

12.3 Complaints

The ASA receives hundreds of complaints each year regarding advertisements for holidays and travel which mainly relate to omissions of price and other offer restrictions and misleading descriptions of holidays.

easyJet

An example of such complaints relates to an internet advertisement for flights that could be booked through easyJet's website. The complainant was quoted £68 for flights to and from Aberdeen but was unable to book them because of a problem with the easyJet site. The claimant was told in a telephone call with easyJet that the flights were not available at the prices quoted on the website. The complainant challenged the availability of flights at the advertised prices.

easyJet argued that the complaint referred to their online booking engine and that it did not constitute advertising. The ASA held that, because the complaint concerned web pages that were accessed before the customer entered into a transaction, those pages constituted an advertisement. However in this case, easyJet provided the ASA with documentation showing that it had sold seats at the advertised prices on the flights the complainant had tried to book. Therefore in this case, the complaint was not upheld.

13. Spamming

The sending of unsolicited e-mails is an intrusive way of advertising and marketing and has various privacy and data protection implications. The main restrictions on spamming are set out below.

13.1 Privacy and Electronic Communications (EC Directive) Regulations 2003

The Privacy and Electronic Communications Regulations provide that explicit consent is required from consumers before sending unsolicited marketing communications by e-mail or SMS, except in respect of the so-called 'soft opt-in' exemption where the e-mail address or mobile phone number is obtained in the course of the sale or negotiations for the sale of a product or service similar to that which is being marketed. The Regulations also require that each unsolicited e-mail or SMS message must contain a simple means of opting-out of further messages free of charge (except for the costs of the transmission of the refusal). Please refer to chapter 3 for a comprehensive discussion of the Regulations.

13.2 Data Protection Act 1998

E-mail marketers are also required to comply with the Data Protection Act

1998 ('the DPA'). (Please refer to chapter 3 for a comprehensive discussion of the provisions of the DPA.).

13.3 CAP Code

The ASA regulates the use of personal data for direct marketing purposes as well as the content of mailings. The CAP Code covers three principal areas related to personal information:

- *Obtaining personal information*: The advertiser's name and general purpose for which a person's details are being collected should be made obvious at the time the information is requested from that individual. If there is an intention to make the individual's details available to third parties or if the data may be used for a significantly different purpose, this should be clearly stated. The explicit consent of consumers is required before sending marketing communications by e-mail or to mobile devices, save that advertisers may send unsolicited marketing about their similar products to those whose details they have obtained in the course of, or in negotiations for, a sale.
- *Corrections*: Advertisers are required, where requested, to correct any inaccuracies to an individual's personal information.
- *Accuracy and deletion*: Advertisers are required, on request, to delete a name from their mailing list and to stop future mailings to that individual. Mailing lists should be kept accurate and up to date.

The CAP Code has specific rules to ensure that the above principles are adhered to by advertisers. For example e-mail advertisements must state the full name and address of the advertiser so that it can be retained by the addressee.

13.4 E-commerce Directive

The E-commerce Directive requires that the following provisions should be met in respect of e-mail marketing:

- all e-mails must give the name, geographic address, e-mail address of sender and the details of any 'supervisory authority' to which it belongs, so that recipients can readily take action to avoid receiving such communications in the future;
- all unsolicited marketing e-mails must be identifiable as such and must identify the person on whose behalf it was sent;
- all unsolicited marketing e-mails must be clearly identifiable as such as soon as they are received so that they can be deleted without having to read them;

- senders of unsolicited marketing e-mail must consult regularly and respect any opt-out registers.

13.5 Direct Marketing Association

The Direct Marketing Association (DMA – the direct marketing industry watchdog) has a Code of Practice for electronic commerce, which sets out the standards of ethical conduct and best practice for e-commerce which their members must adhere to ('the DMA Code of Practice').

The DMA Code of Practice for electronic commerce has the following specific provisions in respect of unsolicited e-mail:

- unsolicited e-mails must be clearly identifiable as such;
- random untargeted commercial e-mails must not be sent;
- appropriate e-mail preference services must be used and e-mail communications must not be sent to individuals who have registered an objection to receiving such communications;
- unsolicited e-mails must include a mechanism for the addressee to register an objection to receiving further unsolicited communications;
- unsolicited e-mails sent as a result of a scheme must make clear to the recipient that their personal information has been obtained through such a scheme.

14. Advertising financial promotions

14.1 FSMA

Issuing a financial promotion in the UK that has not been approved by a person authorised by the Financial Services Authority (FSA) under the Financial Services and Markets Act 2000 (FSMA), may be a criminal offence punishable by imprisonment, a fine or both.

The FSMA contains a wide definition of what constitutes a 'financial promotion'. Material on the internet could be defined as a 'financial promotion' if it invites people to engage in investment activity or if it is likely to lead people directly or indirectly to engage in or offer to engage in investment activity. The scope of the FSMA/FSA regulatory regime has also been expanded to include certain mortgage products from 31 October 2004 and general insurance business from 14 January 2005.

Promotions of financial products over the internet from other countries may also be caught by the UK financial promotion restrictions under the FSMA if the promotion is directed at persons in the UK.

Factors taken into account in determining whether or not a promotion has been directed towards UK persons include explicit statements that the promotion is not directed at, nor should be relied upon, by UK persons or the prevention of UK persons entering into the investment activity.

Various exemptions and exclusions apply and the circumstances of each case will be taken into consideration when determining whether the advertisement is considered 'a financial promotion' and whether any exclusions or exceptions apply. Apart from committing an offence under the FSMA, breach of the Act can also lead to civil proceedings by the FSA for an injunction and for recovery of any money paid by investors.

14.2 Consumer Credit (Advertisements) Regulations 2004

The Consumer Credit (Advertisements) Regulations 2004 set out certain requirements in respect of credit advertisements which are not regulated under the FSMA/FSA regime. In particular all credit advertisements must:

- use plain and intelligible language;
- be easily legible; and
- specify the name of the advertiser.

In addition if the credit advertisement includes certain types of information this will automatically trigger a requirement to include other types of information (including in some circumstances a requirement to state the 'Typical APR'). Publishing a credit advertisement online which breaches these requirements may be a criminal offence punishable by imprisonment, a fine, or both.

14.3 Disclaimer

Although a disclaimer posted on the site in respect of a financial promotion may make clear that the promotion is not directed at, nor should be relied upon by the UK, such a disclaimer may not alleviate the risk of committing an offence under the FSMA and/or the Consumer Credit (Advertisements) Regulations as it is only one factor which is taken into account when considering whether the advertisement is unlawful.

14.4 Distance marketing

As mentioned, the Distance Marketing Directive has been implemented in the UK by virtue of the Distance Marketing Directive Instrument 2004 and the Financial Services (Distance Marketing) Regulations 2004. Please refer to section 7.6 above for further details.

Trident case

In November 2001, the Financial Services Authority successfully took legal action against an offshore firm trading as Trident Market Advisors, which targeted UK investors. Trident used mail shots to attract UK customers' interest and offered customers share dealing and investment advice services, although it was not authorised to undertake such business by the FSA.

The FSA stopped Trident's unauthorised business at the end of 2000 and in November 2001 successfully won a High Court case against the company whereby the court declared that Trident had issued an investment advertisement in the UK without the required approval from the FSA.

This case illustrates the importance of recognising that special rules may apply in respect of the service advertised and the importance of taking legal advice on the legality of the advertising in each target country.

15. Consumer Guarantee Directive

The Directive on the Sale of Consumer Goods and Associated Guarantees was implemented in the UK by the Sale and Supply of Goods to Consumers Regulations 2002 which runs alongside the existing Sale of Goods Act 1979 (as amended). The Directive aims to harmonise consumer protection laws in the European Union for those customers who purchase defective goods.

15.1 Consumer rights period

The Regulations provide a two-year period in which a consumer who purchases goods with defects present at the date of delivery from the supplier, may be entitled to a repair, replacement or price reduction or a refund within that two-year period.

The Regulations also place a burden on the supplier to prove that, if a defect appeared within the first six months after purchase, the product was sold without that defect.

15.2 Sellers' obligations

Sellers must deliver goods to consumers that conform with the contract of sale under the Regulations. Goods must therefore:

- comply with the description given by the seller and have the qualities ascribed to the goods by way of sample or model;
- be fit for the purpose for which the consumer requires the goods (and which he told the seller about when the contract was made);

- be fit for the purpose for which the particular goods are normally used;
- be of the quality and performance which are normal in goods of that type and which the consumer can reasonably expect given the nature of the goods and taking into account any public statements on the specific characteristics of the goods made about them by the seller, the producer or his representatives, particularly in advertising or on labelling.

The Regulations will not change the current law in the UK in respect of misleading descriptions in advertising, but will serve as additional ammunition for consumers and consumer representative bodies, such as Trading Standards.

Therefore online advertisers should be particularly careful in describing goods and/or services advertised.

16. Some cases highlighting risks

In this section a few recent cases are summarised to indicate how things can go wrong for online advertisers.

16.1 Keeping competition websites updated

In March 2001, Free Money Limited's rules of entry of its competition website stated that a daily prize of £1,000 could be won and that winners were drawn every day. A complaint was received by the ASA on the basis that daily prizes had not been given for a long time and that Free Money had not updated their 'previous winners' page.

The ASA noted that the daily £1,000 draw had been unavailable for a long period of time. This was referred to on Free Money's home page. However the rules of entry to win a daily prize of £1,000 were still accessible on the site and the frequently asked questions section also referred to the daily prize of £1,000.

The ASA concluded that the claims referring to the daily £1,000 prize were invalid and in breach of the CAP Code as they were misleading and not true.

The lesson to be learned from this adjudication is to keep website material current and updated to make sure that any claims which are no longer valid are immediately removed.

16.2 Specific products and their rules

In June 2000, the ASA received a complaint in respect of a website advertising magnetic products. One of the products advertised was a magnetic wristband which the advertisement claimed could give relief for various medical conditions, including eczema, blood pressure and asthma.

In respect of the magnetic wristband, the complainant challenged whether it could give relief for the advertised medical conditions.

The advertisers said that they had intended to list the benefits of the products and encourage sufferers from the advertised medical conditions to try their products. The advertisers had not provided the ASA with any written evidence to substantiate their claims. The ASA concluded that the advertisers' claims were not substantiated and upheld the complaint. It asked the advertisers to remove the advertisement from their website and to seek advice from CAP's Copy Advice Team before advertising again.

The CAP Code provides specific rules for the advertising of health and beauty products. Broadly speaking, these state that any medical and scientific claims made about such products must be backed by evidence. They also state that advertisers should not offer medical advice or a diagnosis or treatment unless this is conducted under the supervision of a qualified health professional. An advertiser should always check whether there are any specific rules, either under the CAP Code or any statutory rules, which may apply to the products advertised.

16.3 Industry complaints

The ASA ruling in respect of Design Holidays' claim to be the largest and longest established tour operator for a particular resort in Spain illustrates how claims made on an advertiser's website may lead to an industry complaint from a competitor.

In June 2000, a competitor of Design Holidays challenged the claim because they believed that they were in fact the largest tour operator for the resort and that they had been selling holidays to the resort for longer than the advertisers. The complaint was upheld and the advertisers amended their claim to being 'one of the largest and longest established operators'. Advertisers should not use a claim in respect of their products or services unless they can supply documentary evidence to prove the claim, as this may lead to complaints not only from consumers but also from within the industry.

16.4 Text messages

In November 2001, the ASA received a complaint about a mobile phone text message sent by a computer games company. The message stated 'please report to your local army recruitment centre for your second tour of duty. Commandos 2 on PC, it's more Real than Real Life – out today from Eidos'. The recipient's mobile phone identified the sender as 'SNBS'. The complainant, who was a man and an ex-member of the British Army, objected to the message on the grounds that it could cause undue fear and distress.

The advertisers had not intended to insult their customers and apologised for any distress caused by the insensitivity of the text message. The ASA upheld the complaint and considered that at first glance the text messages could distress recipients.

Direct marketers should consider the appropriateness of their messages to unprepared recipients, as not only could it cause anxiety and distress to customers, but they could be made to discontinue their marketing campaign.

17. Limiting liability for unlawful adverts

Depending on the type of liability, both the advertiser and the ISP may be liable for unlawful adverts. (An ISP may be able to limit its liability to the advertiser through its terms and conditions, see chapter 2.)

The online advertiser may, by contract with its ISP, be obliged to ensure compliance with relevant legislative and regulatory provisions and may have to indemnify the ISP for any unlawful adverts it carries on the advertiser's behalf. An advertiser's first step in minimising liability is to include a disclaimer on the site.

Of course, if an advertiser's banner ad is placed on a third-party website, it may not be possible to include such a disclaimer.

17.1 Disclaimer

A disclaimer may help to reduce the risk of legal action but in cases of strict liability (for example in defamation) it may not alleviate liability.

A disclaimer could include wording to the effect that:

- the goods and services advertised are supplied on standard terms and conditions to which English law and jurisdiction apply;
- the goods advertised on the site are primarily marketed to a particular country (or countries) and orders from other consumers will not be accepted;
- all liability is excluded to the fullest extent allowed by English law.

Legal advice should be taken before including any disclaimers in respect of the validity and ambit of such disclaimer.

17.2 Checklist

Secondly, a legal compliance checklist will assist the advertiser to identify and check relevant areas where legal or regulatory liability may arise.

The checklist below sets out some key areas to consider and may help to minimise the legal risks of webvertising.

✅ CHECKLIST

→ obtain legal advice in respect of the advertising.

→ ensure that any statements made in relation to the products or services advertised are accurate and not misleading.

→ ensure that any prices quoted are clearly stated, accurate, complete (no hidden charges), and that any terms and conditions which may apply to the price are clearly stated.

→ ensure that the information relating to the advertisement is kept up to date.

→ ensure that any promotion is removed after it has run its course.

→ ensure that any sales promotion is well planned and can be fulfilled for all customers who have responded to it.

→ ensure that consent is obtained for any direct e-mail marketing.

→ ensure that all statutory requirements such as Distance Selling Regulations have been complied with.

→ ensure that any special rules for the goods or services advertised have been checked and are complied with.

→ ensure that the advert will not be offensive or controversial in the countries where the marketing or advertising is aimed at.

→ ensure that any designs, logos, pictures and other creative materials used in the advert have been cleared.

→ if a disclaimer is used, ensure that it has been checked by legal counsel.

→ obtain indemnity insurance for when things go wrong.

---

18. Overview

Advertising online may be a cost-effective way to communicate your marketing message to a large audience but there are additional legal risks inherent in using the internet as a marketing medium.

This chapter has aimed to set out the main legal risk areas of webvertising. It is advisable to take legal advice in respect of online adverts and marketing, especially when the target group extends over various countries.

CHAPTER 7

Domain Names and Dispute Resolution

Introduction

This chapter discusses domain names and explains the dispute resolution procedures that have been put in place where a dispute concerning domain names arises. It also provides practical tips for resolving disputes, and uses mini-case studies to provide illustrations.

⚖️ CASE STUDY I

Company A has recently decided to take part of its business online. The Director has sought legal advice and realises he must carry out various tasks in order to achieve his goal. The first thing he must do is obtain an appropriate domain name.

---

1. The name

1.1 Terminology

Every website on the internet is identified by a unique number comprising of four groups of digits, these are known as Internet Protocol Numbers. In essence this is a domain name in its original form. However, strings of digits are difficult to remember, and so domain names are used and domain name servers translate the domain names back into Internet Protocol Numbers.

1.2 Technical information

Domain names are categorised into various levels:

1. The top level domain (TLD) is at the top of the naming hierarchy in the

Domain Name System (DNS), for example the .com or .uk part of the domain name. TLDs are divided into generic TLDs (gTLD) and country code TLDs (ccTLD).

- Generic TLDs, for example .com (generally used for commercially focused sites), .net (commonly used by Internet Service Providers) and .aero (used by the air transport industry) are not country specific.
- Country code TLDs, such as .uk or .jp indicate a geographical connection (.uk for the UK and .jp for Japan). They are broken down further into second level domains (SLD). Examples are .co.uk (which should indicate a commercial site based in the UK) and .org.uk (which should indicate a non-profit making organisation's site based in the UK).

2. The next element of a domain name is found to the left of the TLD. Using the example of the author's domain name, this would be the 'osborneclarke' section. This is sometimes also called the second level domain. It is this level that enables businesses to carry over their branding to the web and it is the combination of this and the TLD that most people normally refer to as being 'the domain name'. Consequently, this is the part of the domain name that gives it its true value. There can only be one osborneclarke.com, though by comparison there could hypothetically be a number of businesses or individuals trading under the name Osborne Clarke. Those businesses could even have registered 'Osborne Clarke' as a trade mark in different classes of goods and services and in any number of territories.

3. Finally, particular pages of a website are identified by the information which appears to the right-hand side of the TLD, for example the '/home' in www.osborneclarke.com/home. This part of the domain name is not registered.

1.3 Value

Normally the owner of a website will be seeking to attract as many visitors as possible. There are a number of ways in which this can be done, and choosing the appropriate domain name is often high on the list of priorities.

In attempting to find a website, a user will often use a search engine such as Google or Yahoo. A problem associated with using a search engine is that they will frequently list a number of websites that match the search criteria. This can be frustrating for a user and result in potential visitors giving up the search at this stage. In recognition of this, website owners often strive to obtain a domain name that their visitors/potential visitors can easily recall.

Businesses have been particularly keen to obtain domain names that will make e-commerce as easy as possible. A business will often seek to obtain a domain name that corresponds with their brand positioning, for example, by using a domain name that includes their corporate identity and trade marks. By doing so, businesses increase the chances of their customers/potential customers being able to find their websites.

The differences between domain names and trade marks is important. A number of different businesses may register the same trade mark in different classes of goods or services and in different territories. In contrast, each domain name is unique and registration of a particular name gives the domain name owner the ability to establish a presence on the web that can be viewed by anyone having access to the internet irrespective of their location. Additionally, registration of a domain name is not contingent on classes of goods or services. Unlike the position with trade marks, once a domain name has been registered, it cannot be registered by anyone else until the contract for registration has lapsed.

 CASE STUDY II

Company A has decided to purchase the domain names 'companya.co.uk' and 'companya.com'. They are of the opinion that the domain names will be of value to them and correspond with their market branding. They have decided to obtain both the .co.uk and the .com domain names because they are a commercial enterprise in the UK, and although they don't have a US branch, it is quite possible that they will have in the near future.

The first thing they must do is find out whether the names are available.

---

2. The domain name system

2.1 Internet Assigned Numbers Authority

The Internet Assigned Numbers Authority (IANA) is responsible for allocating top level domain names, such as .com and .uk.

2.2 Internet Corporation for Assigned Names and Numbers

The Internet Corporation for Assigned Names and Numbers (ICANN) manages and co-ordinates the Domain Name System to ensure that every address is unique and that all users of the internet can find all valid addresses. It does this by overseeing the distribution of unique IP addresses and domain names, although it deals only with domain names which have generic TLDs, such as .com or .net.

ICANN's involvement in the actual assignment of domain names is limited. It does not:

- actually assign gTLD based domain names (eg. *Osborneclarke.com*). It authorises various Registrars such as VeriSign Global Registry Services to carry out this function (see section 2.3 below); or
- oversee ccTLD domain names. ccTLD domain names are assigned and managed by Country Code Managers and a list of current Country Code Managers is at www.iana.org/cctld/cctld-whois.htm. The Country Code Manager for the UK is currently Nominet UK (see section 2.4 below).

2.3 gTLD Registrars and registration companies

Various organisations manage and assign domain names which are based on gTLDs. For example, VeriSign Global Registry Services operates the .com and .net TLDs and the .org TLD is operated by the Public Interest Registry. A list of accredited Registrars is available at www.icann.org/registrars/accredited-list.html.

Registrars for each gTLD (such as VeriSign) have authorised other companies to carry out the actual registrations of gTLD based domain names. A list of these registration companies is at www.internic.net/regist.html. A user therefore registers its domain name using one of these registration companies.

2.4 Registration of domain names base on ccTLDs – Nominet UK and registration agents

As stated above, ccTLD domain names are assigned and managed by Country Code Managers.

Since August 1996, Nominet UK has been the Country Code Manager responsible for allocating UK (e.g. .uk) domain names. Nominet UK categorises the .uk domains as

- co.uk – for commercial enterprises;
- me.uk – for personal domains;
- org.uk – for non-commercial organisations;
- net.uk – for the host machines of ISPs;
- sch.uk – for schools only;
- ltd.uk and plc.uk – for use by registered companies only.

Whilst it is in some circumstances possible for a user to register a .uk domain name direct with Nominet UK, in general, the actual registration is carried out through a registration agent (which Nominet UK calls an Internet Service

Provider). A non-exhaustive list of registration agents (which are members of Nominet UK) is at www.nominet.org.uk/Members/ListOfMembers/List OfMembers.html.

 CASE STUDY III

By carrying out WHOIS searches (through ICANN http://www.internic.net/ whois.html and Nominet http://www.nominet.org.uk) Company A establishes that companya.com is available but that companya.co.uk has already been registered by a third party.

Company A therefore registers companya.com through an ICANN accredited Registrar. As regards companya.co.uk, Company A is prepared to purchase the domain name from the current owner at an appropriate price, and enters into negotiations. Negotiations are successful and the domain name companya.co.uk is re-registered as being owned by Company A. Unfortunately, things do not always go as smoothly as this.

---

3. Disputes and dispute resolution

3.1 Why dispute?

In the late 1990s domain names became the centre of an increasing number of disputes in the UK and internationally. The main reason for this phenomenon was the value that can be attached to this new form of property. At the height of the internet boom the value of certain domain names spiralled into astronomical sums.

Although the amounts of money now attached to domain names can generally be said to have decreased, their value is still sufficient to justify action against infringement.

In contrast to actions such as trade mark infringement, there is no cause of action for domain name infringement. By registering a domain name, one does not acquire the monopolistic rights that attach to a trade mark. As a result, a business will often attempt to register all the possible variants of TLDs to prevent registration by third parties. By registering companya.com and companya.co.uk, Company A has made an attempt at doing this in the case study above.

3.2 Options for resolving a domain name dispute

Where a domain name dispute cannot be resolved by commercial negotiation, the two options for resolving it are essentially: (i) to use the relevant dispute resolution procedure which applies to the disputed domain name; or (ii) to commence court proceedings. Which option is available and appropriate will depend on the facts of the case.

ICANN has developed various dispute resolution policies relating to gTLD-based domain names. These are set out at www.icann.org/udrp/. Nominet UK has its own Dispute Resolution Service policy for .uk domain names.

The most commonly used policies for businesses in the UK (and the policies which we focus on) are the ICANN Uniform Domain-Name Dispute Resolution Policy www.icann.org/dndr/udrp/policy.htm (which is used to resolve .com disputes) and the Nominet Dispute Resolution Service policy www.nominet.org.uk/DisputeResolution/DrsPolicy/DrsPolicy.html (which is used to resolve .uk disputes).

Sections 3.3 to 3.6 below set out:

- for each of these policies, an overview of the policy, the corresponding procedure, practical tips for both complainant and registrant and the approach taken by the adjudicating panels (see sections 3.3 and 3.4);
- an overview of the basis for commencing court proceedings (see section 3.5);
- an overview of the litigation process (see section 3.6); and
- comments on the respective merits of the ICANN/Nominet procedures and court proceedings (see section 3.7).

We have not commented on the 'sunrise' dispute resolution procedures which are often put in place when new TLDs are introduced. They are designed to try and minimise the improper registration of domain names following the launch of the new TLD (such as the .eu TLD). Those dispute resolution procedures are closely linked to the application procedure and are only in effect for a relatively short period.

3.3 ICANN Uniform Dispute Resolution Policy

The policy

At present there are four ICANN approved dispute resolution providers, namely:

- the World Intellectual Property Organisation (WIPO);
- the National Arbitration Forum;
- the CPR Institute for Dispute Resolution;
- the Asian Domain Name Dispute Resolution Centre.

The four 'providers' follow ICANN's Uniform Dispute Resolution Policy (the UDRP) (see www.icann.org/dndr/udrp/policy.htm) and it is worth noting that the UDRP has been adopted by all competitive registrars in the .com, .org and .net TLDs. This means that when someone now registers a gTLD, they are agreeing to be bound by the UDRP. It may also apply to ccTLDs where the registrar for the country in question has signed up to the UDRP.

As with all forms of alternative dispute resolution, there are both benefits and drawbacks. While the procedure is quicker and cheaper than traditional litigation, the remedies available are less extensive. For example, the most that a successful party can hope to achieve will be a cancellation or transfer of the domain name in question. The arbitrators will not award damages to the complainant, whose rights may well have been infringed.

In summary, the complainant must show that the registration of the domain name is an 'abusive registration'. An abusive registration is one that meets the following criteria:

- the domain name must be identical or confusingly similar to a trade mark or service mark in which the complainant has rights; and
- the domain name holder must have no rights or legitimate interest in the name; and
- the domain name must have been registered and used in bad faith.

Under the UDRP, the following circumstances will be taken to be evidence of bad faith for the purposes of the last bullet point above. It is not an exhaustive list:

- the registration was made for the purpose of selling, renting or otherwise transferring the domain name registration to the complainant who is the owner of the trade mark or service mark or to a competitor of that complainant, for valuable consideration in excess of the registering party's documented out-of-pocket costs directly related to the domain name; or
- the domain name was registered in order to prevent the owner of the trade mark or service mark from reflecting the mark in a corresponding domain name (provided that the registering party has engaged in a pattern of such conduct); or
- the domain name has been registered primarily for the purpose of disrupting the business of a competitor; or
- by using the domain name, the registering party has intentionally attempted to attract, for commercial gain, internet users to its website or other on-line location, by creating a likelihood of confusion with the complainant's mark as to the source, sponsorship, affiliation or endorsement of the registered party's website or location, or of a product or service on its website or location.

The UDRP also sets out a non-exhaustive list of factors which the registrant can use to support a claim that the domain name was registered in good faith. These factors are:

189

- before receiving notice of the complaint, the registering party has used, or made preparations to use, the domain name or a name corresponding to the domain name in connection with a bona fide offering of goods or services; or
- the registering party has been commonly known by the domain name, even if it has acquired no trade mark or service mark rights; or
- the registering party is making a legitimate non-commercial or fair use of the domain name, without intent for commercial gain, to misleadingly divert customers or to tarnish the trade mark or service mark at issue.

The procedure

Full details of the procedure are set out on ICANN's website at www. icann.org/dndr/udrp/uniform-rules.htm. The four dispute resolution providers also have their own supplemental rules (covering issues such as fees) which can be found on their individual websites. A model complaint and model response can be obtained from WIPO (see their website at www.arbiter.wipo.int/ domains/filing/udrp/index.html).

The ICANN procedure will proceed through the following major stages:

- a written complaint is filed with one of the providers;
- the registrant responds in writing within 20 days;
- an Administrative Panel of one or three persons is selected (the 'Panel');
- the Panel makes its decision and notifies the Registrar within 14 days;
- the Registrar notifies the parties within three days of receiving the decision from the Panel.
- the Registrar implements the decision.

The procedure sets out how the parties can choose to have a single or three person Panel decide the dispute. It also details how the costs of the Panel will be borne between the parties, depending on which party elected for which type of panel.

There will only be an in-person hearing if the Panel decides, in its sole discretion, that a hearing is necessary. Most disputes are decided without this.

The procedure does not prevent either party from issuing proceedings. However, if court proceedings are commenced prior to or during the procedure, the Panel can decide, in its sole discretion, whether to suspend or terminate the procedure or whether to proceed to a decision. If one of the parties commences court proceedings, it must notify the Panel promptly.

Practical tips for a complainant

The first issue to consider is whether the domain name has been registered in bad faith such that it is an abusive registration (as set out above). If it has not been registered in bad faith, then the procedure will not be appropriate and traditional litigation should be considered as an alternative.

The list of factors set out above which are indicators of bad faith is not exclusive. There may, of course, be additional matters that support an allegation that a registration has been made in bad faith and is abusive. For example, any evidence that the registrant has registered other domain names of other brand owners in similar circumstances may serve to influence the Panel against them.

It may also be worth checking variants of the domain name under different TLDs; for example, if the domain name in dispute is *brandx.com* a 'whois?' search should be made for *brandx* under other TLDs such as *brandx.co.uk*, *brandx.net* etc. A registrant who has warehoused names in such a manner may find it hard to convince the Panel that the registrations were not made in bad faith.

Practical tips for a registrant

When challenging a complaint, the starting point is obviously to produce as much evidence as possible either to counteract or explain the evidence contained in the document sent to the Panel by the complainant.

One particular area of difficulty that may arise for a respondent is whether or not to offer to sell the domain name to the complainant. Often this may be the most practical solution to disputes of this nature, particularly when the registrant is prepared to establish a web presence under a different domain name. One needs, however, to be very careful when making offers to sell, particularly when the asking price is likely to be a great deal more than the costs of registration and transfer. If possible, the party making the complaint should be manoeuvred into a position whereby they make the first offer.

Evidence of trade mark searches made prior to the domain name registration may also assist. The WIPO Panel decision in *allocation.com* showed that the Panel will not expect a registrant to have made exhaustive searches, but negative searches within the territories targeted by any proposed website may amount to powerful evidence to counter an allegation of bad faith.

Registrants may be tempted to consider avoiding the complaint by looking to sell the domain name on to a third party as quickly as possible. It should be noted however that there are restrictions on transferring domain names whilst the procedure is ongoing (or within fifteen days after the Panel's decision). Those restrictions also apply for as long as court proceedings are pending (unless the party to whom the domain name is being transferred agrees to be bound by the court's decision).

What approach have the Panels been taking?

A visit to the WIPO website at www.arbiter.wipo.int/domains/decisions/ index.html may be time well spent if one is contemplating either filing a complaint or is required to respond to one. It would be a Herculean task to read them all in any detail but a consideration of a number may pay dividends insofar as they show the approach that the Panel tends to take.

As shown in the *One in a Million* case (see section 3.5 below) the mere registration of the domain names, without anything further, was enough for the Court of Appeal to deprive the registrants of the domain names. The WIPO Panel now seems to take a similar approach. Initially, it held that even where a domain name is registered in bad faith, it could not take any action because the domain name was not being used (see *BuyVuarnetSunglasses.com*). However, in the more recent cases, including for example the *annsummers.org* case, the Panel found that the registration amounted to bad faith (see also *telstra.org* where passive holding of a domain name was found to amount to 'being used in bad faith'). This approach by WIPO in many ways mirrors the attitude of the Court of Appeal to cyber squatters.

However, the decision in *speedup.com* provides an illustration of situations where the complainant may be best advised to issue proceedings. In this case the complainant was the owner of the trade mark (and traded under the name) 'Speed Up' in various territories and operated a website at *espeedup.com*. The registrant had registered the service mark 'Speed Up' and had taken steps towards using the domain name *speedup.com* in the US. The Panel held that the complainant had not established a registration in bad faith, even though the complainant's trade mark registrations pre-dated the registrant's. It is likely that the complainant would have been more successful if it had opposed the registrant's service mark application or had (if possible) applied to have the registrant's service mark revoked.

Where the domain name is considered to be generic, the 'first come, first served' maxim will apply (see *concierge.com*).

Respondents may also do well to produce evidence showing that the complainant has previously acquiesced in the use of their mark (see the *militec.com* and *drawtite.com* decisions concerning distributors), though if such use is in breach of an agreement with the complainant this may amount to bad faith (see *heelquick.com*).

3.4 Nominet Dispute Resolution Service (DRS) Policy

The policy

Unlike some national registries, Nominet has not adopted the ICANN Uniform Dispute Resolution Policy. Details of the Nominet policy are at www.nominet.org.uk/DisputeResolution/DrsPolicy/DrsPolicy.html (the 'Nominet Policy'). The current Nominet procedure was introduced in September 2004 and applies to all disputes filed on or after 25 October 2004. Nominet can only transfer, suspend, cancel or otherwise amend the disputed domain name. Given that Nominet does not have the power to make awards of damages or give orders for legal costs to be paid, there will be times when the court remains the most appropriate forum in which to commence proceedings.

One feature of the Nominet Policy is the early attempt at mediation, which is not part of the UDRP. The mediation is facilitated and driven by Nominet. It is in keeping with the Civil Procedure Rules in the English courts which encourage parties to resolve disputes (and minimise costs) by negotiation and other alternative dispute resolution procedures.

If the dispute is not resolved by mediation, it will be determined by an expert (and we comment on the procedure below). Under the Nominet Policy the complainant must establish that the registration of the domain name is an abusive registration. The Nominet Policy lists factors which may be evidence that a registration is abusive and these factors are very similar to the indicators of an abusive registration and bad faith under the UDRP (see above).

The Nominet Policy also lists factors which the respondent may rely on to indicate that a registration is not abusive. These are again similar to the corresponding factors in the UDRP. The list of 'legitimacy' factors under the Nominet Policy are however wider than those under the UDRP. They provide, for example, that a tribute site may amount to fair use and that if a domain name is generic or descriptive, use of that domain name may be fair.

The procedure

Once a complaint, which must not exceed 2000 words, has been submitted to Nominet, the following procedure will apply:

- The complaint is sent to the respondent within three days of receipt by Nominet (assuming that it complies with Nominet's rules).
- Once the respondent is deemed to have received the complaint he will have fifteen days to submit a response. The response must not exceed 2,000 words.
- Within three days following receipt of the response, Nominet sends the response to the complainant.
- Within five days of receiving the response from Nominet, the complainant may submit a reply. This must not exceed 2,000 words.
- The matter is then referred to informal mediation (in a manner which Nominet in its sole discretion considers appropriate). The negotiations conducted during this mediation are confidential and will not be shown to any expert who is subsequently appointed if the mediation does not resolve the dispute.
- If the dispute has not settled through mediation within 10 days then Nominet will send a notice to the parties saying that they will appoint an expert provided that the complainant requests that the matter be referred to an expert and pays, within 10 days of notification, the necessary fee

(currently £750 plus VAT for disputes between the same parties concerning up to five domain names).

- Within five days of receipt of the referral request and fee, Nominet will appoint an expert (Nominet holds a list of approved experts).
- In the absence of any exceptional circumstances, the expert should forward his decision to Nominet within 10 days of his appointment. The decision will be in writing and should give reasons.
- Within three days of receipt of the expert's decision, Nominet will send a full text of the decision to each of the parties. The decision will also be published on Nominet's website.
- If the expert decides that the domain name registration should be cancelled, suspended, transferred or amended then the decision will be implemented within 10 days (unless within that 10-day period either party appeals or issues court proceedings).

Nominet's DRS Procedure also sets out the procedure to be followed if the expert's decision is appealed:

- The appellant must give notice of an intention to appeal within 10 days of receiving the expert's decision.
- This must be followed within 15 days by an appeal notice (which must not exceed 1,000 words) and payment of the fee of £3,000 plus VAT.
- The respondent has 10 days to file an appeal notice response (again limited to 1,000 words).
- Nominet will then appoint an appeal panel of three experts who should make their decision within 30 days.

In the event that one of the parties issues court proceedings concerning a domain name prior to or during the course of proceedings under the DRS, Nominet will suspend its proceedings pending the outcome of the court case.

Nominet has included a sanction against the practice of 'reverse hijacking' of domain names. If the expert finds that a complaint has been brought in bad faith, and the complainant has been found on three separate occasions within a two-year period to have brought a complaint in bad faith, then Nominet will not accept any further complaints from that complainant for a period of two years.

Practical tips for complainants and registrants

Whilst there are some differences in detail between the UDRP and the Nominet Policy, they both operate with very similar concepts of what is an improper registration. The practical tips set out above in respect of the UDRP are therefore equally relevant to dealing with disputes under the Nominet Policy.

One notable difference is that the Nominet DRS has an appeal process. A party who disagrees with the first, single expert decision can therefore have a second bite at the cherry in a forum which is likely to be cheaper than pursuing the matter through litigation in the court.

What approach have Nominet DRS experts been taking?

Under the UDRP, there are a large number of decisions. Reviewing all of the decisions would be a very large undertaking. However, reading a selection of the decisions gives a potential claimant or registrant some guidance on how the DRS experts are deciding cases.

Where it is clear that the registrant has registered the domain name in order to try to make a profit by selling it to the complainant or is warehousing domain names, the usual result is that the domain name is transferred (see the *allianceandleicster.co.uk*, *allianceanleicester.co.uk*, *alliance-ieicester.co.uk*, *alliance-leiceste.co.uk*, *allianceandleciester.co.uk* and *allainceandleicester .co.uk* cases).

The decisions show that, even where the registration is not made with a view to extracting money from the complainant, domain names will be transferred if the registration is likely to cause confusion. In the *englishheritage.co.uk* case, the registrant registered the domain name and linked it to English Heritage's official website. Users were therefore taken from the disputed domain name to the official English Heritage site. The expert held that the registrant registered the domain name in a manner which took unfair advantage of, and was unfairly detrimental to, the complainant's rights (which included four registered trade marks). The registration was abusive and the domain name was transferred to English Heritage.

A more complicated situation is where the registrant has registered a domain name which is the same as the complainant's trading name but where the registrant uses the domain name for its own business and that business is in a different sphere to the complainant's. In the *isopportunities.co.uk* case the registrant, which had full knowledge of the complainant's IS Opportunities magazine (aimed at IT sales and marketing professionals), registered *isopportunities.co.uk* and operated a software industry recruitment website through that domain. Each page of the website included a statement that it was not connected with the IS Opportunities magazine. Whilst the complainant did not have a registered trade mark for IS Opportunities, the Nominet Policy provides that a complainant's rights which must be considered include any enforceable rights, such as goodwill rights acquired in a name. The expert held that the complainant had established relevant rights in the IS Opportunities magazine. However, the expert held that the registrant had not used the domain name in a way which was unfairly detrimental to the complainant's rights and refused to transfer the domain name.

The decision in each case will obviously depend on the facts of that case. Where the registrant's registration has been speculative or the domain name is not being used for a genuine purpose, the complainant should stand a good chance of securing a transfer. However, where the registrant is operating a website through the disputed domain name in good faith, it may well be difficult for a complainant to establish that the registration is abusive, even where the complainant can establish relevant rights.

3.5 Court proceedings relating to domain names

An option to recover disputed domain names is to use litigation in the civil courts.

Basis of claims – infringement of registered trade mark and passing off

Claims for the recovery of disputed domain names are generally on the basis of infringement of registered trade mark or passing off. We set out below a summary of key issues.

Infringement of trade mark

To establish infringement of a registered trade mark a claimant must prove that the defendant is using in the course of trade a mark which is:

- identical to the claimant's mark, in relation to goods or services which are identical to those in respect of which the trade mark is registered; or
- similar to the claimant's mark, in relation to goods or services which are identical or similar to those in respect of which the trade mark is registered such that there is a risk of confusion on the part of the public; or
- identical or similar to the claimant's mark, in relation to goods or services which are not similar to those in respect of which the trade mark is registered, where the trade mark has a reputation in the UK and the use of the mark without due cause takes unfair advantage of or is detrimental to the distinctive character or the repute of the registered trade mark.

In *Musical Fidelity Ltd* v. *David Vickers (T/A Vickers Hi-Fi (A Firm))* [2002] EWCA Civ 1989, the claimant, which developed and manufactured hi-fi equipment, owned the registered trade mark MUSICAL FIDELITY in respect of sound recording apparatus. The defendant registered the domain name *musicalfidelity.co.uk*. Some of the claimant's customers complained since users who typed into a browser *musicalfidelity.co.uk* were taken to the defendant's website, which was part of the defendant's hi-fi retail business. The Court of Appeal held that the defendant's registration and use of *musicalfidelity.co.uk* infringed the claimant's registered trade mark. The defendant was using an identical mark in respect of similar goods and there was a risk of confusion.

Passing off

To establish passing off a claimant must prove that:

- it has developed a reputation/goodwill in the relevant name or mark;
- there is a misrepresentation by the defendant which has deceived or is likely to deceive people who would be customers for the relevant product or services; and
- the claimant's reputation/goodwill has been or is likely to be damaged as a result.

In the *Musical Fidelity* case the court found that, in addition to trade mark infringement, the defendant was liable for passing off since there was relevant confusion.

Cybersquatting – The *One in a Million* case

The archetypal situation where a defendant is liable for infringement of trade mark and passing off is where they are actually carrying out acts (or threatening to carry out acts) which will confuse customers and enable the defendant to benefit from the claimant's goodwill and reputation. The *Musical Fidelity* case, where the defendant used the domain name to attract customers to his business, is a good example of this.

However, it is possible for someone to register a domain name that is identical or similar to the corporate identity or brand of a business, even though they have no intention of trading under that domain name. This is known as 'cyber squatting' and is generally carried out in the hope that a domain name purchased at market rates can be sold on to a business at an inflated price for a profit. This activity does not fall squarely into the traditional formulations of trade mark infringement and passing off.

The leading case on this issue is the Court of Appeal decision in *British Telecommunications Plc* v. *One In A Million Ltd and others* [1999] FSR 1. Here, the defendants had registered a significant number of domain names comprising well-known names and trade marks (including those of Marks & Spencer Plc, J.Sainsbury Plc Ltd and Ladbrokes Plc). The defendants argued that there were a number of ways in which they could make their intended profit, including selling the domain names to third parties who may have legitimate rights in the names or even to the owners of the goodwill.

The question before the court was twofold. First, did the defendants' conduct amount to passing off? Second, had there been trade mark infringements under section 10(3) of the Trade Marks Act 1994?

At first instance the High Court granted an injunction to restrain the defendants from passing off and from infringing the claimants' trade marks. They were also ordered to transfer the domain names to the owners of the goodwill, the court having found that the defendants had clearly threatened to infringe the claimants' rights in the future. The Judge also observed:

> '*Any person who deliberately registers a domain name on account of its similarity to the name, brand name or trade mark of an unconnected commercial organisation must expect to find himself on the receiving end of an injunction to restrain the threat of passing off, and the injunction will be in terms which will make the name commercially useless to the dealer.*'

The Judge did not, however, find that the mere registration of the domain names, without something more, amounted to passing off.

Taking the matter to the Court of Appeal, the defendants argued that the domain names that they had registered could be used for purposes that were legitimate.

Whilst upholding the first instance decision regarding trade mark infringement, the Court of Appeal went even further with regard to the issue of passing off. In summary it found that:

- a name which would, by reason of its similarity to the name of another inherently lead to passing off was an instrument of fraud;
- as well as granting an injunction where passing off was established or threatened, the court would grant an injunction where the defendant equipped himself with or intended to equip another with an instrument of fraud;
- the registration of a distinctive name (such as 'marksandspencer') made a representation to persons who consulted the register that the registrant was connected or associated with the name registered and thus the owner of the goodwill in the name – this amounted to passing off;
- the registration of such a distinctive name as a domain name eroded the exclusive goodwill in the name which damaged or which was likely to damage the owner of the goodwill;
- domain names comprising distinctive names were also instruments of fraud. Any realistic use of them as a domain name would result in passing off;
- it was the value of the goodwill in the 'household names' (and not the fact that they could be used in some way by a third party without deception) which had caused the Appellants to register the names. The registrations were made with the purpose of appropriating the respondents' property.

Lord Justice Aldous explained when a domain name is considered to be an instrument of fraud:

> '*The Court should consider the similarity of the names, the intention of the defendant, the type of trade and all the surrounding circumstances.*

If it be the intention of the defendant to appropriate the goodwill of another or enable others to do so, I can see no reason why the court should not infer that it will happen, even if there is a possibility that such an appropriation would not take place. If, taking all the circumstances into account the court should conclude that the name was produced to enable passing off, is adapted to be used for passing off and, if used, is likely to be fraudulently used, an injunction will be appropriate.'

Cybersquatting – subsequent decisions

One in a Million is viewed by some as taking the law of passing off too far (particularly since the court was prepared to draw an inference that passing off would take place simply because of the defendants' alleged intentions). However, when the claimants subsequently relied upon the Court of Appeal judgment in a subsequent interim injunction application in *MBNA America Bank NA & anr* v. *Freeman*, they were largely unsuccessful.

In this case, Mr Freeman had registered the domain name *mbna.co.uk*. He explained to the judge that the letters stood for 'marketing banners for net advertising' and were part of a plan to sell banner advertising on websites. Mr Freeman's website was not actually operational.

MBNA were conducting business from their site at mbna.com and began proceedings against Mr Freeman for trade mark infringement (on the grounds of taking unfair advantage of the mark) and passing off. The claimants relied on *One in a Million* in support of their argument that if Mr Freeman's intention had been to use the domain name to take advantage of MBNA's goodwill, with a view to increasing the number of visitors to his website, the court should infer that an appropriation of their goodwill would take place.

While the court granted an interim injunction preventing Mr Freeman from disposing of the domain name pending trial, it did not restrain the operation of the site. Although the outcome may have been different had the claimants shown that there was a risk that they would suffer financial loss or damage before the trial, the fact that Mr Freeman had a proposed legitimate use for the name would appear to have saved him.

In *One in a Million*, the defendants did not appear to have any such 'legitimate proposals'. Moreover, they had threatened to sell some of the domain names to third parties and also to involve the media; such tactics worked against them.

The court will probe any evidence by the defendant that it has 'legitimate proposals' for use of the disputed domain name. In *Britannia Building Society* v. *Prangley & Others* HC 2000 01406, the defendant gave evidence that he intended to use the domain name *britanniabuildingsociety.com*, which he had registered, to supply British building workers to Iran. The court did not find his evidence credible, held that he was liable for passing off (following *One in a Million*) and ordered that the domain name be transferred to the claimant.

Use of a domain name can still amount to an instrument of fraud, even though its use does not inherently lead to passing off. In *easyJet Airline Co Ltd & ors* v. *Tim Dainty (t/a easyRealestate)* [2002] FSR 6, the defendant had registered the domain name easyRealestate.co.uk and created a site using a get-up in plain white lettering against a bright orange background. easyJet applied for summary judgment and for an injunction to restrain the defendant from passing off and for an order that the domain name be transferred to easyJet. The defendant argued that easyJet should not be entitled to exclusive use of the word 'easy', that easyJet did not as far as he knew have any estate agency business and finally that he had no intention of taking advantage of easyJet's goodwill.

easyJet succeeded in obtaining summary judgment on the basis that although they were not entitled to appropriate the word 'easy' there was a likelihood of deception because of the get-up of the website. In other words, it was not the registration of the name itself but rather the get-up of the site that would probably lead to passing off.

Even if a domain name is descriptive of the type of goods or services being offered, it is not necessarily the case that the courts will tolerate its use. If another party has established goodwill in a similar domain name, and the defendant's use of its own domain name is likely to cause confusion, then the court may intervene. By way of example, in *Lawyers Online Ltd* v. *Lawyeronline Ltd* (Ch.D Birmingham District Registry 29/9/00), the claimant, who operated a website at lawyersonline.co.uk, succeeded in obtaining an interim injunction to restrain the defendant's use of lawyeronline.co.uk despite the fact that the domain name was descriptive. The court was satisfied that there was an arguable case that goodwill attached to the domain name and that there had already been confusion.

Following *One in a Million* and the other cases referred to above, the days of the blatant cybersquatter (who simply seeks to hold a brand to ransom) are probably over. Domain name disputes are now much more likely to occur where more than one party believes that it has some legitimate right to use the name. However, as the *Britannia Building Society* case indicates, the court will look carefully at whether the alleged legitimate use is genuine.

3.6 Litigation procedure

This section gives a short overview of litigation procedure for non-legally qualified readers.

The courts

Claims for infringement of registered trade mark and passing off must be brought in the Chancery Division of the High Court, the Patents County Court or a county court where there is also a Chancery district registry.

Injunctions

Where the matter is urgent, the claimant can apply for an interim injunction. The court hears such applications on both:

- a without notice basis, where no notice of the application is given to the defendant; and
- an on-notice basis where the defendant has notice of the hearing and can attend to oppose the application.

To obtain an interim injunction the claimant must prove that it has a good arguable claim on the merits, that damages will not be an adequate remedy and that the balance of convenience favours granting the injunction. In assessing the balance of convenience the court will take into account both the claimant's and the defendant's interests and whether granting or not granting the injunction will cause the least damage overall.

Where the court grants an interim injunction, the claimant will be required to give an undertaking to the court to pay damages to the defendant if the injunction is later overturned and the defendant has suffered loss as a result of the injunction. If the injunction is granted at a without notice hearing, there will be a return hearing shortly after it has been served on the defendant at which the defendant has the opportunity to seek to discharge the injunction.

When the injunction is in place, the case will progress through the normal litigation steps to trial (see below). However, it is common for the parties to negotiate a settlement after an injunction has been granted since in granting the injunction the court has indicated, albeit at an early stage, the strength of the claim.

Ordinary proceedings

The alternative (and more common) way in which domain name dispute cases are commenced is by the claimant issuing a claim form and serving it on the defendant with particulars of claim which set out details of the claim.

The defendant then has 28 days in which to file its defence (and any counterclaim). This period is extendable by a further 28 days by agreement. The claimant may serve a reply within 14 days of service of the defence. The court then gives directions for the future conduct of the case at a case management conference. The case progresses through disclosure (i.e. exchange of documents which are relevant to the dispute), exchange of witness statements and exchange of any expert evidence to a pre-trial review and then the trial. The trial date will depend upon court availability but will usually take place between nine and 18 months after the claim has been commenced. At the trial the court will hear evidence and legal argument from both parties and will make its decision.

In some cases the claimant may apply for summary judgment either before or shortly after the defence has been served. The claimant will need to prove the defendant's defence has no real prospect of success and that there is no other reason why the matter should proceed to trial. The evidence before the court on a summary judgment application is set out in witness statements. A successful summary judgment application can resolve a claim far more quickly and cheaply than by proceeding all the way to trial. It is also possible for the defendant to apply for summary judgment (to strike out the claim) on the basis that the claim has no real prospect of success.

Remedies

The remedies which the court can grant to a successful claimant include:

- an order that the defendant transfer the domain name to the claimant;
- a permanent injunction to prevent the defendant from infringing the claimants' rights or from carrying out other specified acts in the future;
- delivery up or destruction of infringing material (such as marketing literature containing the disputed domain name);
- an order for damages compensating the claimant for the loss which it has suffered as a result of the defendant's infringements or, at the claimant's option, an account of the defendant's profits. An account of profits is an assessment and order for payment to the claimant of the profit which the defendant made as a result of its infringing activity.

Costs

Litigation can be expensive. The general rule on costs is that the loser pays the winner's costs and the winner's costs will be assessed by the court if they cannot be agreed. A costs order in a party's favour does not give them a full indemnity for their costs and the court has wide discretion to penalise a party in costs if it has acted unreasonably during the litigation.

3.7 Relative merits of ICANN UDRP and Nominet DRS procedures compared with traditional litigation

Whether a complainant pursues a claim under the ICANN/Nominet procedures or through litigation will depend on a variety of factors including the strength of the claim, the evidence available, where the registrant is situated, the importance of the disputed domain name to the complainant and the budget available for the dispute.

Points in favour of using the ICANN and Nominet procedures as against commencing court proceedings include:

- the speed of the process (usually concluded in as little as two months);
- cost – the fees (excluding any professional legal fees) range from £750–£3,000 depending on whether the ICANN or Nominet procedure is followed and the number of panelists;
- lack of formality;
- the experience of the Panel;
- convenience; there is no need to attend any hearings (which may be particularly advantageous when you or your client are in a different country to the Panel).

A disadvantage of proceeding with an ICANN or Nominet claim is that the losing party can still commence litigation.

There will also be occasions where using the litigation process will be more appropriate. The benefits of litigation include:

- interim injunctions are available (and, in appropriate cases, can be obtained within a matter of days);
- the scope of issues which the court can consider is wider – it is not limited to considering whether the registration is abusive;
- the parties have a greater opportunity to influence the conduct of the proceedings;
- litigation can be a useful method of applying pressure to an opponent to reach a negotiated solution;
- the court can award a wider range of remedies, such as injunctions and orders for damages/account of profits;
- the successful party is likely to obtain an order that its opponent pays its legal costs (although such an order will not be a complete indemnity).

4. Conclusion

The growth of the internet as a business medium has led to a new range of disputes relating to the registration and use of domain names.

There were initial difficulties with opportunist 'cyber squatters' who warehoused domain names and effectively blocked the registrations of legitimate users. The courts were able to deal with that type of activity. The online community (in the guise of ICANN and Registrars like Nominet) also responded and appropriate dispute resolution policies were developed. Although the days of the successful cyber squatter would appear to be over, at least in the United Kingdom, whenever new TLDs are created there is generally a rise in the number of cyber squatting disputes. There is also greater risk of confusion where the domain name will be aimed at numerous countries that have different languages, for example the new .eu (European) domain names.

When disputes do arise, consideration should be given to whether or not the matter is suitable for some form of alternative dispute resolution, such as the ICANN or Nominet procedures. Resolving matters in this way may prove to be the most cost effective way of achieving your objectives or those of your client. However, there will be situations where such methods are unsuitable and proceedings should be issued.

 CHECKLIST OF PRACTICAL TIPS

→ Select a domain name that corresponds with the nature of your/your client's business.

→ Having selected a domain name conduct (and record) trade mark searches in the territories to which the website will be targeted.

→ If other businesses have trade mark rights in a particular territory, consider including a notice on the website making it clear that the target audience is restricted geographically (see *Euromarket Designs Inc.* v. *Peters and another*).

→ Make sure that the domain name is used.

→ If a certain type of goods or services is suggested by the domain name, try to ensure that this corresponds with the actual goods or services being sold.

→ Be cautious about making offers to sell the domain name, particularly to parties who may arguably already have rights in the name and particularly for extortionate sums.

→ Register variants of your/your client's domain name to prevent confusion amongst clients and customers (links could even be established from those sites to the main website, thereby maximising the number of hits).

→ Do not stockpile domain names that have no connection with your/your client's business.

→ If you discover that another party is infringing your/your client's trade mark, be wary of the consequences of 'threats actions' when writing letters before action (see *Brain* v. *Ingledew, Brown, Bennison & Garrett* [1996] FSR 341 and *Prince Plc* v. *Prince Sports Group Inc.* [1998] FSR 21).

8 Employment and Human Rights

Introduction

This chapter considers the employment issues which arise when a company such as Trading Company Limited (chapter 2), decides to provide e-mail and internet access to its employees. In addition to the obvious problem of reduced productivity amongst employees who engage in lengthy e-mail conversations or surf the web to find the best holiday deal, an employee's abuse of the e-mail and internet systems may lead to claims against the company as diverse as libel, discrimination (on a number of grounds such as sex, race, sexual orientation, disability etc) or breach of copyright.

To stand a chance of *legally* defending such claims, the company will have to show that it has taken all reasonably practicable steps to prevent the abuse perpetrated by its employees. This will only be possible if the company has provided clear guidance to all employees on the appropriate use of the systems through a comprehensive IT policy. In addition, the company needs to manage the situation actively on an ongoing basis, checking that employees are complying with the policy by monitoring their use of the systems and taking the requisite disciplinary action against those who breach the policy. However, the company needs to ensure that the monitoring of employees' e-mail and internet use is done lawfully, within the applicable statutory provisions and without infringing an individual's right to privacy under Article 8 of the Human Rights Act 1998.

From a more practical perspective, it is also worth noting that an individual may make a request for the disclosure of e-mails which contain 'personal data' relating to him/her pursuant to the Data Protection Act 1998. Although the scope of this right has been curtailed to an extent by the Court of Appeal decision in *Durant* v. *Financial Services Authority* [2003] EWCA Civ 1746, it is still a useful litigation tactic for individuals and one that can be very costly to employers who have allowed abuse to take place over their e-mail system. Damaging e-mails may put the employer in an embarrassing position in the courtroom, and give an individual additional bargaining power in relation to settlement of the dispute.

1. E-mail abuse

The issues that a company may face as a result of the misuse of e-mail by its employees are many and varied. At one end of the scale this could entail dealing with a practical joker who has sent a compromising e-mail from a colleague's PC. At the other, the company could find itself on the losing end of a high-value claim for defamation or it could be vicariously liable for discrimination.

This section looks at issues that could have a significant financial impact on the company.

1.1 Defamation

What is defamation?

Defamation is used as a generic term for libel and slander. If a defamatory statement is made in print, for example in a newspaper, or in some other permanent form (which is likely to include e-mail), the individual who is the subject of the statement may have a claim for libel. If the defamation is verbal only, the claim will be for slander.

A defamatory statement is one that lowers the standing or reputation of a person in the estimation of right-thinking members of society generally or which would cause that person to be avoided, ridiculed or to be disparaged, whether personally or professionally.

In order to bring a claim, the defamatory statement must have been 'published' which means that it must have been communicated to someone other than the person who is the subject of the statement.

There are a number of defences that a defendant to a defamation claim could raise. These include:

1. *Justification* – on the basis that the statement is true or substantially true.
2. *Fair comment on a matter of public interest* – on the basis that the statement consists of comment or opinion, the opinion is capable of being honestly held and relates to facts which are true or privileged and the defendant is not motivated by malice.
3. *Qualified privilege* – on the basis that there is a sufficient common interest between the maker and recipient of the statement or an obligation on the maker to communicate the particulars of the statement. For example, if a manager with supervisory responsibility for an under-performing employee sends a report in the context of a performance management procedure to the Human Resources manager, explaining the employee's particular deficiencies. The defendant must again not be motivated by malice.
4. *Innocent dissemination* – on the basis that the defendant does not have primary responsibility for the offending statement. For example, the printer of a book which contains a defamatory statement.

5. *Innocence (referred to as Offer of Amends)* – on the basis that the defendant, who published the offending statement innocently and in good faith, made a prescribed form of offer of amends, including an offer to publish a correction and apology and to pay damages. If this is not accepted by the defamed party, it provides a defence for the defendant at trial.

A company or other corporate body may also have a right to sue for libel or slander when a defamatory statement is published or spoken (as appropriate) which is damaging to its business.

How it applies to e-mail

The law of defamation applies to e-mail and information posted on the internet, in much the same way that it applies to more traditional forms of publishing. Businesses have always been subject to the risk of their employees committing libel, for example by defamatory statements contained in internal memoranda or employee newsletters, but the risk appears to be much greater with e-mail. This increased risk is partly due to the ease and speed with which e-mail messages can be transmitted to large numbers of recipients, both internally and externally. Also, people adopt a more casual approach in e-mail communications than they do in written correspondence, treating it more like the spoken rather than the written word.

Examples

Take a disaffected employee who has sent an e-mail to a few of his colleagues which contains vociferous criticism of his manager and casts aspersions on the manager's private life or his ability to do his job. Before e-mail, the employee may have had the same conversation with his colleagues, but it would not have been committed to print. The offending e-mail may be transmitted onwards to the whole workforce by the touch of a few keys, either in error or purposely to cause mischief. The manager who is the subject of the e-mail may well have a claim for libel for the damage caused to his reputation.

In 1997 Norwich Union paid out £450,000 and made a public apology in the High Court to Western Provident Union after some of its employees circulated an e-mail internally which said that Western Provident was in financial difficulties and that it was being investigated by the Department of Trade and Industry. Such a statement could clearly be very damaging to its business.

The company's liability

As the provider of the e-mail facility through which an employee's defamatory statement is circulated, the company may be liable for publishing the statement. The employee who made the statement will be jointly liable, but as the company will generally have more funds, the defamed individual or business is more likely to pursue the company.

The company may have a defence on the basis that it unwittingly provided a conduit through which the defamatory statement was published but it will have to show, amongst other things, that it took reasonable care in relation to the publication of the defamatory statement. If the company has not provided clear guidance to its employees on the correct use of e-mail, including an express prohibition on making defamatory statements, and does not undertake at least some degree of e-mail monitoring, this may be a difficult requirement for it to satisfy.

The company may also be liable by way of vicarious liability for the defamatory statement if the employee who sends the e-mail containing the offending statement is deemed to be doing an authorised act in an unauthorised manner. It is easy to see how an employee who uses e-mail in their work will be considered to be carrying out an authorised act, albeit in an unauthorised way.

1.2 Harassment

What is harassment?

A claim of harassment may be brought by an individual in the context of the Sex Discrimination Act 1975, the Race Relations Act 1976, the Disability Discrimination Act 1995, the Employment Equality (Sexual Orientation) Regulations 2003, or the Employment Equality (Religion or Belief) Regulations 2003.

Harassment on grounds of race, ethnic, national origin, disability, religion, religious belief or similar philosophical belief and sexual orientation is subject to a statutory definition (set out in the relevant legislation for each such ground) as follows:

> 'unwanted conduct which has the purpose or effect of...violating [a person's] dignity or . . . creating an intimidating, hostile, degrading, humiliating or offensive environment for [that person]'.

There is no statutory definition of harassment where the harassment is alleged to be on grounds of sex, colour and nationality. However, it is well established that harassment on these grounds amounts to unlawful discrimination where:

- it is unwanted, unreasonable and offensive *to the recipient*;
- it creates an intimidating, hostile or humiliating working environment for the recipient; and
- it places the recipient at a detriment.

Harassment may consist of physical, verbal or non-verbal conduct. For example, sexual attention becomes sexual harassment if it continues after the recipient has made clear that he or she regards the conduct as offensive.

However, a one-off incident may constitute sexual harassment if it is sufficiently serious.

It is important to note that an essential characteristic of harassment is that it is unwanted by the recipient and that it is for each individual to determine what behaviour is acceptable and what is considered to be offensive. The motive or intention of the individual carrying out the unwanted conduct is irrelevant. What may appear to be a harmless joke and amusing to one person may constitute harassment to another.

Under the most recent Employment Equality Regulations, harassment on grounds of sexual orientation is prohibited. This could be harassment of a heterosexual or a homosexual employee by reason of their sexual orientation, or even harassment of a person because of their association with a heterosexual or homosexual person. Under the Sex Discrimination and Gender Reassignment Regulations 1999 (SI 1999 No. 1102)), discrimination on grounds of 'gender reassignment', where an individual decides to undergo medical treatment in order to change their sex, has now been included within the definition of 'sex' in the Sex Discrimination Act 1975 and consequently harassment on such grounds will be unlawful. Harassment on grounds of religion, religious belief or similar philosophical belief is also outlawed; however, whilst fringe religions are included, political opinion is excluded.

Looking forward, the Equal Treatment Amendment Directive which is due to be implemented in the United Kingdom in 2005, contains two new definitions of harassment with respect to conduct related to sex and conduct of a sexual nature. These new definitions are essentially the same as those found in the existing UK legislation prohibiting harassment on grounds of race, nationality, sexual orientation etc and which are referred to above.

The problem with e-mail

E-mail has become a means by which harassment can be perpetrated in the workplace. It may be used by an employee as part of a concerted and calculated campaign of harassment against another employee, with large numbers of unwanted and offensive e-mails hitting the victim's inbox over a prolonged period. Alternatively, it may be a one-off incident, perhaps with only one e-mail, containing a thoughtless joke or remark, causing the problem.

As with defamatory statements, the risks are increased by the fact that the offending e-mails may be forwarded to a much wider audience than originally intended and in a very short space of time.

Example

In 2001, a black secretary working at a City law firm handed in her resignation, saying that she had accepted the offer of a job elsewhere. Shortly afterwards, two of the male lawyers for whom she worked engaged in an e-mail exchange about her departure and a possible replacement. One of the lawyers wrote something to the effect of:

> '*Can we go for a real fit busty blonde this time? She cannot be any more trouble and at least it would provide some entertainment!*'

The secretary saw the e-mail and brought a claim against the two lawyers and the law firm for sex and race discrimination.

Liability of the company

The company has a legal obligation to protect its employees from harassment and to provide a safe working environment. If the employee who sends the offending e-mails is doing so in the course of employment, whether or not it was done with the employer's knowledge or approval, the company will be vicariously liable for the harassment unless it can show that it took all reasonably practicable steps to prevent it.

There are a number of actions an employer could take to assist in establishing this statutory defence. For example, dissemination of an e-mail and internet policy to all employees, making sure that the employees are aware of the consequences of breach and of the potential for liability through misuse of e-mail and the internet (we look later at other uses for such a policy); dissemination of an equal opportunities policy (warning employees that harassment will not be tolerated); training for employees and managers on all policies; amendment of existing disciplinary procedures so that any form of harassment (including downloading from the internet potentially sexually explicit, sexist, homophobic, racist or religiously offensive material or material which is potentially offensive to disabled people) is defined as gross misconduct, potentially resulting in immediate dismissal; ensuring that the grievance procedure is appropriate to deal with complaints of harassment. More importantly, it is imperative that these policies are in fact implemented in practice. These actions are not guaranteed to provide a defence to an employer faced with a claim for harassment but should go some way to help the employer to establish that it took all reasonable steps to prevent it.

1.3 Disclosure of confidential information

During their employment, all employees are under a duty to protect the confidential information of their employers. This is part of the duty of fidelity which employees owe to their employers and which is implied into all contracts of employment. In addition, the company's employees may be subject to an express clause in their contracts of employment or employee handbook which prohibits the use and/or disclosure of the company's confidential information.

210

The clause may give examples of the sort of information which the company considers to be confidential, for example customer lists, pricing information and databases.

The introduction of e-mail and the fact that employees tend to have access from their desktops to the company's databases and computer files, increases the risk of commercially sensitive information being disclosed to its competitors or used by its employees for their own purposes.

Examples

An employee is considering resigning and establishing himself in competition with the company. He has access from his desktop to all the company's databases and sensitive files, including documents containing client contact details and tenders for new work. The employee sends a whole range of documents as attachments to otherwise innocuous looking e-mails to his wife at home. If the employee does set up on his own, the information will be invaluable to him.

In 2000, the Conservative Party's head of marketing and membership leaked a speech by a senior member of the shadow cabinet to journalists by e-mail. The e-mail was found on his system and he was asked to leave Conservative Central Office shortly afterwards.

1.4 Inadvertent contracts

An agreement by e-mail is capable of forming or varying a contract in the same way as a paper document. The case of *Hall* v. *Cognos Limited* (17 February 1998, Case No. 1803325/97) illustrates the dangers of employees inadvertently forming contracts on behalf of the company, or alternatively varying existing contractual terms, to which the employer is then bound.

In this case, Mr Hall's right to claim for reimbursement of expenses was subject to detailed rules, which formed part of his contract of employment. Having missed the deadline for submitting a particular expenses claim, he e-mailed his line manager to ask whether he could enter it late. The manager replied by e-mail, saying '*yes, that is OK*', following which Mr Hall submitted his claim. Cognos Limited refused to pay these expenses. It relied on a clause in Mr Hall's contract which said that any amendment or modification to his contract had to be in writing and signed by both parties if it was to have effect. Mr Hall claimed breach of contract in the Employment Tribunal.

The tribunal considered two issues:

1. Whether e-mail correspondence was capable of constituting a document which was in writing and signed by both parties.
2. Whether Mr Hall's line manager had ostensible authority to agree to a variation of the terms of the contract relating to expenses.

In answer to the first issue, the Tribunal held that once an e-mail had been printed out, it was in written form and as each e-mail contained the christian name of its author, it was also signed. It is worth noting that most commentators would argue that e-mail constitutes writing even *without* being printed out.

On the second issue, the Tribunal held that as it was Mr Hall's line manager who had agreed to him submitting the late claim, Mr Hall was entitled to rely on the manager's apparent authority to vary the terms of his contract. Cognos Limited was, therefore, bound by the variation agreed by the line manager.

2. Internet abuse

This section considers some of the problems which a company may face in connection with its employees' abuse of the internet.

2.1 Personal surfing during work time

Providing internet access to employees from their desktop may have an unwelcome impact on productivity levels. With access to a large array of entertainment, the ability to shop for holidays and to download pirate software, it is easy to see how staff can be enticed away from their work

In the UK in 2003, Phones4U employees were banned from using e-mail at work altogether in an attempt to prevent time being wasted on unnecessary or personal e-mail. Phones4U claims that this has resulted in a saving of three hours a day per employee, which equates to £1,000,000 per year.

In the UK, excessive time spent on the internet or on personal e-mail is likely to constitute misconduct and could lead to an employee's dismissal.

Examples
In 2000 the Xerox Corporation in the US sacked forty employees for 'inappropriate visits to websites'. Some of these employees were recorded as spending up to eight hours a day on the internet visiting non-work-related websites.

In the case of *Mrs L. J. Franxhi* v. *Focus Management Consultants Ltd* (29 July 1999, Case No. 2102862/98), Mrs Franxhi claimed unfair dismissal and sex discrimination after she was dismissed by Focus for extensive use of the internet during working hours for the purposes of booking her holiday. When challenged about this by her boss, Mrs Franxhi initially lied, saying that she had used the internet once only during her lunch hour. At the time of her dismissal, Mrs Franxhi was already subject to a written warning for using the company's stamps for personal postage. Mrs Franxhi alleged that her dismissal was due to her being pregnant.

The Employment Tribunal rejected this allegation and held that Mrs Franxhi's conduct constituted misconduct justifying her dismissal. The Tribunal said that Mrs Franxhi's use of the internet was more than the occasional fleeting one that might conceivably have been regarded as open to all employees. The Tribunal also held even though there was no express prohibition on using the internet for personal purposes, as a senior employee she must have known that her prolonged use was unacceptable, just as extensive use of any other company asset for private purposes would be unacceptable.

2.2 Pornography

A number of surveys have been carried out by web-monitoring companies which reveal that a significant proportion of internet activity in the UK relates to pornography.

The number of cases and news reports relating to employees who have been dismissed for accessing pornography on the internet during working hours suggests that this is a widespread problem for employers. For example, in 2004 the Department of Work and Pensions sacked 16 employees and disciplined 227 after an internal investigation, which involved monitoring computer use for eight months, revealed that two million pages of pornography had been accessed from work computers.

However, it would appear that the fact that an employee has used a work computer and possibly even work time to access pornography does not necessarily give grounds for immediate dismissal. In a 1997 case brought by an employee who had been dismissed for downloading obscene material, the Employment Tribunal observed that in the absence of an express provision or policy which stated that unauthorised use of the internet constituted gross misconduct, the mere use of the internet by an employee for unauthorised purposes (including pornography), would not generally justify summary dismissal. This decision illustrates the importance of having comprehensive rules on what is acceptable in terms of internet use. Helpful guidance as to what should be included in such a policy is given in the Information Commissioner's Code of Practice, published in 2003 and which is discussed further below.

Downloading pornography is clearly an inappropriate activity during working hours and a waste of company resources and could potentially be dealt with through the employee's normal disciplinary or poor performance procedures. It is strongly recommended, however, that a policy is put into place that deals specifically with the use of the internet and e-mail in relation to offensive and inappropriate material.

Harassment claims may also arise as a result of employees accessing pornographic sites in the office, as the case of *Mrs M. Morse* v. *Future Reality*

Ltd (22 October 1996, Case No. 54571/95) illustrates. Mrs Morse shared an office with several men who spent a considerable amount of time viewing sexually explicit and obscene images, which they had downloaded from the internet. Mrs Morse accepted that the men's activities were not directed at her personally and that the circulation and discussion of the images generally went on in the background. However, it made her feel uncomfortable and she resigned, claiming sex discrimination. She cited the offensive pictures, bad language and general atmosphere of obscenity in the office as the basis of her complaint.

The Employment Tribunal held that the activities of the men had a detrimental effect on Mrs Morse and as such their conduct constituted sexual harassment. Future Reality Ltd was held liable because it had not taken any action to prevent the harassment. The award for injury to feelings in this case was only £750 and Mrs Morse received an additional three months' compensation for loss of earnings. If the conduct of the male employees had been directed personally at Mrs Morse, the awards would have been significantly higher.

Recent case law has confirmed this approach. In the case of *Moonsar* v. *Fiveways Express Transport Ltd* [2005] IRLR 9, Mrs Moonsar's male colleagues downloaded and viewed pornographic images on their computer screens. Mrs Moonsar was not sent the pictures nor was she addressed in their banter over the images; however she was aware of what was happening and although the behaviour was not directed at her, it had the effect of causing an affront to her dignity. She did not complain to the employer at the time, only later raising it in an unrelated claim for unfair dismissal. The Employment Appeal Tribunal held that such behaviour was degrading and offensive to Mrs Moonsar and found that she had been the subject of sexual harassment.

Criminal liability

There is also potential criminal liability for an employee who downloads and/ or circulates pornographic material. Under the Obscene Publications Act 1959 it is an offence to send material that could deprave or corrupt the recipient. Under the Telecommunications Act 1984, it is an offence to send through a public telecommunications system, a message or other matter that is grossly offensive or is of an indecent, obscene or menacing character. Under the Protection of Children Act 1978 it is an offence to possess or download child pornography.

An employer could also be found liable under these provisions if the employee's activities are found to have been carried out with the consent or connivance of the employer, or the activities are found to be attributable to the neglect of the employer. If the company knowingly allows employees to download pornographic material relating to children and circulate it around the office by e-mail, it will clearly be guilty of an offence. However, if it merely fails to provide any guidelines on the appropriate and inappropriate use of the internet and fails to monitor employees' use of the internet, it could be found liable due to neglect.

2.3 Breach of copyright laws

If employees download copyrighted materials from the internet, the employer may be vicariously liable for the breaches of copyright committed by its employees.

3. Monitoring employees

So far, this chapter has identified the most common risks associated with the inappropriate use of e-mail and the internet by employees. To defend itself against the various claims which may arise, the company will need to show that it has taken all reasonably practicable steps to prevent the offending behaviour of its employees. In order to satisfy this requirement, the company needs to be aware of what is being sent by way of e-mail and internet traffic by its employees. This will involve monitoring employees. This section considers what the company can do lawfully in terms of monitoring its employees' e-mail communications and internet use.

The company must strike a balance between protecting its business interests and respecting the rights of its employees to privacy, as conferred by the Human Rights Act 1998, the Data Protection Act 1998 and the Regulation of Investigatory Powers Act 2000.

3.1 Human Rights Act

The Human Rights Act 1998 incorporates into UK law the European Convention on Human Rights ('the Convention'). The Human Rights Act 1998 ('the Act') applies directly to public bodies and so they will be directly liable for breaches of the act. Its provisions also affect private employers because the courts and tribunals, as public bodies, need to enforce and uphold the Act and interpret legislation in accordance with it.

Article 8 of the Convention confers the right to privacy of individuals both at home and at work. It is relevant in this context as it has an impact on a company's ability to monitor its employees' e-mail and internet use.

Article 8 (1) provides that:

> *'Everyone has the right to respect for his private and family life, his home and his correspondence.'*

215

The European Court of Human Rights (ECHR) has made clear that the notion of 'private life' includes an individual's working life. The right to respect for correspondence clearly encompasses e-mail, telephone calls and other forms of communication and this includes personal correspondence at work.

The case of *Alison Halford* v. *United Kingdom* [1997] IRLR 471 ECHR concerns the interception of an employee's telephone calls at work by her employer. Ms Halford was an Assistant Chief Constable with Merseyside Police. In 1997 she brought a claim, alleging that her employers had tapped her telephone calls at work in order to obtain information about a sex discrimination claim she had brought against them in the Employment Tribunal. Ms Halford argued that the interception of her calls constituted a violation of Article 8.

The ECHR found that because Ms Halford had not been given any prior warning by her employer that her telephone calls from work were liable to be intercepted, she would have had a reasonable expectation of privacy for such calls. Consequently, the interception was an unlawful breach of Article 8. Ms Halford was awarded £10,000 as compensation for invasion of privacy.

As Ms Halford was employed by a public authority, she was able to lodge a claim based directly on a breach of Article 8 of the Convention. Employees of a company such as Trading Company Limited (which is a private employer) do not have direct, free-standing rights under the Convention (nor under the Human Rights Act 1998 which now incorporates the Convention into UK law). An employee would need to bring a claim against the company under some other domestic legislation and rely indirectly on Article 8, reminding the court or tribunal of its duty to act in a manner compatible with Convention rights. For example, if an employee was dismissed for gross misconduct after monitoring by the company revealed that he was sending offensive messages by e-mail, the employee could bring a claim for unfair dismissal in the Employment Tribunal, arguing that in breaching his right to privacy, the company had acted unreasonably and his dismissal was consequently unfair. To succeed in his claim, the employee would have to show that he had a reasonable expectation of privacy in relation to his e-mail communications.

The corollary of the *Halford* decision would appear to be that an employer is able to monitor communications if it makes clear to its employees that they should have no expectation of privacy in the workplace. On this basis, if the company has a clear policy, which states that the e-mail system is not private and will be subject to regular monitoring, it should be able to avoid liability. However, because of the potential for infringement of human rights associated with workplace monitoring, the legislature has introduced the Regulation of Investigatory Powers Act 2000 and, more importantly for the company as an employer, the Telecommunications (Lawful Business Practice) (Interception of Communications) Regulations 2000.

3.2 The Regulation of Investigatory Powers Act 2000 and the Telecommunications (Lawful Business Practice) (Interception of Communications) Regulations 2000

The Regulation of Investigatory Powers Act 2000 (RIPA) creates a statutory tort of unlawful interception of communications on a private network. Broadly speaking, a person who has the right to control the operation or use of a private telecommunication system must not intercept any communication in the course of its transmission, unless he has lawful authority to do so. In this context, a private telecommunication system will include the company's e-mail system (unless it is wholly internal and has no capacity for sending or receiving e-mails via an outside telephone line). An employer will have lawful authority to intercept if it has the consent of both parties to the communication. An unlawful interception could give rise to a claim by the sender or recipient of the e-mail intercepted, with the injured party being entitled to make a claim for damages. It may also give rise to criminal liability.

RIPA contains provisions that enable the Secretary of State to introduce statutory regulations dealing specifically with work-place monitoring. Pursuant to these provisions, the Secretary of State has introduced the Telecommunications (Lawful Business Practice) (Interception of Communications) Regulations 2000 (the 'Regulations').

As explained above, in order to comply with RIPA, the company needs the consent of both the sender and the recipient of an e-mail before it can legitimately intercept it. This causes obvious practical difficulties. How does the company go about obtaining consent from a potential recipient of an e-mail from one of its employees?

The Regulations assist the company in overcoming this problem by permitting monitoring and recording of communications by employers in a variety of circumstances *without* the need for the consent of their employees.

Regulation 3(1) provides that employers may monitor or record their employees' communications for the following purposes:

- to protect national security;
- to prevent or detect crime – for example, to detect fraud or offences under the Obscene Publications Act 1959, which would include downloading and circulating pornography;
- to investigate or detect the unauthorised use of the telecommunications system – for example, to check that employees are not sending abusive, defamatory or discriminatory e-mails;

- to ascertain or demonstrate standards which are achieved or ought to be achieved by employees using the system in the course of their duties – that is, for quality control and staff training;
- to establish the existence of facts – for example, to verify that a contract has been entered into by telephone or e-mail;
- to ascertain that employees are complying with external or internal regulatory rules or guidelines – for example, the rules of the Financial Services Authority; or
- to ensure the effective operation of the system – for example, to detect viruses.

Employers may monitor *but not record* employees' communications for the following purposes:

- to determine whether communications are relevant to the business – for example, checking e-mails and voicemails of employees who are absent on holiday or due to sickness;
- to monitor communications to a confidential counselling or support service.

The circumstances in which an employer may intercept communications, as set out above, are wide-ranging and cater for most circumstances in which an employer would want to monitor its employees. However, the Regulations stipulate that any interception must be carried out solely for the purpose of monitoring or recording communications that are relevant to the employer's business. At first sight, this would appear to exclude the interception of an employee's private communications. However, if an employee's private e-mail breaches an express company policy on the use of e-mail or internet because, for example, it contains pornographic images or discloses confidential information to a third party, then it is certainly arguable that the communication is relevant to the business.

The Regulations also place an obligation on the employer to make all reasonable efforts to inform every person who may use the telecommunication system that their communications may be intercepted. In relation to employees, this can be effected by including a provision in the company's e-mail and internet policy, which states that monitoring of e-mail will occur on a regular basis. It is a more difficult prospect to inform all third parties who send e-mails to the company that their communications may be monitored. The company should consider including an automatic statement at the foot of all out-going e-mails, advising recipients that their communications may be monitored. This will not solve the problem if the e-mail communication is initiated by the third party. Having said that, the employer is only required to make '*all reasonable efforts*' in this regard and it would have a strong argument that it was impracticable, if not impossible, to inform all third parties that their incoming communications may be monitored.

3.3 Data protection

The Data Protection Act 1998 applies to any e-mail that is monitored, recorded or stored if that e-mail contains information about an identifiable living individual. Data protection is considered in detail in chapter 3.

In 2003, the Information Commissioner issued the third part of his Code of Practice entitled 'The Employment Practices Data Protection Code: Part 3: Monitoring At Work', which deals specifically with employee surveillance, including monitoring e-mail and internet use. Part 3 is supplemented by a guide for small employers offering a simplified version of the Code's requirements as well as supplementary guidance to assist employers with a more in depth understanding of the issues involved.

Whilst the Code does not impose legal obligations, it will be taken into account by the courts when considering whether an employer's actions are lawful under the Data Protection Act 1998. The Code confirms that the Data Protection Act does not prevent an employer from monitoring workers as long as the monitoring is done in a way that is consistent with the Data Protection Act and any other relevant legislation. It expressly recommends that the employer bears in mind Article 8 of the European Convention on Human Rights (see above) and that any policy of work rule is interpreted in accordance with this Article.

Indeed, compliance with the Code will also assist the employer in complying with its legal obligations, particularly under the Regulation of Investigatory Powers Act 2000, the Telecommunications (Lawful Business Practice) (Interception of Communications) Regulations and the Human Rights Act referred to above.

The Code makes clear that employers should monitor only where there is a genuine business need and where the methods used to carry it out are proportionate to the legitimate aims of the employer and do not unduly intrude upon an individual's privacy. Essentially, a balance must be struck between the interests of the business and the legitimate expectations of employees.

Impact assessments

In order to determine whether the intended monitoring is fair and lawful under the Data Protection Act 1998, the Code recommends that employers carry out an impact assessment prior to carrying out any workplace monitoring. A properly conducted impact assessment will make it easier for an employer to establish its business needs and legitimate aims which it seeks to rely on as justifying the monitoring. While the Code does not prohibit 'informal' impact assessments, it would be prudent for employers to record their reasoning in case the monitoring is scrutinised by a court at a later stage.

The Code sets out five steps to be followed when conducting an impact assessment:

(a) identify the purpose(s) of monitoring and benefits it is likely to deliver;
(b) identify any likely adverse impact on workers or other third parties who might be affected such as customers or clients;
(c) consider alternatives to monitoring or less intrusive ways in which it could be carried out (such as better supervision of workers or targeting monitoring in high risk areas);
(d) take into account obligations that arise from monitoring (such as notifying workers about monitoring arrangements, keeping information secure and giving individuals rights to access copies of information collected through monitoring); and
(e) judge whether monitoring is justified when weighing up the benefits against an adverse impact to ensure that any intrusion into individuals' private lives is no greater than necessary.

An impact assessment will balance the benefits to the employer and others against the degree of intrusion to the worker. If the same ends can be achieved in a less intrusive manner, the form of monitoring chosen may not be proportionate, and therefore be unlawful.

The Code indicates that employers who can justify monitoring on the basis of a formal or informal impact assessment do not need the consent of individual employees to process their data, except where sensitive personal data is involved. However, the obligation to inform workers that monitoring is taking place and the nature, extent and reasons for it remains (save in exceptional cases).

Once the employer has carried out an impact assessment, it will be necessary to consider the particular method of monitoring and the corresponding provisions of the Code in more detail.

E-mail monitoring

In relation to e-mail monitoring, the Code of Practice provides that employers should always take account of the privacy of those sending and receiving e-mails. A ban on personal communications does not of itself justify monitoring communications. More specifically, the Code provides that:

- An employer should not monitor the content of e-mail messages unless the business purpose for which the monitoring is undertaken cannot be achieved by simply looking at the record of e-mail traffic on the system. For example, if the business reason for monitoring is to address time-wasting, then reviewing data traffic should be sufficient to achieve this objective. On the other hand, if the aim of the monitoring is to detect harassment, bullying or other discriminatory behaviour, then reviewing data traffic will not help and the employer should be justified in scanning the content of e-mails.
- If an employer intends to check its employees' e-mails in their absence due to

sickness or annual leave, it should notify them in advance that this will occur and should restrict such monitoring to identifying work-related e-mails and ensuring that the business responds properly to its customers and other contacts. The employer should not open messages that are clearly personal.

Internet monitoring

The Code permits monitoring of internet usage provided workers have been informed of the nature and extent of internet monitoring, as well as the extent to which information about internet usage is retained and for how long.

Supplementary guidance to the Code recognises that employers face particular problems in relation to discrimination and harassment where workers misuse the internet to view and download pornography or other offensive materials. The Code also acknowledges that employers are legally obliged to take active steps to prevent harassment in the workplace. However, rather than carrying out random checking, employers are recommended by the Code to restrict monitoring to those employees suspected of misconduct.

In particular, the Code of Practice provides that:

- Employers should explain clearly and precisely to employees any limits or prohibitions on their use of the internet for non work-related reasons and should not monitor the sites visited or content viewed by employees unless it is clear that the purpose for which the monitoring is undertaken cannot be achieved by simply recording the amount of time spent by the employee on the internet.
- As far as possible, a company policy on internet use should be enforced by the use of technology designed to restrict access, rather than by monitoring employees' use of the internet. For example, there are software products available that can detect excessive amounts of skin tone in an image and thereby prevent the display of pornographic material.

There are further specific provisions relating to monitoring and pornography. For example:

- the information obtained by the employer from the monitoring process should be disregarded unless it reveals that the downloading of pornography poses a significant risk to the employer; and
- in using the results of monitoring to take disciplinary action against employees, the employer should bear in mind the ease with which websites can be inadvertently accessed by employees through unintended responses of search engines, unclear hypertext links, misleading banner advertising or mis-keying.

These provisions appear rather lenient to employees who access pornographic material at work and it is important to remember that an employee who is subjected directly or even indirectly in the workplace to a pornographic image that is not legally obscene may nevertheless have grounds for claiming sex discrimination (see *Morse* v. *Future Reality Limited* above) or, indeed, some other form of discrimination.

General

The Code suggests that as far as possible, employers should target those employees who it reasonably suspects of being guilty of certain types of misconduct, rather than monitoring all employees.

Many employers carry out occasional spot checks as a way of monitoring employees and the Code makes it clear that if more general monitoring is necessary, then spot checks or audits are preferable to continuous monitoring. Without spot checks, an employee who has not otherwise come under suspicion (and who will not therefore be subject to targeted monitoring) could make defamatory remarks or disclose confidential information without detection. These are unlikely to be picked up simply by examining traffic data or by software applications.

It is arguable that an employer who does not carry out spot checks is not fulfilling its duty to do everything reasonably practicable to prevent harassment, defamation, breach of copyright and so on by its employees. In that case, the employer is unlikely to succeed in defending itself against such claims. Also, provided employees are warned that they will occur, spot checks support one of the key aims of monitoring which is prevention of misuse rather than detection.

In summary, in response to the Code employers should:

- Draft a monitoring policy or review their existing one so that staff are clear about when they may or may not use the e-mail or internet systems. Employees should understand clearly when information about them is likely to be obtained, how the information will be used and to whom it will be disclosed. The policy should give guidance on the type and extent of personal use allowed. Policies are discussed further below.

- Before monitoring is carried out, they should undertake an 'impact assessment' to decide exactly what will be done and how, and to consider whether monitoring is a 'proportionate' response to the problem. Any adverse impact on employees must be justified by the benefits to the organisation.

- Nominate someone senior to authorise and oversee the monitoring of employees and ensure that the nominated person is aware of the organisation's responsibilities.

- Avoid using any personal information collected through the monitoring for purposes other than those for which the monitoring was introduced – unless it is clearly in the employer's interest to do so or it relates to an activity that they could not be expected to ignore, e.g. criminal activity.

222

In conclusion, it is important to remember that the company must identify the specific business purpose for which any monitoring is introduced. All forms of monitoring should be carried out sparingly and in proportion to the harm which employees could cause to the business.

4. Drafting and implementing an e-mail and internet policy

It is clear, in relation to all the issues we have discussed in this chapter, that a well-drafted and comprehensive policy on e-mail and internet use is essential to minimise the significant legal risks faced by a company as a result of providing access to e-mail and the internet to its employees.

On the one hand, the company faces liability as a consequence of its employees' misuse of the systems, for example if they send defamatory e-mails or e-mails which are offensive and deemed to constitute harassment of the recipient. On the other hand, the company faces claims from those same errant employees, if the monitoring it carries out is unlawful or if it dismisses employees in circumstances which are deemed to be unfair.

Provided the policy is effectively implemented (which essentially means disseminated and communicated), it should assist the company in its defence to a claim that it is vicariously liable for its employees' actions by demonstrating that it has taken all reasonably practicable steps to prevent the harassment, defamation or other misconduct.

In drafting the policy, the company needs to make sure that the right balance is struck between protecting its legitimate business interests, restricting employees' activities and invading their privacy.

4.1 The scope and content of the policy

There should be a general policy statement which explains the rationale for the policy and raises awareness of the potential consequences for the company of misuse by employees. One of the objectives of the policy should be to promote a culture of caution in relation to e-mail and internet use.

The policy should set out the extent to which employees are permitted to use e-mail and the internet for private purposes. The policy should warn employees that their e-mail communications and internet activities may be monitored, thereby removing their expectations of privacy and satisfying the requirement of RIPA in relation to the company making all reasonable efforts to inform those who may use the system that their communications may be intercepted. Details should be given on the purpose, extent and means of any monitoring in the workplace.

The policy must set out clearly the consequences for employees who misuse the systems. It should warn employees specifically of those offences that will be regarded as constituting gross misconduct. For example, if the company wanted summarily to dismiss an employee who was found to be accessing and downloading pornography in the office, it must make clear that such conduct will be considered as gross misconduct and that the employee will be dealt with in accordance with the company's disciplinary policy.

If the company engages independent contractors or agency workers who have access to its e-mail and the internet, it should ensure that the policy applies to them also or that the agency who provides the workers applies equivalent rules and guidance relating to e-mail and internet activities.

 CHECKLIST

Provisions to include in the policy
The e-mail and internet policy should contain clear rules on the following issues:

In relation to e-mail:

➡ Personal use – whether personal e-mail messages are prohibited or allowed on a limited basis. If personal use is permitted, guidance on what the company considers is reasonable use should be provided, for example only during lunchtime or after working hours.

➡ E-mail style – for example, employees should draft e-mails with the same formality as hard copy letters or memos, they should not use capital letters (which is considered to be the equivalent of shouting) and for external e-mails they should include appropriate signature files with relevant contact details and appropriate disclaimers.

➡ Inappropriate messages – for example, a prohibition on messages which may be offensive to the recipient(s) on the grounds of sex, race, disability, religion and sexual orientation, and a prohibition on responding to or forwarding chain letters, humorous stories and jokes.

➡ Defamatory e-mails – for example, a prohibition on e-mails containing criticisms or disparaging remarks of colleagues, other individuals or organisations.

➡ Confidential information – for example, rules on using encryption when sending confidential information by e-mail and a ban on e-mailing confidential information to home computers. Examples of alternative forms of communication for confidential material should be set out. For example, is it more appropriate for certain information to be sent via an internal post system or by hand?

➡ Contractual commitments – for example, rules relating to the negotiation of contracts by e-mail and a warning about inadvertently entering into contractual commitments.

In relation to the internet:

→ Personal use – specifying whether accessing the internet for personal use is prohibited or allowed on a limited basis, for example only during lunchtime or after working hours and for a maximum of 30 minutes in a day.

→ Downloading inappropriate material such as pornography, pirate software or computer games. Specific guidance along with examples of what materials can or cannot be viewed or copied from the internet should be included. A blanket ban on 'offensive material' will not be specific enough on its own. In relation to pornography, there should be a warning that this may constitute a criminal offence as well as gross misconduct.

→ Breach of copyright – for example a statement that employees must take care not to breach copyright laws when downloading material and/or forwarding it to others.

→ Posting information on the company's website, for example, any information must be accurate and up to date. It may be advisable to restrict the ability to amend or add to the website to a small group of individuals.

The policy should also contain a warning that the e-mail system is not private. It should explain the extent to which e-mails and internet access will be monitored, for example, whether the content of e-mails and sites visited will be monitored in addition to recording e-mail traffic and time spent on the internet. It should also contain details of the practice relating to back-up and retention of e-mails on the system.

There should be a clear statement to the effect that breaches of the policy will be treated as disciplinary offences under the company's disciplinary procedures. It should also give an indication of the penalties to be applied for such breaches, specifying in particular which breaches will constitute gross misconduct and warning that the appropriate penalty for gross misconduct is summary dismissal.

The company may also wish to include information on how employees should report inappropriate use of e-mail or the internet (including provisions for anonymous reporting) and rules designed to safeguard the security of the system, for example, rules relating to the use of passwords, security of work stations and the use of floppy disks and CD-ROMs.

4.2 The implementation of the policy

The effective communication of the policy is vital if it is to be effective in educating employees of the risks, creating a culture of caution and assisting the company in its defence of any claims.

The principal means of promoting the policy are likely to include:

- induction training for new employees and regular training for existing employees, perhaps with a presentation by an IT professional which explains the contents of the policy and the consequences of breaching the policy. It would also be advisable for the company to ask employees to sign and return a copy of the policy, confirming that they have read and understood its contents;
- training for managers who will have responsibility for implementing the policy;
- occasional features in the company's in-house publications and/or global e-mails reminding employees of the policy;
- discussions in team meetings of particular problem areas which have arisen.

Further, it is imperative that any policy introduced is enforced. It is practice rather than the policy itself which will be used to determine whether any monitoring is enforceable and also whether any action taken against an employee is 'fair' in all the circumstances.

The recent case of *Brearley* v. *Timber Tailors* (2005) *The Times*, 8 February highlights the importance of having a clear e-mail/internet policy. Helen Brearley was dismissed for gross misconduct after sending more than 300 explicit personal e-mails to her girlfriend. The Tribunal ruled that she had been unfairly dismissed because the employer had not warned her that such behaviour was unacceptable. Ms Brearley was awarded £26,245 as compensation.

4.3 Managing employees who breach the policy

In order to avoid unfair dismissal claims, the company must ensure that it deals with those employees who breach the policy consistently and in accordance with the company's normal disciplinary procedures. If the company turns a blind eye to inappropriate use of e-mail for the first six months after its introduction and then decides to dismiss an employee for similar misuse of the system, the dismissal may be deemed unfair. Not all breaches of the policy will justify dismissal. In many situations it will be appropriate for the company to impose informal and formal written warnings before considering dismissal.

In cases of gross misconduct where dismissal may be appropriate, the company must have investigated all relevant facts adequately with the result that it has a reasonable and genuine belief in the employee's culpability. As well as satisfying any Employment Tribunal that it followed the correct statutory procedures introduced by the Employment Act 2002 (and set out in the Employment Act 2002 (Dispute Resolution) Regulations 2004) when dismissing the employee, the company must also be able to satisfy any Employment Tribunal that it acted reasonably in treating the reason for dismissal as a sufficient reason for dismissing the employee. For example, if an employee is found to have accessed and downloaded pornography from the internet, the tribunal will consider whether the company's decision to dismiss him falls within the band of reasonable responses to the employee's conduct which a reasonable employer could adopt.

If the company's policy specifically states that accessing and downloading pornography constitutes gross misconduct for which the appropriate sanction is dismissal then, subject to complying with the correct statutory procedures, the tribunal is likely to conclude that the company acted reasonably in dismissing the employee. This may not be the case if the policy does not contain such a provision. In *Dunn* v. *IBM UK Ltd* 1 July 1998, Case No. 2305087/97, Mr Dunn admitted accessing pornographic sites at work but had not been warned that this could result in disciplinary action. There was no company policy which prohibited this conduct and the tribunal found that his summary dismissal was unfair. It did, however, reduce his compensation by 50 per cent on the grounds that he had significantly contributed to his dismissal.

As indicated above, the tribunal will take into account not only whether the company had reasonable grounds for dismissing the employee, but also whether it complied with certain statutory steps and more generally adopted a fair procedure. In brief, the company should investigate any allegations. This may involve monitoring and so as not to prejudice the fairness or otherwise of any subsequent decision to dismiss, this should be carried out in accordance with the legislation and guidance issued by the Information Commissioner in the form of the Code, set out above. Consideration should also be given to an employee's right to privacy under Article 8 of the Human Rights Act. If the investigating company officer considers that, following the investigation, it is appropriate that the matter is considered more formally at a disciplinary hearing, the company must inform the employee in writing, setting out the detail of the case against the employee and inviting him to attend a disciplinary hearing. In addition, the company must inform the employee of the basis of the allegation, for example, by providing the employee in advance of the disciplinary hearing with copies of any documents on which it relies, such as copies of relevant e-mails. At the hearing, the employee should have an opportunity to explain his side of the story and/or make representations in mitigation. The employee should also be given the opportunity to appeal to a higher level of management against any finding and/or sanction imposed. The employee is entitled to be accompanied at the disciplinary and appeal hearings by a union/employee representative or colleague of his choice.

The danger of jumping to conclusions and not allowing the employee an opportunity to put forward his or her side of the story is well illustrated by a US case in which a police officer was dismissed after his employers had carried out a review of his computer records and discovered that he had visited whitehouse.com, a pornographic site. The officer claimed that he had typed the address in error and that he had actually intended to visit the official site for the White House at whitehouse.gov.com. He successfully sued his employer and was awarded $100,000 in damages.

Group dismissals

Many of the news reports about dismissals for misuse of e-mail and the internet relate to groups of employees rather than individuals, no doubt because the dismissal of forty employees by a company for accessing and downloading pornography is far more newsworthy than a story about a single employee engaging in such conduct, unless that employee is a high-profile individual.

If the company reasonably believes that a number of employees in a particular area of the business are guilty of serious breaches of the policy, but despite carrying out a thorough investigation it cannot identify which employees are to blame, it may be reasonable to dismiss all of those who could have been responsible. This situation could arise if, for example, each of the employees identified by the company as having breached the policy, claims that one of his or her colleagues must have accessed their computer when they were out of the room and sent the defamatory e-mail or visited the inappropriate website.

The case of *Monie* v. *Coral Racing Ltd* [1980] IRLR 464, established the principle that where an employer believes that one or more of a number of employees is guilty of an offence and, despite proper investigation, cannot identify which of them is culpable, it may be reasonable for the employer to dismiss all those who could have been responsible.

In the case of *Parr* v. *Whitbread Plc t/a Thresher Wine Merchants* [1990] IRLR 39, the Employment Appeal Tribunal set out guidelines for tribunals faced with such group dismissals. It said that a tribunal should consider whether the acts of misconduct would justify dismissal if they were committed by an individual, whether the employer has carried out a reasonable investigation and whether as a result of that investigation, the employer has reasonable grounds to believe that more than one person could have committed the acts of misconduct. In addition, the employer has to show that it acted reasonably in identifying the employees who could have committed the acts and that it has established that each employee was individually capable of doing so. The employer also has to show that it could not identify the individual perpetrator.

5. Conclusion

Introduce a comprehensive e-mail and internet policy at the outset which stresses:

- prohibited uses;
- rules of etiquette in relation to e-mail;
- disciplinary penalties for breaching the policy;
- the fact that e-mails and internet access are not private;
- the company's policy on monitoring.

Ensure that the policy is communicated to all employees and that they receive training and regular updates on its provisions and implications.

Consider the extent to which monitoring is required in order to protect the company's interests. Take a cautious approach and, in particular:

- establish the specific business purpose for which the monitoring is to be introduced;
- target monitoring on those areas where it is necessary and proportionate to achieving the business purpose;
- carry out spot checks (rather than continuous monitoring of all employees) to assist the company in arguing the statutory defence to discrimination claims and in defending defamation claims;
- make reasonable efforts to inform third parties who use the system that their communications may be monitored.

Take a consistent approach to the management of employees who breach the policy. Ensure that it is properly and consistently implemented. In response to a suspected breach:

- investigate thoroughly;
- do not jump to conclusions, allow the employee to put his side of the story;
- follow a fair disciplinary procedure and make provision for an appeal by the employee against any disciplinary sanction imposed.

9 Taxation

Introduction

Chapter 2 touched on structuring the internet business. This chapter looks at these areas in further detail, and also looks at funding the business, expansion in the UK and internationally, businesses coming to the UK, and finally the disposal of the business.

1. Starting-up the e-commerce business

The choice of business vehicle will have implications for the future tax and non-tax position of the business. For example, if we were looking at a US business setting up in the UK, a company is taxed differently to a branch or agency arrangement. The suitability of these business vehicles needs to be considered against say a partnership (perhaps involving an outside investor), or a form of joint venture (again, involving a third party). Each of these options has its own tax consequences. However, for the purposes of this chapter, we have assumed that the business is trading through a company, incorporated and resident in the UK for tax purposes, although we will also examine the use of branches and the position of non-UK resident entities doing business in the UK.

2. Funding the business

This section focuses on investments in new start-up e-commerce businesses and their tax consequences. This can be done by way of a straightforward loan from a parent company or fellow subsidiary company. Alternatively, where outside investors are being introduced to the business, funding may be provided through a combination of loans and share subscriptions.

2.1 Loan finance

Intra-group loan

The overall tax effect of intra-group loans should be largely neutral. Subject to certain anti-avoidance rules, any interest charged will be taxable as income of the lending company and allowable as a deduction for the borrowing company. Care should be taken where the group is large, as transfer pricing rules may apply to the intra-group loan, such that a market rate of interest will need to be charged. These rules are discussed in more detail later.

Third party loans

As with intra-group loans, the interest on third-party loans will also be deductible for the borrowing company. Where the shareholders invest money in the company, they may be eligible for tax relief on interest paid on any borrowings of their own. If those shareholders are individuals, the company must be 'close' at the time of the loan. In general, a company is 'close' if it is under the control of five or fewer shareholders and their associates. Further consideration of the rules is outside the scope of this book.

2.2 Share capital

Corporate venturing scheme

This scheme is intended to encourage larger trading companies to invest in small higher risk trading companies (see further the discussion of EIS relief below). The investee company (the company in which the investment is made) must not be a 51 per cent subsidiary of another company (so, for example, any investment would have to be in the internet company's parent company).

If the scheme applies, the investing company is entitled to a 20 per cent deduction from its profits in respect of any cash subscriptions for new ordinary shares in the smaller company. However, the investing company can only subscribe for up to 30 per cent of the share capital of the smaller company, and at least 20 per cent of the ordinary share capital of the company must be owned by individuals. The relief will be withdrawn in certain circumstances, for example if the investing company disposes of the shares within three years.

The Enterprise Investment Scheme (EIS)

Broadly, this scheme allows individuals to obtain income tax and capital gains tax relief on cash subscriptions for new ordinary shares in small companies. The EIS is designed to help small, high risk, unquoted trading companies raise start up and expansion finance by issuing full risk ordinary shares to investors.

There are conditions for the investing individual, such as:

- they must not be connected to the company in which they invest;
- they must subscribe for ordinary shares in the company;
- they must not receive any benefits from the company.

There are conditions for the company, such as:

- it must carry on a 'qualifying trade' (or be preparing to do so) wholly or mainly within the UK;
- it must not be quoted on any stock exchange;
- its gross assets before the investment must be less than £15m and not more than £16m after the investment;
- it must use the funds received from the investor for its trade.

Provided the conditions are satisfied, the following tax reliefs are available:

- income tax deduction (at 20 per cent) on the amount invested (of up to £200,000 per tax year);
- relief from capital gains tax on disposal of the shares, provided (generally) that they are held for at least three years after issue;
- relief for most allowable losses on the shares against either income or chargeable gains; and
- deferral of capital gains tax on any chargeable gain from the disposal of any asset where the proceeds are reinvested in the shares.

3. General introduction to the UK tax regime for companies

A brief review of some of the UK concepts of direct tax, together with some basic concepts of VAT are set out below.

3.1 UK direct tax

Income profits

Assuming the internet business is being run through a UK-resident company, the first tax to consider is corporation tax. A company resident in the UK pays corporation tax on the whole of its world-wide profits whether they are trading profits or investment profits, although credit is usually given for any non-UK taxes paid on those profits.

In general, income losses can be set off against income or capital profits for the accounting period in which the loss is made or surrendered to reduce the profits of a company within the same group. Trading losses may also be carried back to be set off against income profits of the preceding accounting period, or carried forward indefinitely against profits from the same trade. Losses can also be 'surrendered' to other group companies to be set against their profits.

Capital profits

A UK-resident company also pays corporation tax on any chargeable gains arising from the disposal of capital assets, e.g. land and other investments. Relief may be available to reduce or postpone these gains.

Capital losses may be set off against capital gains of the same or in future accounting periods. Gains can also be 'surrendered' to other group companies so that they can use any capital losses they may have.

3.2 Start-up and development costs

Creation of intellectual property, information technology and goodwill

Since April 2002, the tax treatment of expenditure on the creation of these assets follows their accounting treatment, which has improved the ability to claim tax relief for the expenditure. The new rules apply to all intangible assets including goodwill, although they will not apply to assets owned before April 2002. Specifically, regard should be had to the following points:

1. Tax relief will be available for the purchase price of intangible assets (including goodwill) as it is written off (amortised) in the company accounts.
2. A tax deferral will be available for gains arising on the disposal of intangible assets that are reinvested in the purchase of other intangible assets.
3. Transactions with related parties will be deemed to have occurred at market value, although intra-group transfers will be treated as made on a no gain/no loss basis.

Capital allowances

The capital allowances regime allows businesses to write off certain kinds of capital expenditure as deductions against income profits. Generally, a capital allowance can be claimed over a period of years and is given by allowing a proportion of the expenditure on the asset to be written off annually. The timing on the amount that can be claimed depends on the type of asset purchased, and the size of the company making the purchase. The types of assets that internet businesses may purchase include office equipment and computer hardware and software.

Usually, the allowance is a 'writing down allowance' set at 25 per cent on a reducing balance basis. For example, where expenditure is £1,000, in the first year £250 is claimed. In year 2, it is 25 per cent of the balance (£750) and so on. However, where plant and machinery is purchased by small and medium-sized businesses, they may claim in the first year an allowance of 40 per cent, rather than the standard 25 per cent.

A 'small business' is defined as one with:

- turnover of less than £5.6 million annually;
- assets worth not more than £2.8 million; and
- no more than fifty employees.

A 'medium-sized business' is defined as one with:

- turnover of less than £22.8 million annually;
- assets worth not more than £11.4 million; and
- no more than two hundred and fifty employees.

Often, the government allows small or medium-sized business more generous first year allowances for short periods, say two years at a time. It is worthwhile checking the position regularly, to ensure maximum allowances are being claimed.

Research and Development (R&D)

Where a business fulfils certain conditions, it is entitled immediately to write off the whole of its capital spending on R&D against income. R&D activities must be creative or innovative and performed in the fields of science or technology and must be undertaken with a view to extending the knowledge of the internet business. However, commercial development without scientific or technological development will not satisfy the tests.

3.3 Transfer pricing

Broadly, the transfer-pricing regime seeks to ensure that transactions between companies under common control are entered into at 'arm's length'. Originally they applied just to international transactions but from April 2004 they also apply to domestic transactions. However, these rules will only apply to large groups of companies (and in certain circumstances, medium-sized groups). The rules should be borne in mind when setting up further group companies.

A small group of companies has:

- less than 50 staff; and
- turnover of less than 10m euros or balance sheet assets of less than 10m euros.

A medium-sized group of companies has:

- less than 250 staff; and

■ a turnover of less than 250m euros or balance sheet assets of less than 43m euros

Under the transfer-pricing rules, companies must impose an arm's length price on transactions between them, and pay tax on those amounts. Companies can be under common control where one person owns just 40 per cent of the issued share capital in the transacting companies. If they fail to charge an arm's length price, they must pay tax as if they did charge that price.

The main difficulty faced by companies in applying the transfer pricing rules is deciding what is an arm's length price. There are numerous methods recommended by the OECD (the Organisation for Economic Cooperation and Development), although the correct method is not always easy to choose and apply. Furthermore, a lack of third party transactions for comparison may also cause problems.

3.4 Value added tax

Value added tax (VAT) is a tax on supplies of goods and services. It is levied on supplies made by a 'taxable person' in the UK in the course or furtherance of a business. The principle behind VAT is that it should be borne ultimately by the consumer of the goods and services supplied. If a company is registered for VAT, then generally it will be able to deduct an amount equal to VAT on supplies made to it from the VAT charged by it on its supplies, and it will account to Customs and Excise for the difference.

Supplies made by the internet business are likely to be either standard rated (in the UK, this is 17.5 per cent) or zero rated (0 per cent), perhaps if the supplies are made to certain overseas customers. The correct VAT treatment of the internet business will depend on the goods or services being sold.

4. Reorganising the business in the UK

It was mentioned in chapter 2 that it may be desirable to transfer (or 'hive down') the internet business to a separate company within the same group, which was illustrated by the use of Trading Company Limited, Trading.com Limited and the parent company Trading Holdings Limited. The tax effects and reliefs available are examined in further detail here.

4.1 Hive down, losses and group supplies

The internet business may consist of a domain name, other intellectual property, existing contracts, computer hardware, trading debts, stock and employees currently owned by Trading Company. Trading.com will pay cash for the internet business, although the amount will probably be left outstanding on inter-company loan account. Trading.com may also pay a management charge to Trading Company for help in running its business. The reliefs etc set out below assume that one company is at least 75 per cent owned by the other, or both are at least 75 per cent owned by a third company, i.e. Trading Holdings.

Taking the main tax issues in turn:

- *Income*: The transfer of stock and similar is likely to be at market value, but an election should be made for the transfer to be made at cost, so that no tax charges arise. Intellectual property created after April 2002 can also be transferred without a charge arising. Intellectual property created before then can be an issue, which must be examined on a case by case basis.

- *Chargeable gains*: Transfers of assets (e.g. land and investments) generally take place on a no gain/no loss basis. Note that any sale of Trading.com within six years of the hive down may trigger a tax charge within the company on the assets transferred and still held at the date of sale.

- *Trading losses*: The internet business should inherit any trading losses attributable to the internet business, which have arisen in Trading Company, unless that company retains liabilities in excess of assets retained. The losses transferred may be used by Trading.com against the future profits of the internet business.

- *VAT*: There should be no VAT payable on the transfer:
  - The transfer of a business as a going concern ('TOGC') is usually outside the scope of VAT. Special rules apply where real property is transferred as part of the TOGC;
  - The transfer of a business within a VAT group is also outside the scope of VAT. To simplify the VAT affairs of the group it may be appropriate to register the three companies as a group, as intra-group supplies are ignored for VAT purposes, and the VAT administration burden is reduced considerably as all supplies are treated as made by a representative member of the VAT group.

5. Expanding the business internationally

First, the broad international direct tax principles will be considered followed by a look at some international VAT issues.

5.1 International direct tax principles

Broadly, the taxation of international transactions is based on concepts of residency: tax authorities have jurisdiction to tax business entities that are resident or operating in their jurisdiction. As a result, businesses will tend to be taxed in the country where they carry on most of their activities. Tax authorities may also tax any income derived in their jurisdiction, for example, royalties on licensing intellectual property rights, although this varies from country to country.

Double tax agreements

Double tax agreements (DTAs) are agreements between two countries governing the tax treatment of transactions effected by business and individuals earning income in those jurisdictions. For example, DTAs will typically determine which jurisdiction has the primary taxing rights where a business is trading in both jurisdictions. DTAs also act to reduce the withholding tax obligations (generally payable on interest, dividends and royalty income).

Taxable presence

A company will generally be resident in the country in which it is registered and/or in which the management and control of that company is located. Generally, that country will then tax the company on its worldwide profits and gains, giving relief where tax has also been paid abroad.

The concept of 'permanent establishment' is often used to decide whether a company has sufficient presence in a country to fall to be taxed there. Under DTAs, business ventures are generally assessed to see whether they constitute a permanent establishment and, accordingly, are taxable in the host jurisdiction to the extent that the profit is derived in that jurisdiction. A basic definition of permanent establishment is a '*fixed place of business through which the business of an enterprise is carried on*'. The maintenance of storage facilities, conducting display and delivery activities or simple marketing activities does not generally constitute permanent establishment. However, the use of an agent can amount to a permanent establishment, although an independent agent will not generally constitute a permanent establishment of the principal business. On the other hand, setting up an office or branch would probably amount to a permanent establishment.

Application to e-commerce

Determining the issue of what amounts to a 'taxable presence' can be tricky when looking at e-commerce. This can best be considered through the example of how a company might make use of a website.

If a website hosted by a non-UK resident merely offers information to prospective customers (that is, it is an advertising medium), then this is unlikely to constitute a permanent establishment, so that the profits are unlikely to be taxed in the UK. The position is likely to be similar if a UK company with a website located in the UK liaises with a customer resident abroad.

However, the position is less clear where the customer actually interacts with the supplier through the website or actually effects purchases through the web site. Consider the following: if the only presence which a non-UK resident has in the UK is an interactive website that is accessible from the UK and upon which UK customers may place orders, it is likely that this is not a sufficient presence to amount to a permanent establishment in the UK (although this will not be conclusive). If the non-resident's physical operations are located outside the UK, it should therefore escape UK tax (but not necessarily the other country's taxes) on its profits, but this will ultimately depend on the facts.

Current OECD thinking seems to suggest that a website is nothing more than software and data and therefore it amounts to intangible property. Accordingly, it cannot be a place of business for the purpose of constituting a permanent establishment (discussed further below). It follows, therefore, if a business has a website accessible from the UK, but has no other presence in the UK, then its profits should escape UK tax. The same arguments should apply for a UK internet business conducting activities abroad.

The position is more complicated when a server is introduced into the equation. If the server is operated from a location in the UK, it adds an element of tangibility, which may be enough to constitute a permanent establishment. This means that the tax authorities may have jurisdiction to charge UK taxes where the server is itself physically located in the UK.

Compare this position to using a third party ISP. The basic considerations will be the same, as the third party ISP may be an agent of the company. However, if it is an independent agent for tax purposes (as discussed above), the operation may fall outside of being a permanent establishment.

If the server was found to be used exclusively by a non-resident in connection with trading activities then it may constitute a permanent establishment and would be taxable in that jurisdiction. Similarly, automatic equipment (operated without human intervention) can be classified as a permanent establishment where it amounts to the conduct of a business. Again, this depends on the facts of each case.

5.2 International indirect tax principles

As noted at paragraph 3.4 above, the correct VAT treatment of the internet business will depend on the nature of the goods or services supplied.

So far as international trade is concerned, there are two general principles that can be stated. First, the export from the UK of goods or services is generally free of VAT, unless made to a non business customer in the case of supplies within the European Union. Second, the import into the UK of goods or services is generally subject to VAT, either by the importer (or its agent) or by the customer. The rules can be complex, and need to be considered on a case by case basis, depending on the nature of the goods and services supplied.

An overseas business may need to register for UK VAT, as noted below. Even if it does not and, say, merely imports goods into the UK, the import agent or the customer may have to account for VAT when the goods come into the UK.

6. Overseas businesses in the UK

A company not resident in the UK, but which has UK source profits, is charged corporation tax on its UK source profits if it trades through a branch or agency in the UK, i.e. if its activities amount to a 'permanent establishment'. Guidance can be sought under the relevant DTA if available. The branch or agency is treated in a similar way to UK-resident companies, so that the UK tax principles discussed above will apply. It is, of course, open to a non-resident company to set up a UK subsidiary rather than a branch. Profits can be repatriated to the overseas parent by way of dividend.

It is also worth noting that a non-UK resident company which does not have a branch or agency in the UK, although not liable to corporation tax, may be liable to income tax on some of its UK source profits (e.g. royalties from the licensing of intellectual property). Much will depend on the terms of any applicable DTA.

If a non-resident company carrying on trade in the UK is able to do so without establishing a branch or agency in the UK, then the profits from the trade will escape UK tax.

The general VAT rules were stated at section 5.2 above. However, it is worth noting that a business that does not have sufficient taxable presence to constitute a permanent establishment for direct tax purposes may still be required to be registered for VAT purposes. Even if it is not required to be registered, if its goods or services are imported into the UK, then VAT may be payable by its customer upon importation. Again, the issues need to be considered on a case by case basis.

7. Selling the internet business

7.1 Sale of substantial shareholdings

There is an exemption from a charge to tax, on any capital gains accruing to a company on the sale of a shareholding in another company, where that shareholding is a 'substantial holding' and both the investor and investee companies satisfy the conditions for the relief.

The basic conditions for full exemption from corporation tax on chargeable gains are:

- the shareholder company must have held the shares for 12 months and must be a trading company;
- the investee company must also be a trading company;
- the shareholder company must have at least a 10 per cent shareholding.

Losses on substantial shareholdings cannot be used for tax purposes. Anti-avoidance provisions apply to ensure that losses cannot be used, and ineligible gains cannot be sheltered.

Business asset taper relief

What about if the company is sold by an individual shareholder or shareholders? Broadly, taper relief is available to reduce the chargeable gain on disposals made after 5 April 1998. Different rates of taper relief apply to business assets and non-business assets. The longer the asset is held, the greater the relief available.

Business assets include shareholdings in unlisted trading companies.

Maximum taper relief is generally available after the asset has been held for two years. A higher rate taxpayer will achieve an effective tax rate of 10 per cent for disposals of business assets held for two years.

Taper relief for non-business assets is significantly less generous in terms of rates and length of ownership than the business asset rates of taper relief.

CHAPTER 10

The Application of Competition Law and E-commerce

Introduction

Competition law has three principal aims:

1. to prohibit anti-competitive agreements;
2. to prohibit the abuse of a dominant position
3. to control anti-competitive mergers.

These aims apply as much to companies active in e-commerce and the internet as they do to those in other areas of commercial activity. The EU and UK competition authorities aim to adopt a flexible approach suited to the fast-moving internet and e-commerce markets by using the established competition law framework and by relying on tried-and-tested economic principles. As there is no new body of competition law or principles to apply, analogies and examples from other sectors can be applied with equal measure to the internet and e-commerce sectors. As described below, the consequences of not considering competition law issues in relation to any proposed agreement or conduct may be very serious. Awareness of the fundamental principles of competition law is important for anyone involved in commercial negotiations or decision-making.

This chapter aims to provide:

- a summary of EU and UK competition law;
- guidance on what types of agreement and behaviour are acceptable and what areas must be avoided;
- guidance on mergers in e-commerce and internet markets; and
- examples of decisions and cases relating to e-commerce and the internet to illustrate the issues raised.

1. EU and UK competition law

This section sets out the key provisions of EU and UK competition law. In practice, many other competition law regimes exist and may be relevant to any particular agreement or conduct. Some comfort may, however, be gained from the fact that most EU member states have regimes that mirror EU law and therefore compliance with the EU regime will generally ensure EU-wide compliance. The possibility remains, however, that some non-EU regimes may be relevant.

1.1 EU competition law

The two fundamental principles of competition law are set out in Articles 81 and 82 of the EC Treaty. Article 81 prohibits anti-competitive agreements and Article 82 prohibits the abuse of a dominant position. These provisions are set out below in full for reference:

> *Article 81(1)*
> *The following shall be prohibited as incompatible with the common market: all agreements between undertakings, decisions by associations of undertakings and concerted practices which may affect trade between Member States and which have as their object or effect the prevention, restriction or distortion of competition within the common market, and in particular those which –*
> *a) directly or indirectly fix purchase or selling prices or any other trading conditions;*
> *b) limit or control production, markets, technical development, or investment;*
> *c) share markets or sources of supply;*
> *d) apply dissimilar conditions to equivalent transactions with other trading parties, thereby placing them at a competitive disadvantage;*
> *e) make the conclusion of contracts subject to acceptance by the other parties of supplementary obligations which, by their nature or according to commercial usage, have no connection with the subject of such contracts.*
>
> *Article 81(2)*
> *Any agreements or decisions prohibited pursuant to this Article shall be automatically void.*
>
> *Article 81(3)*
> *The provisions of paragraph 1 may, however, be declared inapplicable in the case of*
>
> *– any agreement or category of agreements between undertakings;*
> *– any decision or category of decisions by associations of undertakings;*

- *any concerted practice or category of concerted practices;*

which contributes to improving the production or distribution of goods or to promoting technical or economic progress, while allowing consumers a fair share of the resulting benefit, and which does not –

a) *impose on the undertakings concerned restrictions which are not indispensable to the attainment of these objectives;*
b) *afford such undertakings the possibility of eliminating competition in respect of a substantial part of the products in question.*

Article 82

Any abuse by one or more undertakings of a dominant position within the common market or in a substantial part of it shall be prohibited as incompatible with the common market in so far as it may affect trade between Member States.
Such abuse may, in particular, consist in –

a) *directly or indirectly imposing unfair purchase or selling prices or other unfair trading conditions;*
b) *limiting production, markets or technical development to the prejudice of consumers;*
c) *applying dissimilar conditions to equivalent transactions with other trading parties, thereby placing them at a competitive disadvantage;*
d) *making the conclusion of contracts subject to acceptance by the other parties of supplementary obligations which, by their nature or according to commercial usage, have no connection with the subject of such contracts.*

It is clear that, in each case, an effect on trade between member states is essential for an infringement to have occurred. Where no such effect is likely – for example, the agreement is made between two UK-based companies – it is necessary to consider national laws.

1.2 UK competition law

The key provisions of UK competition law are set out in sections 2 and 18 of the Competition Act 1998, and are known as the Chapter I and Chapter II prohibition respectively. They mirror almost exactly the EU provisions with the exception of the reference to trade between member states.

UK competition law has recently been supplemented by the Enterprise Act 2002, which has introduced both changes to the UK mergers and monopolies regime as well as the new 'Cartel Offence' which makes it a criminal offence for individuals to dishonestly agree with a competitor to engage in hard-core cartel activities such as price-fixing, limitation of supply or production, market sharing or bid rigging. However, the substantive provisions of Chapter I and Chapter II have not been changed.

The Chapter I and Chapter II provisions are as follows:

The Chapter I prohibition

Agreements between undertakings, decisions by associations of undertakings or concerted practices which –

a) may affect trade within the United Kingdom, and

b) have as their object or effect the prevention, restriction or distortion of competition within the United Kingdom,

are prohibited unless they are exempt in accordance with the provisions of this Part.

Subsection (1) applies, in particular, to agreements, decisions or practices which –

a) directly or indirectly fix purchase or selling prices or any other trading conditions;

b) limit or control production, markets, technical development or investment;

c) share markets or sources of supply;

d) apply dissimilar conditions to equivalent transactions with other trading parties, thereby placing them at a competitive disadvantage;

e) make the conclusion of contracts subject to acceptance by the other parties of supplementary obligations which, by their nature or according to commercial usage, have no connection with the subject of such contracts.

Subsection (1) applies only if the agreement, decision or practice is, or is intended to be, implemented in the United Kingdom.

Any agreement or decision which is prohibited by subsection (1) is void.

The Director may grant an exemption from the Chapter I prohibition .... if the agreement ... contributes to (a):

improving production or distribution; or
promoting technical or economic progress,
while allowing customers a fair share of the resulting benefit; but (b) does not:

impose on the undertakings concerned restrictions which are not indispensable to the attainment of those objectives; or
afford the undertakings concerned the possibility of eliminating competition in respect of a substantial part of the products in question.

The Chapter II prohibition

Any conduct on the part of one or more undertakings which amounts to the abuse of a dominant position in a market is prohibited if it may affect trade within the United Kingdom.

Conduct may, in particular, constitute such an abuse if it consists in –

a) *directly or indirectly imposing unfair purchase or selling prices or other unfair trading conditions;*

b) *limiting production, markets or technical development to the prejudice of consumers;*

c) *applying dissimilar conditions to equivalent transactions with other trading parties, thereby placing them at a competitive disadvantage;*

d) *making the conclusion of contracts subject to acceptance by the other parties of supplementary obligations which, by their nature or according to commercial usage, have no connection with the subject of the contracts.*

Given the close similarities between EU and UK law, it is appropriate to consider Article 81 alongside Chapter I, and Article 82 alongside Chapter II.

1.3 Article 81/Chapter I

These provisions are exceptionally broadly drafted and could, in principle, prohibit any agreement entered into between two or more persons which contains any restrictions on commercial behaviour whatsoever. This is supported by briefly addressing some of the key concepts of the provisions:

Agreement

This covers any agreement, whether legally enforceable or not, and whether written or oral. There does not have to have been any meeting of the parties, and telephone calls will suffice so long as an agreement was reached. The prohibitions also apply to decisions of trade associations and to concerted practices – where there need be no formal agreement or decision to act in a certain way, merely a consensus as to some form of practical cooperation.

Undertakings

This includes any natural or legal person so long as they are capable of carrying on commercial or economic activities. A sole trader is quite capable of entering into an anti-competitive agreement. The Chapter I prohibition (and Article 81 for that matter) does not apply to agreements where there is only one undertaking, i.e. between entities which form part of a single economic unit or group. In particular, an agreement between a parent company and its subsidiary or between two companies which are under the control of another, will not usually be deemed to be an agreement between undertakings.

Effect on trade

Both EU and UK competition law require there to have been some effect on trade, either between member states or in the case of the UK legislation, within the UK. Where an agreement involves parties based in the UK, then an effect on trade within the UK is almost certain to be found. The more difficult question is to determine whether there has been an effect on trade between member states. In practice, this term is interpreted very widely by the European Commission to include actual, as well as potential, effects on trade. As a consequence, even agreements between parties in one member state have been found to infringe EU law where they have a potential effect on trade, for example, by making it more difficult for companies from other member states to enter a particular market.

It follows that the scope of Article 81 and the Chapter I prohibition is very broad. Given the many millions of commercial agreements entered into each year, it is not surprising that there are a number of measures in place to ensure that only the more serious anti-competitive agreements merit the full sanctions that follow an infringement of the competition laws (see section 1.5 below).

When deciding whether a particular agreement does, in fact, infringe Article 81/Chapter I, it is necessary to consider whether:

- the agreement has an *appreciable* effect on competition;
- any *exemptions* apply to the agreement; and
- the agreement is *excluded* from the prohibitions altogether.

Appreciability

An agreement will infringe Article 81/Chapter I only if it has as its object or effect an *appreciable* prevention, restriction or distortion of competition. This follows from established case law of the European Court of Justice which the Office of Fair Trading (OFT) and the UK courts are bound to follow under section 60 of the Competition Act. Any agreement not having an appreciable effect on competition is unlikely to be of interest to the competition authorities.

In the UK, the OFT has, in the past, taken the view that an agreement will generally have no appreciable effect on competition if the parties' combined share of the relevant market did not exceed 25 per cent (except that the comfort of this threshold did not extend to agreements containing certain hardcore restrictions such as price fixing or resale price maintenance or that the agreement was one of a network of similar agreements having a cumulative effect on the market in question).

However, following recent 'modernisation' changes (see section 1.6 below) to national and EU competition law, the OFT has issued revised guidance, currently in its consultation stage, that indicates that it will follow the

248

European Commission's policy on appreciability in the context of both Article 81 and Chapter I. This policy is set out in the European Commission's Notice on Agreements of Minor Importance (as described below).

The position at EU level has been slightly less generous than that which has historically applied at UK level. The Commission's approach is set out in its *Notice on Agreements of Minor Importance*. This indicates that, in relation to horizontal agreements (i.e. those made between competitors), agreements between persons with a combined market share of less than 10 per cent (in any of the market(s) affected by the agreements) are unlikely to raise competition concerns. In relation to vertical agreements – for example, agreements between suppliers and distributors – a market share of 15 per cent each (in any of the market(s) affected by the agreements) must be reached before there is any likelihood that the agreement will have an appreciable effect on competition. These percentage thresholds are reduced to five per cent where the agreement is one of a parallel network of agreements having similar restrictive effects on the market(s) in question.

Both at UK and EU level, certain hard-core restrictions will always be regarded as having an appreciable effect on competition – in particular price-fixing provisions and export bans.

In practice, therefore, and assuming the absence of any hardcore restrictions, it is likely that many e-commerce agreements, even those containing restrictive provisions, will not be regarded as giving rise to an appreciable effect on competition. This is especially so during any start-up period when market shares will inevitably be low, although the market share of the other party or parties involved in any agreement or concerted practice must of course be considered.

Exemptions

Even when an agreement has an appreciable effect on competition, the law recognises that many such agreements give rise to benefits to consumers and to the market in general. A classic example would be an exclusive distribution agreement, under which a distributor is granted exclusive rights to distribute a particular product in a given territory. The fact that the distributor is, in effect, ring-fenced from competition from other distributors of the same products in its territory makes it more likely that he will invest time and effort (and resources) into ensuring the effective distribution of that product. Hence consumers benefit from an agreement that, on its face, is anti-competitive.

Article 81(3) of the EC Treaty and Chapter I of the Competition Act set out detailed provisions relating to exemptions. (Notably no exemptions are available from the Article 82/Chapter II prohibitions.) Historically, these have been of three kinds:

1. An individual exemption in respect of an individual agreement where the agreement can be shown to contribute to improving production or distribution, or to promoting technical or economic progress, and which allows consumers a fair share of the resulting benefit. Any restrictions contained in the agreement must be indispensable to the attainment of those objectives, and the overall agreement must not afford the possibility of eliminating competition in a substantial part of the products concerned. The relevant agreement had to be notified to the OFT or European Commission in order to receive an individual exemption.

   However, as of 1 May 2004, neither the OFT nor the European Commission will grant formal individual exemptions or comfort letters and the system of notification of agreements for individual clearance has largely disappeared. Whilst agreements notified before this date will continue to benefit from the individual exemption they may have been granted, these residual exemptions are time-limited and will not be replaced or renewed once their time limit expires. Going forward and in the place of formal individual exemptions, parties to agreements (and their legal and economic advisers) will be obliged to self-assess their agreements to determine whether they come within the scope of Chapter I/Article 81 and, if so, whether they satisfy the corresponding general criteria for exemption as also contained in those provisions; or whether they can fall within the automatic safe-harbour of a block exemption (as described below).

2. Block exemptions cover particular categories of agreements that, by corresponding to certain requirements, are automatically considered to meet the exemption criteria set out in Chapter I/Article 81 (without the need for further analysis of their individual competitive effects). An agreement that falls within the terms of a block exemption will be exempt automatically from the prohibitions set out in Chapter I/Article 81. The key block exemptions in force at the date of publication, all of which derive from Community legislation, are those relating to:

   - vertical agreements;[1]
   - technology transfer agreements;[2]
   - motor vehicle distribution and servicing agreements;[3]
   - specialisation agreements;[4]
   - research and development agreements.[5]

   Other block exemptions exist in the air and marine transport sectors and a UK block exemption exists for public transport ticketing schemes.

3. UK law also recognises the application of parallel exemptions whereby agreements which fall within the terms of a Commission block exemption but which are not subject to Article 81 because they do not affect inter-state trade are automatically exempted under the Competition Act.

Block exemptions are time-limited and may be revoked in certain circumstances (although this is very rare). Moreover, whether or not the parties to an agreement qualify for exemption (whether under the specific conditions of a block exemption or otherwise) may change from time to time depending on their individual circumstances, for example, their market share. As a result, it can be important to monitor agreements (and the parties' respective positions within their markets) over time to ensure ongoing compliance.

Exclusions
Under UK law, certain agreements and/or conduct are excluded from one or both of the competition prohibitions altogether. Broadly, these are as follows:

Agreements excluded from the Chapter I prohibition
1. An agreement which is subject to competition scrutiny under the Financial Services and Markets Act 2000, the Companies Act 1989, the Broadcasting Act 1990, the Environment Act 1995 or the Communications Act 2003.
2. An agreement which is required in order to comply with, and to the extent that it is, a planning obligation.
3. An agreement that is the subject of a direction under section 21(2) of the Restrictive Trade Practices Act 1976 (provided no material variation has been subsequently made to it).
4. An agreement for the constitution of a European Economic Area regulated market to the extent that it relates to the rules made or guidance issued by that market.
5. An agreement where it relates to production of or trade in agricultural products as defined in the EC Treaty and in Council Regulation (EEC) No. 26/62, or to farmers' cooperatives.

Agreements and/or conduct excluded from the Chapter I and *the Chapter II prohibitions*
1. An agreement/conduct resulting in a merger or joint venture within the meaning of the Fair Trading Act 1973 or the Enterprise Act 2002.
2. An agreement/conduct resulting in a concentration with a Community dimension and therefore subject to the EC Merger Regulation.
3. An agreement/conduct to the extent to which it is made/engaged in to comply with a specified legal requirement.
4. An agreement/conduct which is necessary to avoid conflict with international obligations and which is also the subject of an order by the Secretary of State.
5. An agreement/conduct which is necessary for compelling reasons of public policy and which is also the subject of an order by the Secretary of State.
6. An agreement/conduct which relates to a coal or steel product within the ECSC Treaty.

7. An agreement made or conduct engaged in by an undertaking entrusted with the operation of services of general economic interest or of a revenue producing monopoly, in so far as the prohibition would obstruct the performance of those tasks.

Practical steps

Having carried out an analysis of whether an agreement is potentially caught by Article 81/Chapter I, it is necessary to consider whether the agreement has an appreciable effect on competition, whether it benefits from an exemption or indeed whether it is excluded from the prohibitions altogether. It should then be possible to reach a view as to whether the agreement in question is at risk of being found to be infringing competition law. There are three options for the parties to an infringing agreement:

1. To disregard the risks and proceed. This is a risky strategy given the consequences of infringement (see below), but may be acceptable where there are good arguments that the agreement does not fall foul of competition law and that an exemption may be available if the agreement ever became the subject of scrutiny.
2. To seek informal guidance from the competition authorities (see 'procedure' below). However, this would only be guidance, not clearance. Moreover, owing to the abolition of the notification system and the move toward the self-assessment of agreements, individual guidance is only likely to be available in very limited circumstances involving novel or previously unresolved issues.
3. To amend the agreement so as to remove the restrictive elements or to redraft them to satisfy the relevant block exemption, etc.

1.4 Article 82/Chapter II

These provisions are both more straightforward and more complex than the Article 81 based prohibition. In essence, there are two stages in deciding whether an infringement of Article 82/Chapter II has occurred:

1. An undertaking must enjoy a dominant position. This has been defined by the European Court of Justice as '*a position of economic strength enjoyed by an undertaking which enables it to prevent effective competition being maintained on the relevant market by affording it the power to behave to an appreciable extent independently of its competitors, customers and ultimately of consumers*' (Case 27/76 *United Brands* v. *EC Commission* [1978] ECR 207; 1 CMLR 429). This definition may not ultimately be helpful in determining whether a company is in a dominant position. The OFT and Commission have therefore indicated that a market share in the

order of 50 per cent will be indicative where there is a dominant position. Such a finding may be rebutted if barriers to entry are low or high buyer power, such that the high market share does not in fact give rise to any real market power. Alternatively a finding of dominance can occur below the 50 per cent threshold, depending on the specific characteristics of the market and the party in question.

2. That undertaking must abuse its position. There is nothing unlawful about having a dominant position, but it puts the undertaking in the delicate position of having to behave in such as way as not to constrain competition in that market, and particularly not to act in such a way as to prevent existing or new competitors from challenging its position. Some of the more commonly found examples of abuse include:

- excessive pricing;
- discriminatory pricing;
- refusals to supply;
- loyalty discounts;
- predatory pricing;
- tie-ins;
- full line forcing.

As stated above, a breach of Article 82/Chapter II is incapable of being exempted and will always be found to have an appreciable effect on competition. The options for any party believing it may be abusing a dominant position are therefore:

1. To continue the abusive conduct – this is a high-risk strategy given the likelihood of complaints from third parties, legal actions for damages and investigations and fines from the regulators (see below).

2. To seek informal guidance in relation to the conduct from the competition authorities. This is only worth doing in those limited circumstances where novel or unresolved issues arise and where there are arguments as to why the conduct should not be seen as unlawful.

3. To cease to engage in the relevant conduct so as to remove any ongoing risk of fines, damages, etc. being imposed. Alternatively to amend the conduct so that the same commercial aims are achieved but in a lawful manner.

1.5 Consequences of breach

The consequences of infringing the competition laws are serious:

1. Financial penalties of up to a maximum of 10 per cent of the worldwide group turnover of the undertakings involved (whether the penalty is applied as the result of a UK or an EU infringement).

2. Any agreement or conduct that infringes competition law is void and cannot be enforced. Where an individual provision in the agreement can be severed from the remainder of the agreement, then it is possible that the remainder of the agreement will remain enforceable.

3. Parties who have suffered loss as a result of any unlawful agreement or conduct have a claim for damages in the national courts. This does not simply extend to a third party who has been prejudiced – a party to an anti-competitive agreement is not itself precluded from claiming damages against the other party depending on the degree of responsibility that the claimant bears for the infringement. In deciding whether to award damages, the ECJ has advised that national courts should take into account the economic and legal context in which the parties find themselves and their respective bargaining powers and conduct. See *Courage Ltd* v. *Crehan* [2001] 5 CMLR 1058, para 32.

4. Under the UK's Enterprise Act 2002, individuals within companies who dishonestly engage in the 'Cartel Offence' as described above, can face criminal prosecution and imprisonment of up to five years and/or an unlimited fine. In addition to any penalty that may be imposed for cartel offences, directors of companies involved in competition law infringements may be disqualified for up to 15 years.

Furthermore, any company found to have infringed EU or UK competition law is likely to suffer bad PR as a consequence. This may not only depress share prices in the short term, but is also likely to make relations with the relevant regulator(s) more difficult in the future.

It follows that a serious infringement of the competition laws can be an expensive mistake. The OFT's first fine under the Competition Act was £3.2 million (imposed on Napp Pharmaceuticals by the decision of 30 March 2001 [No. CA98/2/2001] for an infringement of Chapter II). This fine was reduced on appeal to £2.2million. The OFT has subsequently imposed a number of substantial fines for Competition Act infringements including several fines in excess of £10 million each. The European Commission meanwhile has levied fines in excess of €4.5 billion since October 1999.

1.6 Procedure and modernisation

Both the Commission and the OFT have very significant powers to investigate potential infringements of competition law. Such investigations are often launched as a result of a complaint having been made by an aggrieved competitor or customer. A full description of these powers is outside the scope of this chapter. All that really needs be said is that all companies are now advised to have competition compliance programmes in place to ensure they do not unwittingly find themselves the subject of a Commission/OFT investigation. The advantage of having a competition compliance programme is to ensure that agreements are properly assessed from a competition point of view before they are entered into, to minimise competition risk and to manage the audit trail. Evidence that a competition compliance policy has been implemented may also be a mitigating factor that the competition authorities will take into account in the event of a competition infringement.

Ensuring compliance

As mentioned in section 1.3 above, the procedure whereby the parties to an agreement could actually notify it to the Commission for exemption has been removed (notification also protected the parties from fines in the event that the agreement did not qualify for exemption). This decentralisation is one of the key parts of recent modernisation changes to the way in which competition law is applied within the EU.

As a result of such changes, the risk of whether or not a potentially restrictive agreement satisfies the conditions for exemption as set out in Article 81(3) lies with the parties to the agreement. Therefore, in the interests of certainty, undertakings are advised to draft their commercial agreements so that they comply with the terms of the relevant block exemptions and do not contain any hard-core restrictions i.e. so that they do not need to be separately assessed on their individual merits under Article 81(3). However, because the block exemptions only apply a safe harbour where the market share of the parties concerned falls below a certain threshold, undertakings should remember to keep such agreements under review at regular intervals. If the parties' market shares increase beyond the relevant thresholds, then it is possible for the agreement to lose the protection of the block exemption.

For the small number of cases which fall outside of the block exemptions, a detailed competition analysis of the particular agreement is likely to be necessary. To assist undertakings and their advisers in carrying out the competition assessment, the Commission has published detailed guidelines on the assessment of agreements and conduct. It is important to note that there is no presumption that an agreement which contains restrictions on trade and which falls outside the relevant block exemption is anti-competitive.

Even if an agreement falls outside of the scope of a block exemption, it may be possible to apply some of the rules by analogy (the block exemptions are often accompanied by useful guidance) and, as mentioned above, an agreement which satisfies the individual conditions for exemption under Article 81(3) will be valid. The standard of proof for meeting the requirements of Article 81(3) is quite high and will require detailed evidence of the benefits of the agreement. As in the case of the block exemptions, it is also possible for an agreement to fall outside of Article 81(3), for example, if market conditions change. In order for the parties to an agreement to continue to rely upon Article 81(3), they will need to show that the benefits are ongoing and that they are not outweighed by the damage to competition as a result of any restrictions in the agreement.

National Competition Authorities (NCAs)

Following the recent decentralisation of EU competition law to member states (as set out in Regulation 1/2003), NCAs (such as the OFT) are responsible, alongside the Commission, for the investigation and enforcement of EU competition law. Now, national competition authorities and national courts, as well as the Commission, have the power to decide whether or not parties to an agreement can rely upon Article 81(3) to justify exemption.

The main change with regard to the enforcement of Article 82, which prohibits the abuse of a dominant position, is that national competition authorities will now be able to investigate Article 82 complaints. Unlike Article 81 where restrictive agreements may be justified if they meet the conditions outlined in Article 81(3), an abuse of a dominant position can never be exempted or held to be valid.

Bringing complaints

In the past, aggrieved competitors or consumers who have suffered damage as a result of alleged anti-competitive behaviour have had the option of either bringing their complaint to the Commission or bringing a civil action in the national courts of a member state. Under the new regime, national competition authorities are required to apply EU competition laws as well as UK competition laws, where applicable. Therefore this means that national competition authorities now have the jurisdiction to hear EU competition law complaints.

This change will give complainants greater means of redress against EU competition law infringements and may well result in an increase in competition litigation. In the past, complainants may have been discouraged from complaining to the Commission by the limited resources of the Commission. Secondly, damages have only been obtainable in the national courts and historically very few claims have been successful. Following the introduction of the Enterprise Act in the UK, in the event that the UK competition authorities uphold a competition complaint, the complainant is entitled to claim damages against the infringing party in the Competition Appeal Tribunal.

Powers of investigation and enforcement

The Commission now has enhanced powers of investigation of competition law infringements, for example, the right to search directors' homes, which bring its powers into line with UK powers of investigation.

In addition, where an infringement is being investigated by one or more of the national competition authorities, there is provision for the exchange of information. This issue has been the subject of much discussion and reinforces the importance for companies operating in multiple jurisdictions across Europe (as recently enlarged to include a further ten member states) of having procedures governing audit trails and the protection of documents which are legally privileged.

One of the tools available to companies who wish to protect themselves from the potential consequences of a competition investigation is 'whistleblowing', i.e. informing the relevant competition authorities of anti-competitive agreements or conduct and assisting them with any subsequent investigations. In most EU countries, whistleblowing by an undertaking can either cancel out or reduce the amount of any fine that would be imposed on it by the competition authorities in respect of its own participation in the anti-competitive agreements/behaviour concerned. However whistleblowing in one member state will not be deemed to be effective in another. To cover potential penalties in those jurisdictions, companies will need to have in place procedures to ensure that separate but coordinated notifications may be made (if required).

2. Practical guidance – Agreements and conduct likely to give rise to an infringement

The discussion so far has been on a general basis, without reference to any specific e-commerce agreement or conduct. We now turn to highlight some of the specific types of agreement and conduct, which are likely to give rise to competition concerns and which should, as a general rule, be avoided. As a general rule these observations apply equally to EU and UK law.

2.1 Agreements and concerted practices

The key focus of most competition authorities is to identify, remove and punish, cartel and cartel-like agreements. When we speak of cartels, we mean any number of agreements which have the effect of restricting competition and specifically include agreements to:

- fix prices;
- agree production or sales quotas;
- share product or geographic markets; and/or
- ban exports or imports.

Agreements that contain these kinds of provisions, or are intended to achieve the same effect, are almost certain to fall foul of competition laws and result in fines being imposed. They must therefore be avoided.

Price fixing

Agreements that directly or indirectly fix prices are likely to infringe Article 81/ Chapter I. Such agreements may take many forms, for example:

1. An agreement between two competitors that they will charge the same amount for a particular product or service, or will not charge less than a certain amount, or will stick to a particular range of prices.
2. An agreement between a supplier and a distributor or reseller or wholesaler under which the supplier dictates to the distributor/wholesaler at what price he must sell the goods or services to third parties.
3. Agreements as above, but which relate to fixing discount levels rather than the price of the product/service itself will be equally unlawful.
4. Agreements that relate to elements of the price for a particular product or service, for example transport costs, after-sales costs, credit terms etc will also be regarded as having the same anti-competitive effect as a straightforward price-fixing arrangement.
5. Agreements allowing for the exchange of price lists, or for less formal consultations on pricing levels. Any such agreements should only be entered into after having taken detailed competition law advice.

Since price is arguably the most fundamental reflection of the levels of competition on any market, the agreements discussed above are always regarded seriously by competition authorities. Accordingly, caution should be exercised when drafting any e-commerce agreement in relation to any pricing conditions, especially given the ease with which information can be shared in the context of an internet-based contractual relationship.

Agreements to share markets

Market sharing is another well-recognised form of cartel behaviour: where two or more companies agree to share out a market between them, whether that be in terms of geographic territory, product or customer. Where the parties are actual or potential competitors, such agreements are likely to be regarded as seriously anti-competitive, unless there is a clear justification for the market being divided up in this way. In the context of e-commerce and the internet, it is most likely that any agreement under which markets are shared out, will be unlawful.

Agreements to limit production or investment

An agreement to limit production, or the availability of a particular product or service, is likely to have the effect of reducing supply and thereby increasing prices. Such agreements clearly restrict and distort competition contrary to Article 81/Chapter II. In the context of the internet, such an agreement could arise where two recruitment companies agreed to limit the advertising space to be made available on their particular websites, as a means of driving up prices. Alternatively, two manufacturers could agree to limit their research and development budgets as a means of increasing profits and ensuring the other party does not win an advantage over the other by launching any new products. Another form of agreement limiting output can be found in agreements relating to advertising – specifically those restricting the amount, nature or form of the advertising to be used by the parties.

Collusive tendering

This is really a form of market sharing. Where two or more companies agree which one or more of them should put forward the winning bid to a particular tender, this will amount to an unlawful market sharing agreement. It is unlikely that an exemption would ever be granted for such an arrangement, although the formation of a consortium to bid for a particular project will not normally of itself be regarded as anti-competitive.

Joint buying/selling

Any agreement relating to joint buying or selling may have a similar effect on the market to price fixing. If a number of competitors all obtain a raw material at the same price, this removes one element of competition from the production process and increases the likelihood that there will be less variation in the resale prices offered by those competitors. Likewise, joint selling effectively means a loss of price competition between the parties involved which is likely to have a very significant effect on competition. The Commission has also considered the issue of joint selling in the context of business-to-business (B2B) market places. To avoid the creation of buyer power or the possibility of co-ordination in a downstream market, joint purchasing is only permissible in accordance with the Commission's horizontal guidelines.

Information-sharing agreements

This is a difficult area, but as a general rule, confidential information as to prices, terms of trade, product specifications etc. should not be shared between competitors except on an aggregated and historic basis. Where this kind of confidential information is shared between competitors there is likely to be a very significant loss of competition since any element of competitive surprise brought about by pricing decisions or new product launches will be lost. Such agreements may infringe competition law even where they relate to information that is publicly available. The fact that the agreement facilitates the exchange of information will be sufficient for an infringement to have occurred (see also the *Volbroker* decision).

These broad headings encompass the majority of the types of e-commerce agreements that are likely to give rise to competition concerns. Any agreement will be judged on its effect on competition and not its form. Therefore, it is important to ask what the parties intend to achieve by a particular agreement, rather than hoping that the avoidance of any explicitly anti-competitive provisions will mean the agreement will not fall foul of competition laws.

Examples

In a recent case, the Commission took a strict approach where it considered a company was trying to protect its traditional lines of sale from the pro-competitive effects of electronic commerce. In December 2000, the Commission opened formal proceedings against B & W Loudspeakers Ltd (European Commission press release IP/00/1418, 6 December 2000) as the company was understood to be preventing its authorised dealers from engaging in distance selling such as sales over the internet. It will be recalled that Article 81 specifically refers to agreements which 'limit or control production, markets, technical development or investment' as being unlawful. Attempts by suppliers to control the persons to whom a distributor makes available its goods are therefore likely to be unlawful.

2.2 Abusive conduct

Where a company enjoys a dominant position, a further burden is placed on that company not to infringe the Article 82/Chapter II prohibitions by abusing its position. The following courses of conduct would generally tend to be seen as abusive and should be avoided.

Excessive pricing

The most obvious means for a dominant company to seek to take advantage of its position in the market is to over-charge for its products or services. The European Court has defined excessive pricing as meaning '*charging a price which is excessive because it bears no reasonable relation to the economic value of the product supplied*' (240/96/EC Commission Regulation on the application of Article 85(3) of the Treaty to certain categories of technology transfer agreements).

In practice, there is likely to be an abuse where the dominant company seeks to charge prices that are significantly higher than those charged by its competitors, or where it seeks to charge one set of customers a price which is significantly higher than the price charged to another set of customers (see also price discrimination below). Ironically, where a company is a monopoly supplier of a particular product or service, it may be difficult for the Commission or OFT to carry out any comparisons or to ascribe a fair value to the goods or products concerned.

Apparently excessive prices (and subsequently profits) may be objectively justifiable where a company needs to recoup significant investments, or where such profits reflect a highly efficient operation where high quality products are being supplied at low cost to the supplier. Such prices/profits should be short-term features of the market following which new entry would be expected to be stimulated to compete with the incumbent supplier. Generally, the prices charged need to allow for profits significantly and persistently exceeding the cost of capital before an abuse can be found.

Price discrimination

A dominant company will abuse its position where it applies different prices (or other terms and conditions) to different customers, assuming there is no objective justification for such discrimination. Such justification may derive from the customer's position (e.g. higher prices may be merited if the customer represents a higher than normal credit risk) or where the nature of the product or service means that the volume of the order genuinely has a significant impact on the price that can be quoted.

Predatory pricing

The response of a dominant company to a new entrant is often to engage in predatory pricing. This is when a dominant company reduces its prices to such a level as to ensure that the new entrant goes out of business, following which the dominant company increases its prices to the level they enjoyed prior to the new entrant having appeared on the market. Complex economic analysis (based on the relationship between the prices charged and the costs incurred in providing the product or service) is required in practice to demonstrate that the prices being charged are indeed predatory. Furthermore, evidence of the intent of the dominant company is also often used to strengthen the argument that there has been predatory pricing.

Dominant companies are entitled to react to new entry and compete vigorously; where, however, the response suggests the dominant company is accepting short-term losses in the hope of removing that competitor, then this is likely to be regarded as unlawful. For a start-up company, this area of law may well be used to attack the behaviour of an incumbent dominant operator acting in such a way as to prevent the new entrant being successful.

Tie-in sales and bundling

A dominant company will frequently seek to use its strength in its core market to leverage market share in another market. This is normally done by making customers purchase a secondary product at the same time as a primary product, regardless of whether that secondary product is required. The most high-profile example of this kind of behaviour was seen in the Microsoft investigation in the US and the EU, where Microsoft's inclusion of its Netscape browser software within the Microsoft Office package led to complaints from providers of competing browser software who were effectively precluded from making a significant number of potential sales.

Where possible, dominant companies should ensure that they allow customers to pick and mix from the products and services being offered rather than being required to take any two or more products together – unless there are objective justifications for such bundling. A variation on this abuse is 'quantity forcing' whereby a customer (often a retailer) is required to purchase a specified volume of products. This will often have the effect of ensuring that the retailer is unable to offer competing products for sale since there will be insufficient shelf/storage space for such products.

Discounting

The use of discounts must be handled with care by companies in a dominant position. A straightforward volume-based discount is unlikely to give rise to concerns, but the use of fidelity or loyalty discounts – where the customer receives discounts based on the proportion of its sales which come from the supplier, are more than likely to be regarded as an abuse since their intention is clearly to put pressure on the retailer not to sell competing products. Compare the straight volume discount, which might indirectly have the same effect but would not result in any penalty were competing products to be purchased and subsequently sold. In practice, discounts tend to be drafted in subtly different ways and a careful analysis will be needed as to the effect of that discount on competition.

This is not a comprehensive list of unlawful abuses. Any behaviour which prevents or unfairly hinders new entry, or which exploits customers may well be found to be an abuse. In practice most abuses will fall into one of the above categories or the same principles will be applicable by analogy.

3. Practical guidance – Agreements that are unlikely to raise concerns

We have so far concentrated on those agreements that are likely to give rise to competition concerns. In practice, the overwhelming majority of e-commerce and internet agreements will not give rise to any such concerns and will be fully enforceable (from this perspective at least). This section seeks to highlight those agreements where the parties can be confident that, unless particular characteristics apply, there need be no competition concerns. In addition to what is said below, reference should be made to the concepts of appreciability, exclusions and exemptions above.

The fundamental distinction made for the purposes of classifying agreements in this chapter is between horizontal and vertical agreements. Horizontal agreements being those made between two or more companies at the same levels in the market (e.g. at the same level of production or distribution), and vertical agreements being made between companies at a different level of the production or distribution chain. This is not a watertight distinction however, since a vertical agreement made between two competitors will need to be assessed as both a horizontal and vertical agreement.

3.1 Horizontal agreements

The following types of horizontal agreements:

- cooperation between non-competitors;
- cooperation between competing companies that cannot independently carry out the project or activity covered by the cooperation; and
- cooperation concerning an activity which does not influence the relevant parameters of competition,

will fall within Article 81/Chapter I only if they involve companies with significant market power and they are likely to make it harder for third parties to enter one or more relevant markets.

Furthermore, the Commission has indicated that where a horizontal agreement is made between two or more competing companies it will not be likely to infringe competition law where the market shares of the parties do not exceed 10 per cent. Recent guidance from the OFT suggests that the same figure will apply to agreements which only affect trade within the UK. In both cases, competing companies will not be able to rely on these thresholds where they have included price fixing or market sharing provisions in the agreement. Therefore, many agreements entered into by smaller start-up companies are unlikely to give rise to competition law infringement.

Example
As explained above, agreements between parties with higher market shares may also be permitted where they give rise to benefits for consumers outweighing their anti-competitive effects. A good example of this was the *Covisint* joint venture (European Commission press release IP/01/1155, 31 July 2001). This was an agreement between the world's five leading car manufacturers, to establish a business to business exchange in the automotive components market through a single portal on the internet. The Commission approved the venture after being satisfied that there was no discrimination against certain classes of users leading to foreclosure of the market; adequate data protection was in place to ensure that users did not have access to market-sensitive information; and the agreement did not allow for joint purchasing between car manufacturers for automotive products. This was the first major business-to-business exchange to be examined under Article 81.

The Commission also considered the Volbroker.com joint venture (European Commission press release IP/00/896, 31 July 2000) under Article 81. This concerned the creation, by six large banks, of an electronic brokerage for the trading of foreign exchange options. Initially, the transaction was thought to restrict competition. Once again, the Commission was primarily concerned with ensuring the protection of sensitive information and the possible threat of foreclosure of the market. However, it issued a comfort letter following a host of undertakings from the parties designed to avoid the exchange of commercially sensitive information and an assurance that the parent companies would allow voice brokers, acting as principals, to partici-pate in the venture.

3.2 Vertical agreements

Both the EU and UK competition authorities recognise that in general, vertical agreements are less likely to give rise to detrimental effects on competition. It follows that there are more generous thresholds applying to these types of agreements.

The Commission will not regard a vertical agreement as giving rise to concerns unless the market shares of the parties exceed 15 per cent, and provided it does not contain price fixing provisions or an export ban.

For agreements entered into by parties with more than a 15 per cent market share, it may often be possible to rely on the Vertical Agreements Block Exemption (2790/99/EC Commission Regulation on the application of Article 81(3) of the Treaty to categories of vertical agreements and concerted practices). This exempts from Chapter I/Article 81, vertical agreements where the supplier's market share falls below 30 per cent, again subject to certain provisos, being:

- the agreement must not be between competitors, unless it is non-reciprocal and either: the turnover of the buyer falls below €100 million, or the supplier manufactures and distributes the products whereas the buyer only distributes them;
- the agreement must not contain any price fixing provisions;
- the agreement must not restrict the persons to whom the buyer can sell on the goods or services (although it is permissible to impose an active sales ban in relation to customers based in territories exclusively reserved for other distributors or the supplier). For example, where a manufacturer has appointed an exclusive distributor to act as the only outlet for its products in a particular territory, say Germany, the Commission has indicated that it is perfectly acceptable for the distributor to set up a website over which it can sell the products to customers in a territory covered by another exclusive distributor, say France. This is because the distributor is engaging in passive

selling, whereby it is not actively selling its product in France. If, however, the website specifically targeted the French market, for example if it was in French and listed contact numbers for customers based in France, this would be regarded as active selling and would not be permissible;

- the agreement must have any exclusive provisions limited to a five-year term;
- where the agreement contains an exclusive supply obligation, the relevant market share is that of the buyer – whose market share must fall below 30 per cent.

Meanwhile, in the UK, all vertical agreements are currently excluded from the prohibitions in the Competition Act, other than those containing price fixing provisions (See the Competition Act 1998 (Land and Vertical Agreements Exclusion) Order 2000. However, this Order is being repealed with effect from 1 May 2005. In its place the EU regime will apply by means of parallel effect.

In practice, this means that whilst the vast majority of e-commerce vertical agreements (e.g. all agreements for the supply of goods or services) will be regarded as benign under EU and UK competition law, those that may have previously been confined to the UK will nevertheless need to be reviewed to ensure compliance with the relevant EU block exemption.

4. Merger control

The laws discussed above have referred to agreements and conduct, in other words the day-to-day commercial activities of companies in the e-commerce and internet sector. Merger control laws apply where an agreement gives rise to a change of control of an undertaking and certain specified turnover, asset value or market share thresholds are met. There are many examples of co-operation in the e-commerce and internet sector which have given rise to merger situations requiring the clearance of one of more merger control authorities.

Almost 100 countries worldwide now have merger control laws in place. This text refers only to the EU and UK regimes. One key point to note in respect of merger control laws, is that most merger control regimes impose a mandatory filing requirement if the merger meets certain qualifications or thresholds. Thus, the first question to be asked in assessing any agreement is (a) is this a merger? If so, (b) does it fall within any one or more merger control regimes? If so, (c) are there any mandatory filing requirements?

4.1 EU merger control

Merger Regulation 139/2004 (the Regulation) requires that certain large-scale mergers ('concentrations having a Community dimension') must be notified to the Commission for clearance and, subject to certain very limited exceptions, cannot be the subject of parallel merger inquiries under the domestic merger control provisions of EEA (that is EU and EFTA) member states. (The EFTA member states are Norway, Iceland and Liechtenstein.)

'Concentration'

The concept of a concentration includes full and partial mergers, some joint ventures and acquisitions of control.

Control is defined by the Regulation as the ability to exercise *decisive influence* over an undertaking by, in particular, the ownership or right to use all or part of its assets or the existence of rights or contracts conferring decisive influence on the composition, voting or other commercial decisions of the undertaking. For example, an undertaking can acquire control over another when it holds 50 per cent or less of the other's voting shares, but nevertheless has the *de facto* ability to affect strategic decisions of that undertaking. Where a minority stake gives rise to decisive influence, the acquisition of such an interest may result in the creation of joint control whereby two or more undertakings are able to exercise decisive influence jointly and thereby share control. This is normally the situation in a joint venture.

'Community dimension'

A concentration will have a Community dimension if:

- the combined aggregate worldwide turnover of all the undertakings concerned is more than €5 billion; and
- the aggregate Community/EFTA-wide turnover of each of at least two of the undertakings concerned is more than €250 million;

unless each of the undertakings concerned achieves more than two-thirds of its aggregate Community-wide turnover within one and the same member state. (Only concentrations with a Community dimension are referred to in the remainder of this section.)

A concentration also has a Community dimension if:

- the combined aggregate world-wide turnover of all the undertakings concerned is more than €2.5billion;
- the aggregate Community-wide turnover of each of at least two of the undertakings concerned is more than €100 million;
- in each of at least three EU member states the combined aggregate turnover of all of the undertakings concerned is more than €100 million; and
- in each of at least three of these member states the aggregate turnover of each of at least two of the undertakings concerned is more than €25 million;

unless each of the undertakings concerned achieves more than two-thirds of its Community-wide turnover within one and the same member state.

There are complex rules setting out how turnover should be calculated.

Joint ventures

The creation of a joint venture performing on a lasting basis all the functions of an autonomous economic entity (i.e. a 'full-function' joint venture) constitutes a concentration for the purposes of the Regulation. Accordingly, full-function joint ventures which satisfy the turnover thresholds are subject to the Regulation.

Joint ventures that are not full-function are subject to Articles 81 and 82 of the EC Treaty and possibly also to national merger control laws. Full-function joint ventures which do not satisfy the turnover thresholds and which have as their object or effect the coordination of the competitive behaviour of undertakings that remain independent will also be subject to Articles 81 and 82 and possibly also to national merger laws. Full-function joint ventures that do not satisfy the turnover thresholds but which also do not have this object or effect will fall subject only to national merger laws (where they apply).

Procedure

Any concentration with a Community dimension must be notified (on Form CO) to the Commission, at the latest, one week after the earliest of the conclusion of the agreement, the announcement of the bid or the acquisition of control.

The concentration may not be put into effect before notification and is automatically suspended until a decision of compatibility with the common market (see below), unless the Commission has waived the suspensory requirement.

In straightforward cases, a concentration will be cleared within a month, or six weeks where undertakings are negotiated. In difficult cases raising competition issues, the Commission's timetable may extend to five months in total.

Will the whole transaction be covered by the Regulation?

A clearance of a concentration under the Regulation will, by implication, include clearance of all 'ancillary restrictions'. These are contractual terms or arrangements which might restrict competition but which are 'directly related and necessary to the implementation of the concentration'.

The difficulty lies in the Commission's construction of the words 'directly related' and 'necessary'. Restrictive arrangements not considered to be ancillary to the concentration will need to be assessed separately under Articles 81 and 82.

The approval process

In assessing a concentration, the Commission will determine whether it will significantly impede effective competition in the common market, or in a substantial part of it, in particular as a result of the creation or strengthening of a dominant position in the relevant market. If this is the case, the concentration must be declared incompatible with the common market. Unlike EU law on dominant positions (Article 82 EC Treaty), there is no requirement for abusive conduct; the mere creation of a dominant position with foreseeable competition risks will by itself be sufficient (although a finding of dominance is no longer a prerequisite to the finding that a merger is incompatible with the common market as it was under the previous merger regulation). In making this assessment, the combined market share of the merged undertakings within the relevant product and geographical markets will be an important factor, as will the magnitude of barriers to entry and expansion, procurement patterns and the existence of any vertical links between the parties.

The Regulation contains provisions allowing the Commission to attach conditions to the clearance of a merger, either after the initial period of inquiry or following a full investigation. Such requirements could include commitments on the part of the acquirers to divest certain parts of the target undertaking with a view, for example, to reducing market share or eliminating other competition concerns.

Third party comments

The procedures under the Regulation make full accommodation for third party comments. Competitors and customers will be sent questionnaires by the Commission, and a notice will be published in the Official Journal seeking any additional third party comment. Finally, it would be open to a party that could establish a legitimate interest to appeal a Commission decision to the European Court of Justice.

Examples

The dominance test as set out in the Regulation has provided an effective means of examining the impact of mergers in many hi-tech sectors such as telecommunications, the internet and the media. Generally speaking, the Commission aims to develop an environment, which allows an open and competitive internet/New Media market to flourish.

The Commission has addressed competition concerns in cases where it has considered that access to networks is essential for the provision of other services leading to the so-called 'Gatekeeper effect', where the dominant party is able to dictate the conditions in the market. Many of the cases concern potential dominance in the infrastructure used for electronic commerce or the control of upstream content.

The prohibited MCI Worldcom/Sprint merger (Case No. COMP/M.1741 MCI Worldcom/Sprint, 28 June 2000) was an example of a case where the Gatekeeper effect was produced by a horizontal overlap (i.e. the combination of two operators' networks). The Commission was primarily concerned that the concentration would create an entity with such a strong lead in the market for top-level connectivity providers that its competitors and consumers would be unable to exert any competitive constraint upon it. The Commission was equally concerned that control over such an important infrastructure could be used to leverage the parties' positions into related markets.

The same theme arose in the case of Vodafone/Mannesmann (Case No. COMP/M.1795 – Vodafone Airtouch/Mannesmann, 12 April 2000). The parties intended to merge their national mobile networks to form a pan-European network. The Commission was concerned that the accumulation of the various networks would create a company of such magnitude in the market for the delivery of pan-European services that it would have an anti-competitive effect. The Commission allowed the concentration but required the entity to open up its integrated network to its competitors for three years. This ensured that the company's strong position in one market could not be used to strengthen its position in the related service market. The time limit recognised the fact that competitors were likely to try to build an alternative infrastructure in the future.

The Gatekeeper effect has also arisen in the context of vertical integration (i.e. the combination of services at different levels of the supply chain). A clear example is the AOL/Time Warner case (Case No. COMP/M.1845 – AOL/Time Warner, 11 October 2000) in which the Commission considered that the concentration would result in the vertical integration of AOL's service provision with the media and entertainment content of Time Warner and Bertelsmann. The new entity would probably be dominant in the online music delivery market by becoming a Gatekeeper and being allowed to dictate the terms for the distribution of music over the internet. The Commission eventually cleared the merger on the basis that AOL / Time Warner would divest itself of Bertelsmann. Perhaps more surprisingly, the Commission has since approved the joint venture between Sony and Bertelsmann (Case COMP/ M.3333 — Sony/BMG). The case included an examination of the joint venture's impact on the emerging market for online music licences as well as online music distribution. The Commission also looked at the vertical relationships between Sony BMG's recorded music and Bertelsmann's downstream TV and radio activities in a number of member states. Although it concluded the absence of serious competition problems, the Commission observed that it would be keeping a close watch on future concentration in the music industry

Vertical integration concerns also emerged in the proposed Vizzavi joint venture between Vodafone, owner of the Mannesmann group, and Vivendi, owner of Canal + (Case NO COMP/JV.48 – Vodafone/Vivendi/Canal+). The parties intended to create an internet portal service designed to group together information and transactional services on one convenient site accessible via computers, televisions and mobile phones. However, the Commission was concerned that the parties' existing strong positions in the infrastructures of pay television and mobile networks could be leveraged into the internet portals market. To remedy this, the Commission's approval was conditional upon the parties granting third parties the same access to their facilities as the joint venture would enjoy.

The emergence of popular web-based business to business trading and business to business electronic marketplaces promises to create a more transparent, cost-effective and efficient means of conducting business. Essentially, buyers and sellers of similar products are able to carry out procurement activities using computer systems. The Commission has cleared a large number of electronic marketplaces in a variety of industries. For example, the Commission gave the green light to MyAircraft.com (Case No. COMP/M.1696 – UTC/Honeywell/12/MYAIRCRAFT.COM, 8 August 2000), a joint venture between UTC and Honeywell for the one-stop provision of shopping and supply management functions to all aerospace participants. The Commission found there were no competition concerns as alternative modes of conducting business were available to third parties and it was likely that the venture would face competition from other existing or planned business to business market places in the same sector.

Similarly, the Commission approved the Emaro joint venture between Deutsche Bank and SAP, providers of software (press release IP/00/783, 14 July 2000. 7. Press release IP/00/1775, 10 December 2001). Emaro is an electronic trading platform allowing suppliers of office equipment to conduct business online with their suppliers. The Commission was satisfied that there was no overlap between the parent companies' activities in any of the markets relevant to the concentration.

The Commission also cleared the creation of Eutilia and Endorsia electronic marketplaces. Eutilia is a joint venture between eleven European electricity utilities to provide business to business services in the area of procurement of goods and services to utilities in the electricity sector, including auctions, buy/sell enquiries and supplier database services. Endorsia is owned by five manufacturers of machines and industry components. It is designed to support the buying and selling requirements of manufacturers, distributors and end-users for branded industrial goods and services by acting as an electronic interface between individual sellers and their customers. In both cases, the Commission found that the internet portals would be open to all potential users on a non-discriminatory basis without forcing exchange members to use the portal as their only means of conducting business. There was also sufficient protection to avoid commercially sensitive data from being disclosed between competitors.

A number of useful lessons can be learnt from the Commission's assessment of business to business marketplaces so far. Any companies wishing to establish an e-marketplace without infringing EU competition rules should consider the following guidelines if they wish to avoid the potential pitfalls that the Commission has identified in the past:

1. Ensure secure data protection and put in place safeguards against the exchange of information to protect against the exchange of sensitive information between competitors.
2. Joint purchasing is only permissible in conjunction with the Commission's horizontal guidelines so as to avoid the creation of buyer power or the possibility of coordination on the downstream market.
3. Ensure open and non-discriminatory access to the exchange from all interested parties in order to reduce potential market foreclosure concerns and ensure open access to the marketplace.
4. Ensure separation between the exchange venture and its parents supported by a Chinese Wall structure to address the problem of only a handful of privileged market participants having access to certain information due to their status as market owners;
5. Ensure that no attempts are made to lock users into the proposed exchange. This safeguards against the threat of market dominance by one exchange.

4.2 UK merger control

UK merger control legislation is primarily contained in the Enterprise Act 2002 (although the Fair Trading Act 1973 (FTA) still applies to newspaper mergers). The Enterprise Act applies to actual or proposed mergers where:

(a) two or more 'enterprises' (at least one of which is carried on in the UK or by or under the control of a company incorporated in the UK) cease to be distinct (i.e. are brought under common control or ownership); and
(b) either one or both of the following criteria is satisfied:
  – as a result of the merger, the merged enterprise will supply 25 per cent or more of goods or services of a particular description in the UK or a substantial part of it ('the share of supply test'). This is sometimes referred to as 'market share' test. However, it is potentially narrower than a market share test as more than one type of product may comprise the relevant market); or
  – the annual value of the UK turnover of the enterprise being taken over exceeds £70 million ('the turnover test').

The target company will be 'brought under common control or ownership' in the following circumstances:

- when one party acquires a controlling interest in the other party (legal control); or
- when one party acquires the ability to control the policy of the other (*de facto* control); or
- when one party acquires the ability materially to influence the policy of the other. (Such an ability may arise from a shareholding as low as 15 per cent, and even in the absence of any shareholding, the existence of significant contractual relations between the parties may exceptionally give rise to such an ability.)

Procedure in dealing with the OFT – guidance and filings

Unlike other jurisdictions where prior clearance is mandatory, there is no obligation under the Enterprise Act to seek prior clearance of a merger which is subject to the Enterprise Act ('a qualifying merger') from the authorities either before or after the merger takes place.

The OFT is, however, obliged to keep itself informed about mergers which may qualify for investigation, and may seek information from the parties to any such qualifying merger.

There are two possible procedures for obtaining a 'clearance' (i.e. a decision by the OFT that it will not refer a qualifying merger to the Competition Commission (CC)) and two methods of seeking guidance from the OFT before a proposed transaction is formalised.

Seeking confidential guidance

Confidential guidance may only be sought before a proposed acquisition becomes public knowledge. It is particularly useful in acquisitions where public disclosure of the parties' proposals would raise sensitive commercial issues.

Confidential guidance may be sought informally from the OFT. This will normally involve a meeting with the OFT preceded by a briefing paper and can be arranged at relatively short notice.

A formal application for guidance will require a fuller submission to be sent to the OFT which will then evaluate the merger as if it were a published case.

Under both procedures, the OFT is precluded from seeking the views of the interested third parties and is entirely dependant on published information or information supplied to it by the applicant. Consequently, in certain cases the OFT may feel unable to give confidential guidance.

Seeking clearance using a Merger Notice

There is no obligation under UK law to seek clearance for a merger. However, two means exist for doing so. The first is the statutory Merger Notice under which a merger is pre-notified to the OFT on a standard form following which the merger will (subject to the possibility of extension) be deemed to have been cleared (subject to some exceptions) by the OFT twenty working days after submission of the Notice unless at or before that time it has been referred to the CC. The OFT may request further information and may seek one extension of time of ten working days.

Seeking clearance without a Merger Notice

The 'traditional', non-statutory way of seeking clearance from the OFT exists alongside the statutory procedure. This is the submission, in a bespoke format, of relevant information and market analysis, together with a request for clearance.

This route remains most appropriate for difficult or controversial cases (e.g. contested takeovers or mergers with significant market overlaps where the statutory timetable may not give the OFT time to reach a view).

The OFT aims to provide clearance from the Secretary of State within forty working days from the receipt of a satisfactory submission in 90 per cent of cases.

Fees for merger clearance

Fees are payable for obtaining clearance. The amount of the fee depends on the value of the annual turnover of the enterprise being acquired.

Reference to the CC

Save in relation to public interest cases (in which cases references will be considered by the Secretary of State following OFT advice), the OFT will refer qualifying mergers to the CC for further investigation if it has a reasonable belief, objectively justified by relevant facts, that there is a realistic prospect that the merger will lessen competition substantially.

Remedies

There is a statutory procedure for avoiding a reference to the CC under which the acquiror agrees to enforceable undertakings to the OFT. Such undertakings are typically to dispose of the part of a business which gives rise to competition concerns, but can also relate to conduct.

If the CC concludes that a merger has resulted or may be expected to result, in a substantial lessening of competition within any market or markets in the UK for goods or services, it may prohibit the merger or allow it to proceed subject to conditions.

5. Summary – what the risks are and how to be compliant

Competition law seeks to encourage commercial activity and not to stifle it. Large corporations with market power are expected to act more carefully in ensuring their agreements and conduct do not harm or restrict competition. However, a newly-formed company will not need to concern itself with whether it has abused a dominant position, nor will merger control laws generally apply to any small acquisitions it makes. All companies do, however, regardless of their size, need to ensure they do not enter into agreements which fix prices, share markets or which create actual barriers to trade across EU member states' boundaries. Such restrictions, regardless of the size of the parties, will be unenforceable and may result in fines being imposed, or damages being sought by third parties.

Many companies, of all sizes, seek to limit their exposure to competition law by putting in place competition law compliance programmes, which are effectively audits of a company's agreements and practices coupled with training for senior management so as to ensure both past and future agreements and conduct reflect an awareness of competition law. Both the OFT and Commission have publicly stated that the existence of a compliance programme, along with evidence that it was observed and taken seriously, will be a factor in assessing the size of any fine to be imposed, should an infringement come to light. Such an awareness within the company will also help senior management to identify where competitors, suppliers or even customers are acting unlawfully and where it may be possible to make a complaint to the OFT or Commission or even to bring an action for damages, where loss has been suffered.

Notes

1. 2790/99/EC Commission Regulation on the application of Article 81(3) of the Treaty to categories of vertical agreements and concerted practices.
2. 772/04/EC Commission Regulation on the application of Article 81(3) of the Treaty to categories of technology transfer agreements.
3. 1400/02/EC Commission Regulation on the application of Article 81(3) of the Treaty to categories of vertical agreements and concerted practices in the motor vehicle sector.
4. 2658/2000/EC Commission Regulation on the application of Article 81(3) of the Treaty to categories of specialisation agreements.
5. 2659/2000/EC Commission Regulation on the application of Article 81(3) of the Treaty to categories of research and development agreements.

Appendix: Useful Sources of Information

Entity	Internet address
Chapter 1	
OFTEL (for unfair contract terms)	www.oftel.gov.uk
International Chamber of Commerce	www.iccwbo.org
European Commission	www.europa.eu.int
Chapter 2	
Whois domain name searches	www.whois.net
ICANN (registration of domain names)	www.icann.org
Nominet UK (domain name services)	www.nic.uk
Internet Service Providers Association	www.ispa.org.uk
Royal National Institute of the Blind's 'See It Right' campaign	www.rnib.org.uk
The National Computing Centre (Escrow services)	www.ncc.co.uk
W3C Web Accessibility Initiative	www.w3.org/WAI/resources
RNID	www.rnid.org.uk
Chapter 3	
Information Commissioner's Office	www.dataprotection.gov.uk/
E-mail Preference Service (site includes preference service facilities for fax, e-mail, telephone and SMS)	www.emailpreferenceservice.co.uk/
Direct Marketing Association	www.dma.org.uk www.dma.org.uk/shared/lgl_code.asp
DMA Codes of Practice	www.dma.org.uk/shared/lgl code.asp
Financial Services Authority	www.fsa.gov.uk
Marketing Law website	www.marketinglaw.co.uk
Chapter 4	
European Commission	www.europa.eu.int/comm/index_en.htm
UK Trade Marks Agency	www.patent.gov.uk/tm

Entity	Internet address
Chapter 4 *continued*	
Office of Harmonisation in the Internal Market (OHIM)	www.oami.eu.int/en
Financial Services Authority	www.fsa.gov.uk
Council of Europe's Cybercrime Convention	www.conventions.coe.int/Treaty/EN/cadreprincipal
Internet Services Providers Association	www.ispa.org.uk
Chapter 5	
National Outsourcing Association	www.noa.co.uk
Chapter 6	
British Codes of Advertising and Sales Promotion	www.cap.org.uk – select 'The Codes' option on list of options.
Advertising Standards Authority (ASA)	www.asa.org.uk
The Interactive Advertising Bureau UK	www.iabuk.net
Admark scheme	www.admark.org.uk
Patents Office	www.patent.gov.uk
Office of Fair Trading	www.oft.gov.uk
Federal Trade Commission	www.ftc.gov
Cigarette Code (on ASA site)	www.asa.org.uk/index.asp?bhjs=1&bhsw=1024&bhsh=768&bhswi=1004&bhshi=602&bhflver=4&bhdir=1&bhje=1&bhcold=24&bhrl=-1&bhqt=-1&bhmp=-1&bhab=-1&bhmpex=&bhflex=4,0,28,0&bhdirex=8,0,0,206&bhcont=lan
E-mail Preference Service	www.emailpreferenceservice.co.uk
Direct Marketing Association	www.dma.org.uk
Marketinglaw.co.uk	www.marketinglaw.co.uk
Department of Trade & Industry	www.dti.gov.uk
Federal Trade Commission	www.ftc.gov
UK Intellectual Property	www.intellectual-property.gov.uk
Chapter 7	
The Internet Assigned Numbers Authority (IANA)	www.iana.org
The Internet Corporation for Assigned Names and Numbers (ICANN)	www.icann.org
VeriSign	www.verisign.com
Nominet	www.nic.uk

Entity	Internet address
Chapter 7 *continued*	
World Intellectual Property Organisation (WIPO)	www.wipo.int
National Arbitration Forum	www.arb-forum.com
CPR Institute for Dispute Resolution	www.cpradr.org
Eresolution Consortium	www.eresolution.ca
Chapter 8	
European Court of Human Rights	www.echr.coe.int
Information Commissioner	www.dataprotection.gov.uk
Chapter 9	
Business Link	www.businesslink.org.uk
Customs and Excise (e-commerce)	www.hmce.gov.uk/bus/vat/e-comm.htm
Customs and Excise (generally)	www.hmce.gov.uk
Inland Revenue (e-commerce)	www.inlandrevenue.gov.uk/ecommerce/index.htm
Inland Revenue (e-business)	www.inlandrevenue.gov.uk/ebu/index.htm
Inland Revenue (generally)	www.inlandrevenue.co.uk
Inland Revenue Information Centre	www.inlandrevenue.gov.uk/enq/index.htm
Office of the e-Envoy (Part of Cabinet)	www.e-nvoy.gov.uk/ecommerce_index.htm
Small Business Link	www.sbs.gov.uk
UK Online for Business	Www.ukonlineforbusiness.gov.uk
Chapter 10	
Competition Commission	www.competition-commission.gov.uk
Office of Fair Trading	www.oft.gov.uk
Europe Online	www.europa.int
Sources of information from the author	www.osborneclarke.com
	www.ocalliance.com
	www.marketinglaw.co.uk
	www.gamesbiz.net

Osborne Clarke

Osborne Clarke is a firm of solicitors with offices in London, Bristol, Thames Valley, Palo Alto (California), Cologne and Munich; and associated offices in: Paris, Brussels, Rotterdam, Barcelona, Madrid, Helsinki, Copenhagen, Milan, Rome, Brescia, Tallinn and St Petersburg.

Any enquiries should be directed to Simon Rendell, Head of the Commercial Department at the London office or on his e-mail at: simon.rendell@osborneclarke.com

OSBORNE CLARKE UK OFFICES:

Osborne Clarke
London
One London Wall
London
EC2Y 5EB
UK

Tel: 020 71057000
Fax: 020 71057005

Osborne Clarke
Thames Valley
Apex Plaza
Forbury Road
Reading RG1 1AX

Tel: 0118 925 2000
Fax: 0118 925 0038

Osborne Clarke
Bristol
2 Temple Back East, Temple Quay
Bristol BS1 6EG

Tel: 0117 917 3000
Fax: 0117 917 3005

Website: www.osborneclarke.com

Index